GOD THE BLACK MAN AND TRUTH

Ben Ammi

Communicators Press
P.O. Box 26063
Washington, D.C. 20001

Communicators Press is an imprint of
Kingdom Products Inc. International

4th Revised Edition

Copyright © 1982, 1985, 1990, 2000 Ben Ammi
All rights reserved by Kingdom Products, Inc. International

ISBN 0-9620463-1-0
Library of Congress Catalog Card Number 82-50906

The scriptural references used in this book are taken
from the New Scofield Reference Bible

On the Cover

I HAVE 10,000 RECOLLECTIONS," a 111cm x 144cm, collage is on display in the Prince Asiel Center for International Studies at the African Hebrew Israelite Community in Dimona, Israel. Created by first-year graduate students of the New Kingdom School in Holiness (college level), the work was unveiled on April 30, 1987, at a commemorative ceremony.

Capturing no less than 100 of the characters and events, facets and phases of the African American experience, "I HAVE 10,000 RECOLLECTIONS" is a timeless historical reminder, a thought-provoking consciousness raiser and an invaluable teaching aid.

"I HAVE 10,000 RECOLLECTIONS" is available as a 22" x 28" glossy poster.

Contact:
Communicators Press; P.O. Box 26063; Washington, DC 20001
tel: (202) 291-9244; fax: (202) 291-9149; email: dckog@idt.net
www.kingdomofyah.com

Chronological Breakdown of the Captivities of the Nation of Israel and the Migration of the African Hebrews

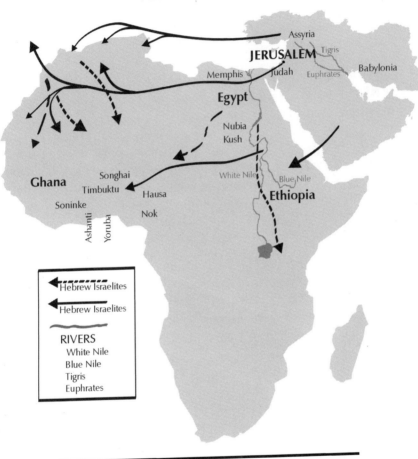

I. The 430 year captivity of the Children of Israel in the land of Egypt under Pharoah until Moses

II. The Assyrian Captivity, 721 B.C. Captivity of the Northern ten tribes of Israel by King Sargon II of Assyria.

III. 586 B.C. the Babylonian Exile—King Nebuchadnezzar came against Jerusalem and carried away captive the Children of Judah to Babylon and razed Jerusalem.

IV. The Romans invaded Jerusalem under the Roman General Titus dispersing all the remnants of the Black Northeastern African tribespeople such as the remnants of the Israelites and Sons of Judah, Babylonians, Persians and Greeks, and Egyptians. This great event took place in 70 A.D. (see map)

This book is dedicated to the word's afflicted people. May the words wipe away your tears and soothe your pain, while assuring you that your salvation is nigh at hand...

> *"For even at this time the Lord God of Heaven has established Him a kingdom which shall never be destroyed. This kingdom did not come at a time of peace, but at a time of great turmoil and trouble to become the vehicle, which shall bring peace unto all men.*
>
> *This kingdom shall not be ruled over by the oppressors of thy soul but it has been given unto you, the word's afflicted. This kingdom shall break in pieces all other kingdoms, for only your kingdom can stand forever."*

Daniel 2:44
(Modified)

Table Of Contents

About The Author

BEN AMMI
("Son of My People")

Ben Ammi (which means "Son of My People" in Hebrew) was born October 12,1939, to Levi and Rena Carter, in an old, dilapidated neighborhood on the near southwest side of Chicago, Illinois. I first met Ben in the fall of 1948, when his family moved into my neighborhood on Chicago's near northwest side several blocks from Lake Michigan. From that day on, our lives have been intertwined, as we never lived far apart. We grew together and shared our hopes and dreams for the future.

Much of our youth was spent a block or so from the old Cabrini (now the notorious Cabrini-Green) housing projects. An extraordinary person from his youth, Ben always had an intense and boundless love for his God, people, and the Creation. In the forty-two years that I have known him, I've yet to see him in any violent, physical confrontation, (which was a phenomenon in our neighborhood), even though he was a statewide wrestling champion. His strength was and is his unique insight and the precision of his tongue. He has an exceptional ability to discern and articulate. In this he has no equal — and I'm not being partial. It seems as though there has always been some "unseen force" watching over him.

Ben attended Washburn Trade School, later transferring to Marshall High where he dropped out during his third year. He joined the U.S. Army, serving on a nearby missile base. Still, he managed to complete his high school education during his military term. Shortly thereafter, he married, and found employment at Howard Foundry, where he became an excellent metallurgist.

It was during this period, that Ben met his first mentor of Hebrew history, the elder Eliyahoo Buie, who taught him in-depth concerning our African Hebrew heritage. Elder Buie confirmed many things passed on to Ben verbally by his parents and relatives, inspiring his avid search into the

Holy Scriptures for the hidden truths concerning the agonizing captivity of the African in America.

Perplexed by the overt racial injustice of American society, and the "privileged position" of Europeans in America, he questioned whether in fact God was somehow partial to them. Looking upon the despair of his people, he reasoned: "If 'thy will be done' indeed means the inevitable manifestation of God's will — then the horrible predicament of the Black man m America must be the Will of God."

Intense meditation, study and research soon convinced him that the problems of African Americans were self-inflicted — the result of *their willful disobedience* and not God's ultimate will. He then set out to strengthen his personal relationship with the God of Israel, seeking to invoke His presence in the struggle for true freedom, on behalf of Black people in America, and all men in general.

A co-founder of the Abeta Hebrew Cultural Center on Chicago's south side, he became one of the center's chief teachers, spokesmen, and organizers. Here he had the vision that an exodus of the Black man from the United States was inevitable, and indeed necessary, if true freedom was ever to be attained.

In 1967, at the zenith of the Black revolt in America, approximately 350 men, women and children left the confines of the United States enroute to Israel, via Liberia, West Africa. After a successful sojourn of two-and-one-half years in the interior of Liberia, where a myriad of negative and unbecoming traits were purged, the remnant of these pioneers moved on to Israel in 1969. Since that time, Ben Ammi and his followers have struggled to establish the long-waited Kingdom of God — on earth!

Ben Ammi has boldly taken on the prophetic mandate to lead all men — in word and deed — back unto God. His burning pursuit of Divine Intellect and wisdom has qualified him to be the master teacher and profound (yet simple) philosopher that he is. Multi-lingual, he communicates the Plan of God to others clearly and effectively with the understanding of the original Hebrew thought. As spiritual leader and Father of the African Hebrew Israelites, Ben Ammi has become the first to *successfully* bring about the repatriation of African Americans. He is beloved by his people, admired by his acquaintances and respected by his foes. His selfless regard for the well-being of others makes him a natural leader. Ben Ammi exudes supreme confidence and composure, seemingly unshaken by opposition and the many obstacles encountered along the way. His record demands the serious attention of all.

All praises to the Most High God of Israel!

- Prince Gavriel HaGadol

Foreword

"And ye shall know the truth, and the truth shall make you free."

St. John 8:32

It is an ironic testimony to the history and phenomenon of the Black Race, that despite the incalculable stumbling blocks that have prohibited our humanization, that there remains an unceasing faith in the existence of God Almighty. Like a determined artist who struggles to be successful no matter how many setbacks, the Black man has persisted in his quest for approval. Yet, although we have suffered perpetual torment at the hands of the forces of evil, we have still maintained a reverence for and fear of the Creator.

Even the worship of God through the vehicles of Christianity, Islam or fetish beliefs still has not elevated the African American out of the abyss of minority, second-class or "underclass" status. No amount of coup d'etats, riots, nonviolent demonstrations, boycotts, sit-ins, or demands for civil rights, human rights or Black power have served to remove the stigmas or lessen the aversion to our people. If you have not diagnosed that the entire African American community suffers from the diseases of continued racism, exploitation and injustice, then you must be visiting from another planet. Neither has piousness or being sanctimonious lifted the African American from the crater of discontent. Somehow, somewhere, something has gone terribly wrong. In a loaded crap game, the winners would exclaim to the Black man that he "couldn't hit a lick."

This book, **GOD the BLACK MAN and TRUTH**, reveals why it is not a coincidence that Blacks the world over have been sliding and stumbling, reaching but still missing, striving yet failing, never able, as Dr. Martin Luther King, Jr. commented, to "transform the jangling discords of our nation into a beautiful symphony of brotherhood."

Why have Reverends King, Jr., Abernathy, Jackson and Young, Bishop Desmond Tutu, the Honorable Elijah Muhammad, Minister Malcolm X, or any of the innumerable "men of God" been unable to turn the nightmare of

Blackness into the dream deferred? Why has the truth about the special tie between God and Black people not been revealed? Why did African civilizations fall from the pinnacle of greatness to the chasm of obscurity? More than four centuries have elapsed since Blacks were taken from Africa and brought to America and we still have not "overcome." Could there be an "unseen force" present which has worked against the success of African Americans and the African and "Third World" nations? On these sacred pages is the message to the Black man as it has never been told, — the staggering revelation about why the African world has remained in the dark about who we are and where we should be going, and why as the 21st century labors to debut, we still are a people who are not truly free.

In **GOD the BLACK MAN and TRUTH**, Ben Ammi gives light to the disheartening realization that we are a people buried in the muck and mire of complacency; a people imprisoned in poverty and ignorance and trapped in the web of religion. **GOD the BLACK MAN and TRUTH** underscores the need for our people to ignite the fires of discontent — this time with new fuel — for it is beyond the time for righteous men to sit idly as the wicked prevail, unmolested in their den of iniquity.

Taking on the risks of fighting the established order, done unflinchingly in this book, will undoubtedly set off warheads among all who dare to read it. Centuries of planned ideologies, ordered beliefs and precise propaganda fall apart with each new paragraph. Waging war on religion while uplifting the Creator is a task few have dared to undertake. Who would dare to question the teachings of Jesus or tell you that the true worship of God does not occur on a specific day with the chiming of a church bell?

What proof is there to the statement that heaven is in your mind, if you choose it to be and not somewhere beyond the clouds? By what authority is the task of redefining the norm — shaming the perpetuators of the Christmas and Easter lies — placed in the hands of ordinary men? And why is the name you wear as vital to your survival as the air you breathe?

This book is not an armchair philosopher's ego trip to never-never land. Whether you read the Bible, believe in God or are Black, gentile or Jew (and believe yourself to be of the chosen race), **GOD the BLACK MAN and TRUTH** will either rejuvenate you or ruin you. For those readers who are Black, the choice is yours. You can continue down the "yellow-brick good-ship lollipop" road to hell or you can read and reread this work, then reexamine your life in America under the influence of the European and decide for yourself which path leads to salvation.

How often in one's lifetime does something come along detailing the means to an end while at the same time allowing one to sample the results before the theory has been dissected? Surely, anyone with eyes to read and a mind to comprehend will appreciate the magnanimous offering that this work is. **GOD the BLACK MAN and TRUTH** should be considered the gift of a lifetime to you. Ben Ammi is giving you the power to redefine all that you thought you were powerless to amend. He is excavating you from the pits of hell — the depraved cavity of the mind — and leading you on God's chartered safari out of the jungles of degradation, bigotry and humiliation.

GOD the BLACK MAN and TRUTH fuels the fire of the struggle of the righteous, outlining the way back unto the same God who chastised His people by sentencing them to a 6,000 year term of pain and suffering.

My fervent prayer is that you hear in these final hours as the chapter of Euro-American dominion and rulership is speedily being closed. Unlike our fathers who scorned the idea, "the end of this world" has come in this generation...your's and mine. Inevitably it had to manifest itself. The physical and spiritual destruction of the Euro-gentile world was sure to come in *somebody's* generation and time.

However, the end of Euro-gentile rule on God's planet does not mean the end of all life. It simply means that the Great <u>Spiritual</u> Magna Carta — the authority and right for the Euro-gentiles to rule God's people and creation — has been nullified. The destruction shall conclude with the Euro-gentile world becoming morally corrupt, spiritually void and physically sick. If you are not aware that the European world is evincing the symptoms of terminal torment then perhaps a little less television and a lot more prayer would be the solution to your myopic state.

Perhaps you are one of those who feels that prestigious position, fine homes, lavish affairs, and rubbing shoulders with the wealthy preclude these troubles and make you exempt from the plight of the African. But do not believe for one moment that your Mercedes Benz, (occupied by your Swedish starlet), will deter the inevitable. Neither will you escape the immutable destruction with the host of readily-available artificial devices or temporary relief mechanisms that cast you adrift from reality.

Jesus warned: "And except those days be shortened; there should no flesh be saved; but for the elect's sake those days shall be shortened." Certainly if any flesh is to be saved, then someone must arrive on the scene with the objective of shortening the destroyer's time. If any flesh is to be saved, then the time has come that we as a people stand up to assume our God-given responsibility as the transmitters of the law (instructions) of God. It is tragically ironic that the Euro-gentile (the European and his descendants throughout the world) knows that his time to exercise rulership and dominion over the earth has come to an end. He is likewise very much aware of who we really are.

We are the true elect and chosen people of God. We must neither be afraid...nor discouraged. We can and need to once again hold our heads high, projecting the majesty and splendor of our Divine heritage wherever we may be found. The stakes are high: winner-takes-all. But truth is the winning hand and God Almighty is the cashier. Now is the time to collect our winnings.

There have been many great sacrifices that have gone into the writing of this book. Valiant knights have fallen, warriors gone astray, princes relieved of their crowns. And, with the unfolding of these truths came tears of travailing, the anguish of misunderstanding and the sorrow of death.

But the truth must be told, every grievous word of it, for the deception has gone on too long. For those who have suffered to make this work a reality, you will be elated as justice prevails and the heartache of the ordeal is lessened.

In the coming days, the actuality of who God is and why He has made His people suffer will be made clear to you; your spirit will come alive. And, the undying faith of the righteous, the woes of our grandmothers with their broken backs and arthritic spirits, and the lamentations of the blues singers will not have been in vain.

You are now at the mountain top; you are awakened to the "Promised Land." You will never be the same upon the reading of this book. Here is praying you are ready and able to accept your fate.

By Odehyah Baht Israel

Introduction:
Who Were... And Are, The African
Hebrew Israelites?

"Keep not thou silence, O God; hold not thy peace, and be not still, O God,

For lo, thine enemies make a tumult, and they that hate thee have lifted up the head.

They have taken crafty counsel against the people, and consulted against thy hidden ones,

They have said, Come, and let us cut them off from being a nation; that the name of Israel may be no more in remembrance."

Psalms 83:1-4

Contrary to the deeply-humiliating debacle and devastation that is the situation today, African Americans are in fact, the Children of God — the direct descendants of Jesus Christ, Mohammed, Abraham, Ishmael, Moses, David and the prophets.

Yet what has happened to the Africa that was the cradle of civilization and birthplace of the original man; that fostered the great empires of Ghana, Mali and Songhai; that developed the high centers of learning and culture at Timbuktu, Jenne and Carthage; that produced leaders such as Hannibal, Tarik, the Queen of Sheba, Chaka Zulu, Jomo Kenyatta and Kwame Nkrumah; that created unrivaled architectural and engineering wonders which still stand centuries later; that rendered a legacy of scientific achievements which baffles the world today; and on and on?

Why do economic woes, political setbacks and catastrophic events disproportionately affect us? Why does the African American continue to wallow in the mire as a permanent underclass, a prey to virtually every new immigrant arrival?

The answer to these questions is surprisingly simple: we disobeyed the laws and commandments of God. We turned our backs on God...and He turned His back on us. As a result of this impasse, we were left vulnerable and exposed to a host of evils, among them a Divinely-authorized-and-sanctioned chastisement at the hands of a terrible enemy.

Stop thinking it is coincidence! Stop shrugging off our devastated condition as fate. To believe that our people are naturally inept at everything is foolish. The complacency and corruption that abounds among the African American as well as Africans globally is not coincidence, but conspiracy — a conspiracy to destroy our knowledge of self, our glorious past, and our way back to God. The conspiracy has so thoroughly succeeded, that we actually find contentment in our rootlessness and deplorable state, allowing the conspirators to maintain their power and control over us.

Slavery, discrimination and worldwide hatred are severe punishments, but we are victims of a cruel plot, an international religious plot, that came about as a result of our disobedience to God. It is hard to imagine that a loving God would subject His children to such punishment, but the Most High is a very jealous and terrible God when angered.

We are a people, who despite continual catastrophies, have a special bond with God. Only a people who have a sacred tie to the Creator of the Universe — an inside connection with "the Man upstairs," could have survived the ordeal.

Accordingly, in His Omnipotent Mercy and Wisdom, God granted us a way back to Him, leaving pieces of the puzzle intact for us to find in our diligent search for Truth.

Let us look to Biblical history to piece the puzzle together. If you acknowledge the archaeological findings that earliest man originated in Northeastern Africa, then what is written in the Bible as it pertains to the creation of man and the Garden of Eden is confirmed. In establishing exactly where the Garden was, the book of Genesis cites the four rivers: Pishon, Gihon (in the land of Ethiopia), Tigris and Euphrates which run through Syria and Iraq. I mention these facts from the Bible because it is that great history text that will clarify any doubts or misnomers of Black people's ancestry. Oddly enough, despite many Blacks' love for the God of Creation, few realize the truths of our beginnings that are contained in the Bible. We are so caught up with religion that we are not seeing what is actually contained in the Bible. The Middle East was previously connected to the continent of Africa prior to the excavation of the Suez Canal in 1859. The countries of Israel, Syria, Lebanon and Saudi Arabia, which we now refer to as the Middle East (a term coined by war correspondents during World War II) prior to 1945 originally comprised the northeasternmost part of Africa.

A *Time* magazine article (Sept. 21, 1981) reported the results of an archeological dig in Ebla, Syria (Ebla was a trading center that attracted ancient Israelites and others in the region) in which tablets (writings) written 45 centuries ago were unearthed which constitute "the most complete record of ancient civilization." I quote from that article by Richard Ostling: "Enthusiasts claim that Ebla could revise theories on the origins of Judaism, Christianity and Islam; alter many scriptural interpretations; make all current Bible translations obsolete; and require scholars to credit the Old Testament with great historical accuracy."

Some of the earliest controversy over the Ebla findings was sparked when famous names in the Bible — Adam, Eve, Jonah and David among them — turned up on the Ebla tablets. This did not mean the same persons were being written about, but indicated that Ebla and the Bible could have come from similar cultural milieus. Especially tantalizing was the appearance of two names which later appear in the Hebrew tradition: Abraham, the spiritual forefather of Jews, Christians and Muslims, and his Biblical ancestor Eber (whose name formed the root of the term Hebrew).

Pettinato (author of <u>The Archives of Ebla</u>, Doubleday) proposed that Abraham was a native of northern Syria. An intriguing Ebla text shows a town named Ur near Haran, the Biblical town in Syria from which Abraham moved into the promised land.

Pettinato writes that in some Eblaite personal names, the syllables ya and el mean "god" and that Ya might have been the proper name of a specific deity. Naturally that brings to mind the later Hebrew names for the one God, Yahweh (Jehovah) and El (Lord). Pettinato also finds in Ebla a possible Flood story, prophets and tribal leaders whose function is reminiscent of the Biblical Judges."[1]

What does all of this have to do with African people? After the Great Flood, the survivors, Noah and his sons Shem, Ham and Japhet, fathered generations of people including Abraham, son of Terah of the city of Ur of the Chaldeans. We know from the findings in the work <u>Hebrewisms of West Africa</u> by Joseph J. Williams that the early Northeast Africans (Middle Easterners), those people like Abraham, were Black. According to Hebrew and Arabic histories, King Nimrod was the son of Cush, grandson of Ham, and the ruler of the kingdoms of Shinar (2450 B.C.), Babylonia, and areas northward along the Tigris River over Assyria. Anthropologist Sir Harry Johnston stated, "the curliness of the hair, together with a negro eye and full lips in the portraiture of Assyria, conveys the idea of an evident negro element in Babylonia."[2] Professor W. Max Miller of Bible Exegesis identifies Cush in the Jewish Encyclopedia as "the ancestor of the Nubians" who inhabit modern Ethiopia and Sudan. The Encyclopedia Americana further substantiates the idea that Nimrod was a "cushite." Abraham's father Terah, was a relative of Nimrod and a minister in his government in Mesopotamia, modern day Iraq.

It is written in Genesis that God directed Abraham, his wife Sarah and his nephew Lot into the land of Canaan, what we now refer to as Israel, saying (in Genesis 15:18): "Unto thy seed have I given this land, from the river of Egypt unto the great river, the river Euphrates..." God also told Abraham (in Genesis 15:13): "Know of a surety that thy seed shall be a stranger in a land that is not theirs, and shall serve them, and they shall afflict them four hundred years." Black people are the seed of Abraham of whom God spoke and it is African Americans (African Hebrews) who as slaves and second-class citizens have lived in service to a strange people for more than 400 years.

Biblical historian Samuel Mercer reveals that in 1650 B.C., Jacob (grandson of Abraham) and his family went into Egypt and lived there about 430 years. This was a great migratory time. Jacob and his family, thought to have been Hyksos (a Semitic people) entered Egypt and ruled the land. Hyksos means "rulers of foreign countries" and suggests a people who came from another land. During this migratory period, many people of Israel were in service to Egyptians. As history tells us, the Hebrew slaves in Egypt were led by Moses to return to Israel.

Many of the descendants of Abraham followed Moses from Egypt, but some remained in Egypt, while others migrated south and westward according to Joseph Williams. Another scholar, Edmond D. Morel, identifies the Fulani of West Africa as "lineal descendants of those Hyksos and Hebrew migrants." Those migrating Hebrews explain why traces of Hebrew culture can be found throughout west, central and east Africa. Many scholars believe the ancestors of the Fulani, Ashanti, Ewe, Yoruba, Bantu and other peoples were in fact early Hebrew Israelites.

Many Israelites were also driven out of their land by the Romans in 70 C.E. and thereby migrated gradually to the surrounding nations of Africa. We know that many West Africans, especially the Ashantis, are direct descendants of the ancient Hebrews because of the strong Hebrewisms that have been identified in Ashanti tribal customs, including similar-sounding words, similarities in marriage and childbirth customs, observance of the Sabbath (Saturday) as well as the name Ashanti from the words "ti," which in the west African tongue means "race of" and Ashan, a town in the domain of Judah (see Joshua 15:42).

In both language and customs, the retention of certain Hebrewisms is evidence of the connection between the two groups. It only supports the contention that African Americans are descended from not only the Ashantis, the Fulani, Ewe, Yoruba and Bantu nations but the ancient Hebrews as well. If we know nothing more about ourselves we do know that we were brought to America from west and central Africa — Senegal, Guinea, the Gambia (land of Kunta Kinte), Ivory Coast, Ghana, Togo, Benin, Nigeria and Cameroon, where these various African people lived.

Not long after the first slaves were taken from Africa by Europeans, Pope Julius II, in 1505, commissioned the painting of certain Biblical works by artist Michelangelo (Buonarroti) and in doing so initiated the concept of God as being white. Included in the painting is the portrait of Mary, mother of Jesus, whose prominent African features were distorted to resemble a Florentine Italian woman. Likewise, in the Michelangelo paintings, the images of the Christ child, the three wise men, the Last Supper, and the Resurrection, were changed until no trace of their original blackness remained. Not only were these images changed, but entire nations, peoples and empires were changed, like the ancient Egyptians, the Israelites, Babylonians, Persians, and Chinese. The features came to resemble those of caucasian ancestry. Thus, we have Michelangelo, Leonardo de Vinci and others to thank for artistically changing the face of the world from black to white. However in Poland, the Pope, Union Solidarity leader Lech Walesa and millions of Catholics pay homage to an ancient portrait of the Black Madonna thought to have been painted by Jesus' disciple Luke. This painting is one of the few remaining works which portray the true features of ancient Israelites, who were an African people.

It is as a result of the dispersion of the Israelites to West Africa and the subsequent enslavement of 40 million Africans to Europe and the Americas that the African Hebrew Israelite Nation of Jerusalem came forth. After years in the Diaspora, African Americans are returning to their homeland, fulfilling the prophecies as they were set down in the Bible, which predicted the return of the Children of Israel to the land of their forefathers, Abraham, Isaac and Jacob.

Dedicated to the establishment of a New World Order and setting the pace for positive examples of Godliness for all people to follow of morality, righteousness and love, the African Hebrew Israelites of Jerusalem are revolutionaries in the literal sense. In the words of one Hebrew: "we have not come forth upon our own accord to do that which is of men and for the glory of men, nor to be seen of men, nor seek power or majesty or riches or earthly glory, for those things are for the glorification of man and man's works."

The spirit of Almighty God inspired 400 African Americans to make an exodus from America during the height of the civil rights era in the late 1960's. When others were marching and singing "We Shall Overcome," 400 Black Hebrews were marching out of 400 years of captivity in America back home to Africa. No others have been successful in bringing nationalism to African Americans in the true sense. What so many others, including Malcolm X, Marcus Garvey, and Martin R. Delaney dreamed about, was fulfilled.

During the Six Day War in Israel in 1967, the African Hebrews journeyed to Liberia, settling 110 miles outside of Monrovia, to purge themselves of the decadence that had been the way of life for them in America. Aside from a grant and unlimited use of the land on which they settled, the pilgrimaging African Hebrews accepted little from the Liberians in the way of "western comforts." Life for these special people was far from easy. Despite extreme difficulties adjusting to the new lifestyle, including adapting to an agricultural existence, these pioneers were determined and above all ordained by God to do His will. Can you imagine going from electrical appliances to virtually no electricity at all, or sisters washing all the clothing by hand after using washing machines all their lives? These were a strong and courageous people. It is difficult to envision chronic T.V. watchers living without sterile electronic entertainment, yet these people subsisted on the love and talent God had given them to maintain their positive spirits, during a time when everything around them was new and alien. After cleansing themselves of the *niggerisms* and negative habits acquired during their captivity in America and after learning to live, love and trust one another like human beings, the Hebrew Israelites had become fit to begin the work of building God's Kingdom.

The African Hebrew Israelites do not subscribe to any religion, allowing for the unifying in principle and righteousness of all men; whereas religion has become a stumbling block to unity. Our mission is Divinely inspired. We have undertaken what may seem to others as an impossible mission, but what is in reality a purposeful, fulfilling endeavor for all those involved. We are determined to build a nation whose people love and follow the God of Israel, as well as love and respect one another.

A Note To Our Readers

You will frequently encounter the use of the term "Euro-gentile" through-out this work. It is a term coined by the African Hebrew-Israelites in keeping with our having seized the "Power to Define," (a concept which will be made clear in the chapter of the same name.)

The suffix "gentile" simply denotes a people or nation that is without the knowledge of the True and Living God of Creation. When using the term "Euro-gentile," (often interchangeably with "Euro-American"), we are in fact referring to the entire European family of nations, i.e., Europe, the United States of America, Canada, South Africa, New Zealand, Australia, etc.

Its usage also reflects the pervasive and powerful social, economic, cultural and political influence these nations have wielded on this planet. As such, though these "Euro-gentile" nations are obviously and unquestionably responsible for having brought all of humanity and creation to the brink of destruction as a result of their continuously evil activities and deeds, no racist or otherwise negative connotations are inferred by the phrase.

You will also notice the capitalization of the word "black," when referring to *race,* as opposed to merely *color.* We are well aware that this usage many not conform to generally-accepted norms of the English language.

While the use of "Black" may thus be deemed inaccurate, it must be recognized that many "Blacks" or "Africans" have not yet arrived to the point of tracing and identifying their particular *nation* of origin, or *nationality.* It is an obvious fact that our skins are black and that "Black Americans" hail collectively from the continent of Africa.

Again, many other words and terms may be capitalized, e.g., "Truth," "Divine," "Love," or "Power to Define." When they appear in such formal usage, it denotes their application as a *principle* "building block" or concept in the New World Order.

The Quest for God

Stop and consider the number of times in a year, or even in a day, that you hear the word "God" used. Are you one of those quick to say "Good God Almighty"; or "God knows"; "God will get you"; or "God help me?" People use the word "God" daily in conversations and numerous times on their day of worship. Unknowingly, you hear the word so much that you naturally assume that those using it are relating to the God of the Bible. Unfortunately, ninety-nine percent of the usage of the word God has very little to do with the true God — the Creator of the Universe. But, men deceivingly use the word enough whereby you think they are identifying with and worshipping the Almighty God. In actuality, there are many who pay homage to false gods, for a god is whomever or whatever you serve and obey.

Where are the detestable false gods we were warned of in the Holy oracles? What do you imagine when you think of a false god? No doubt, because of the heavy influence of images and stereotypes promoted by the Euro-gentile media, when you hear "false god" you think of some primitive man in some primitive society, bowing before a wooden or metal idol. However, the understanding of false gods should be very clear, for the Commandments begin with the words "Thou shalt have no other gods before me." Have the masses been deceived into following false gods? In our quest for God, we must know.

> *And why call ye me, Lord, Lord, and do not the*
> *things which I say?*
>
> **St. Luke 6:46**

The word "Lord" means ruler, master, great teacher, or the one you obey. Jesus complained, asking why they were calling him Lord and not doing as he instructed them. That is to say, if they did not obey him, he was not their Lord. Only those who obey God can be His children, for only they will carry out their moral obligation to Him.

The second Commandment also admonishes you to be careful of false idols and images (gods). In my explaining these truths to you, I will not change the Commandments, but I will explain them in their relevancy to the freedom struggle today.

Satan is cunning in concealing his evil, so that it appears attractive and not deceptive. The idols of the Commandments in the days of the ancients were in most cases made of wood and stone. But satan is too clever to address the people on that level today. Today, these idols or images are men and women in entertainment and politics. There are many celebrities with the ability to persuade who sometimes lead the people, and sometimes impress or influence their actions and thoughts. The Commandments refer to them as vain, graven images who have been presented before the people to bring them the Word of God, appearing as lambs, but who are, in actuality, ravenous wolves. They are the standards (images) placed before you by society, that are "in the know" concerning the way to God or to success. But to just "succeed" is not enough; there now has to be success in Righteousness. The present world institutions have caused success in unrighteousness. They have succeeded in the production of devices that destroy humanity (with weapons), the family structure (through constant television and adult-only movies, etc.) and the fabric of pleasant societies. They have succeeded in destroying the food, the air, the water, and the wildlife, and everyday we read about other "successes" of the same nature.

The graven, vain images or idols pacify the people and justify this cruel, wicked world. They are the ones that created the saying "worship according to the dictates of your own conscience," or in other words, "do what you want to do," for evil is really innocuous!

> *"Not every one that saith unto me, Lord, Lord, shall enter into the kingdom of heaven, but he that doeth the will of my Father, who is in heaven.*
>
> *Many will say to me in that day, Lord, Lord have we not prophesied in thy name? And in thy name have cast out demons? And in thy name done many wonderful works?*
>
> *And then will I profess unto them, I never knew you; depart from me, ye that work iniquity."*
>
> **St. Matthew 7:21-23**

> *"And Jesus answered and said unto them, Take heed that no man deceive you.*

For many shall come in my name, saying, I am
Christ; and shall deceive many."

St. Matthew 24:4,5

Who are these "many" who would come in Jesus' name, not denying him, but acknowledging him as the Christ, sometimes working amazing works, seeming and looking pious as they say all of the "right" words — "Jesus is the Lord"; "believe in Jesus" — but deceiving many? Could this be slave-oriented Christianity, the apostate church, whose roots lead only back to Europe? One thing we can agree on is that to deceive "many" or "multitudes", you must be in a position of recognized authority and power. This is not an innuendo, but I do admonish you to consider the words of Jesus, "take heed that ye be not deceived."

For in truth, the people have not been taught about the God of Creation or the manner in which to worship Him. Therefore, when God's true messengers begin to relate the simple truth concerning God and worship, it sounds completely strange, almost as if it is coming from another Bible. You then become defensive about the truth; you shy away because it sounds strange, never considering that right sounds strange to wrong.

Through various plots and schemes, God's adversaries have attempted to prevent the true worship of God, for without God (the Light), the darkness can remain. For it is in the light that all of the bloodsuckers and destroyers run for cover. They return to their dark holes. They hate light. David in the Psalms said, "The law is the Light." Jesus said, "I am the way, the truth and the light." The light is what allows you to see things clearly without guessing. The light removes the confusion. It allows you to see your way. The light is going to make you see your mistakes. The light will show you the proper path back to God.

The quest for our *true* God, one must realize, is more than a quest for religious identification. As a matter of fact, it has to be removed from the arena of religion altogether, especially since the governments under Euro-theological Christian rulership follow constitutions which call for separation of church and state or religion and government. This is because today's religions are merely socio-political parties. They have an awesome influence on geopolitics, and very little influence on establishing righteous lifestyles for their parishioners. Yet it is absurd to think that one can separate God from government or righteousness from authority. God has to be the thought that produces all substance, because substance can only remain in existence if it is pleasing unto God. It has to be God's (Divine) culture, God's (Divine) political system, God's (Divine) economic system. The first objective is to govern and create in a manner pleasing unto God. Then you will find yourself and your land filled with love and concern for your brother; you will become a Saint, a servant of the people, wanting the best for all the inhabitants of your land and the world.

The world today is openly hostile toward what is right and Godly. No leaders come into office dedicating their lives unto God. Furthermore, they are very careful not to use God's name in speeches, or God's guidelines in planning. It is an adversary approach. World leaders are not equipped with the will, authority or ability to order the fundamental changes required in men's life-style that will prevent the world from becoming a devastated wasteland. To order that change, these leaders would have to acknowledge God and confess this inability to change the course of the world with their own minds. Because of this egotistical mental defect, world leaders refuse to seek the help and the understanding of God. Instead, they have attempted to supplant the need for one another with abundant materialism to give you the missing pleasure of "love ye one another."

Mankind, using its own mind, has failed dismally. This sick world is the result of sick minds. All lands are governed by laws and rules established by the rulers, but God, to whom *all the earth belongs,* does not have even one land governed by His laws.

Law, in the general sense, governs all things in the universe and upon the earth. There is a law that governs man and his relationship to rushing waters; you do not jump into rushing waters because they will sweep you away. There are laws governing man and fire, man and cold, man's body and woman's body. These are God's laws for nature. No man can deny or circumvent these laws and live. Man's attitude of hostility must change to submission unto God, his maker. You must be in the image of God or God-like, which will cause you to like the things liked by God. You will also begin to think like God. For as sons, we must set our goals, to walk like our Father (God), talk just like our Father...as a matter of fact, when one sees the sons, one should see the Father, for we look just like our Father.

Does this sound strange? Well, it should not, for all sons desire to be like their fathers, and we the Sons of God want to be so close to His image until when you see us, you see Him. Our quest for God is the quest for our true culture; our true political system (system of governing and allotting power); our true economic system; the spirit of our art and life. God is spirit, and they that worship Him must worship Him in the spirit and in truth.

The beginning of every substance is thought. Before substance can be manifested there must be thought. Thought is spirit, the unseen, but it does not remain unseen. The thoughts of a man are soon revealed in the substance of deeds which follow those thoughts.

The Euro-gentile gave you the idea of an inferiority complex in your early childhood, even before you could read. Children receive their first worldly images and impressions from pictures. Therefore, before you could read, you opened the Bible, and from the pictures you received your first impression of God and angels, and you have never forgotten what you saw. You saw pictures of a European Jesus on the cross, a European Jesus carrying the cross, and teaching the people on the Mount of Olives. You saw a picture of a European Mary, the mother of Jesus, and you saw pictures of angels in negligees with wings on their backs. You saw many other pictures of Europeans being cast in the surroundings of the Holy Land. As you grew up, you never realized that it was those childhood thoughts of Euro-gentiles as God that started you on the path of attempting to prove yourself worthy and acceptable to Europeans. He has portrayed himself as God having both your future and your destiny in his hands.

They kept those pictures (thoughts) before you all of your life, everywhere you went, in every store, in every home, and on almost every wall of your church. Now you even feel offended when someone suggests that the pictures be taken down and destroyed. When someone mentions the racist connotation of these pictures to European Christians or others, the favorite answer is "God doesn't have any color." And, worse yet, he turns around and implies that the one who raises the question is a racist.

Why is it that the problem of race only enters the picture when we begin discussing positive Black images? How could it be that all of these artists have had such a vivid imagination of all those characters being European, but none of them have ever imagined that those African Hebrews in that African land (Israel) were Black?

Yet had we known, as youngsters, or when we were still projecting an image of ourselves as "bad" or invincible, we would have accepted, in fact *loved,* being considered like God, Jesus or men of God. Instead, we rejected any implication of being Godly: to be righteous or Holy was sissy or weak, not manly and acceptable.

All of those great errors had their origin in European religious dogmas, which include the Ham curse, the belief that the Old Testament has been fulfilled, and the presentation of false images.* Then, it should not come as a surprise that as the nationalistic spirit is kindled in the young, they feel that they must deny God in order to continue the struggle. When someone appears, telling the young the truth in God, they relate the word "God" to the European dogmas, not knowing that they have only heard the word "God," but have not been taught the truth in God. This is the path of despair which religion, in the manner which it has been handed down to Africa by Europeans, has led us. For you have gone out to war my son, but you have taken the wrong banner.

> *"Then shall ye return and discern between the*
> *righteous and the wicked, <u>between him that serveth</u>*
> <u>*God*</u> *and him that serveth <u>him not.</u>"*
>
> **Malachi 3:18**

The time for the fulfilling of that prophecy is *right now.*

Even the winged angel is a stereotype, created for deceptive purposes, so that you would not recognize the true angels when they come *walking* up to your door. In the original Hebrew text an angel was, and is, merely a messenger. In Hebrews 13:2 we read:

> *"Be not forgetful to entertain strangers: for thereby*
> *some have entertained angels unawares."*
>
> **Hebrews 13:2**

Now can you imagine entertaining someone with two big wings on his back — unawares!! My brethren, it is high time that you come to your senses! The time is now to realize who the true deliverers of God's word are. How can this generation of vipers, being evil, speak of good things? That is to say, how can those who are doing everything against God be teachers of the worship of God? "Religion" in some form exists in three-fourths of the world. There are entire countries and societies identified with a specific "religion." Yet, "religion" as we are taught it by the Euro-gentiles (Roman Catholicism and all of its "Protestant" offspring) has yet to come close to producing a righteous society, or even a righteous state, city or community...nay, not even one *individual.* The entire Euro-gentile world is characterized by corruption, immorality and greed; it is plagued by

---

*It is widely accepted that African people are "the cursed seed of Ham." Yet this evil and racist cornerstone of Euro-gentile doctrine has absolutely no basis in truth. Go ahead!...Check your scriptures!

terrorism and other forms of violence, and is beset by confusion and chaos, while the nations and cultures of the the so-called "developing" world rush toward "westernization" as rapidly as their economies will allow. Yet, surely by its fruits we must discern that the Euro-gentile world is completely wrong.

I bring your attention to the state of today's world only to remind you that all human activities can be traced to man's culture: Culture, it has been said, is the barometer used to measure and determine a man's past, present and future. It touches every facet of man's life — either directly or indirectly. It is what distinguishes man from all other species of life on the planet. And the roots of culture are to be found in religion. Yet we can look separately at the numerous facets of culture (education, music and dance, food preparation and consumption, etc.) and see just how far from the quest for God we have gone astray.

Education today is based upon class, aimed at attaining power and fulfilling materialistic desires rather than providing a service to our fellow man. When so-called "higher education" is attained, the recipient is often left with a false sense of boastful arrogance and it leaves a vacuum in his relationship with his people. He is no longer able to socialize with his own people. European education leaves many cold — outwardly and inwardly. When you lose contact with your people, you lose contact with your very soul and the source of your strength. Happiness among the families of those who have attained "higher education" is virtually unknown. A perfect example is the suicide rate among Black American professionals. This rate has increased overwhelmingly in the last decade. The divorce rate among Black Americans, whose relationships with each other were once rooted in the strong African family traditions, is among the highest in the world. An amazing seventy-five percent of those who marry end up divorced. And, no doubt, many of the marriages of the remaining twenty-five percent are held together only because children are involved.

Two of the most coveted professions in contemporary society, that people clamor to partake of — medicine and law — are filled with some of the most immoral and unethical practices known to man. Today's courts and legal systems are a joke. How well you are represented in court depends upon how much cash you can raise. Black Americans comprise over seventy-eight percent (1,110,000) of the population in America's inadequate prison facilities. Only twelve percent of that number are people who can possibly be called "criminals." The other sixty-six percent are victims of inequitable social systems, unscrupulous lawyers and racist judicial systems.

If you have been in a situation which required a lawyer and court proceedings, then it was certainly one of the worst experiences in your life! The present court backlogs are unbelievable; sometimes it takes years before a case is closed. During that time your pockets have been thoroughly gleaned. It is a system built around creating a need for the large number of lawyers turned out of the educational institutions yearly. Thus, through continuances, appeals and retrials these lawyers are kept employed, making a business out of the delaying and denial of "justice."

The lawyer is not the only "professional" trained to swindle the public. Little did you know that once you fill out the card in your doctor's office, that he intends for you to become an active, lifetime clinic member. Like his unscrupulous brother the lawyer, whose intention is *not to keep you out* of the legal problems, *but in them*, the doctor proceeds to systematically treat you in a manner which will require you to visit his office for further treatment! Then, in many cases, operations are performed and drugs dispensed which are neither required nor desired. Being educated by the same system, the doctor and the lawyer possess the same spirit. They use identical unethical methods to keep their practices flourishing. Add to this the fact that the American educational system teaches little of how to prevent illness and maintain health, leaving the average person to be victimized by these scheming practitioners. So it starts with the system; is passed on to your "professionals" who, in turn, pass it on to the people. When the blind lead the blind, they all pay the price, for they all fall into the pit.

Unless you return to a life of righteousness, your life will be consumed with darkness and ignorance as you foolishly plunge deeper and deeper until the ultimate — death — befalls you. Since, as it is written "God is a God of the Living," then it stands beyond a doubt that His entire message would be centered around teaching you how to live. In addition to that, He taught you how to love, respect and honor Him. This is termed worship. Also, He taught you how to love and respect thy fellow man as thyself. This has been the message of the Creator of the Heavens and the Earth since the beginning, but the old devil has so confused and deceived everyone with his teachings of untruths until even the simplest things of God appear complicated. The next question that arises is, how was the Almighty God to reveal Himself? For that, there is no better place to start than the book of **Genesis 1:26,27:**

> *"And God said, Let us make man in our image, after our likeness and let them have dominion over the fish of the sea, and over the fowl of the air, and over the*

cattle, and over all the earth, and over every creep-
ing thing that creepeth upon the earth.

So God created man in his own image, in the image
of God created he him; male and female created he
them."

Certainly from this we can discern that this is the manner in which we were to see God. You were to see Him in those who were made in His image or likeness — His servants. Then we find in **Deuteronomy 18:18**:

"I will raise them up a prophet from among their
brethren, like unto thee, and will put my words in his
mouth; and he shall speak unto them all that I shall
command him."

It was said in **Jeremiah 15:19**:

"Therefore thus saith the Lord, if thou return, then
will I bring thee again, and thou shall stand before
me: And if thou take forth the precious from the vile,
thou shall be as my mouth: Let them return unto you;
but return not unto them."

From this we can certainly deduce that this is the way in which God is to be heard — through His messengers. This you must understand. God has no body, no form; God is a spirit, and they that worship Him must worship Him in Spirit and in Truth. He has created all things, and set them in Divine order. To obey that order is to worship He that set the order. To disobey is to deny God. The men that honored, respected and taught that order are the servants of God, the angels of light. Noah was a servant of God, also Abraham, Isaac, Jacob, Moses, Joshua, David, the Prophets and Jesus. They all had the same message, for to have a different message would be to imply that God the Father has changed. The prophecy states — **Malachi 3:6**:

"For I AM THE LORD, I CHANGE NOT; Therefore
ye sons of Jacob are not consumed."

In the prophecies Isaiah made it clear how to find the servants of God.

"To the law (instructions) and to the testimony: (of
the prophets) if they speak not according to this
word, it is because there is no light (intelligence of
God) in them."

Isaiah 8:20

Now you can see and separate the angels of light from the angels of darkness. Jesus made his relationship to the law and the prophecies explicitly clear when he said, **Matthew 5:17-19**:

> *"Think not that I am come to destroy the law, or the prophets; I am not come to destroy, but to fulfill.*
>
> *For verily I say unto you, till Heaven and earth pass, one jot or one tittle shall in no wise pass from the law, till all be fulfilled.*
>
> *Whosoever therefore shall break one of the least commandments, and shall teach men so, he shall be called the least in the kingdom of heaven: But whosoever shall <u>do and teach</u> them, the same shall be called Great in the kingdom of heaven."*

As you read those instructions from the *Old* as well as the New Testaments, ask yourself, where did the *great lie* start that said the Old Testament had been fulfilled, and there is no longer a need to read or study the contents any more? Without it as your foundation you made yourself a prey for the devil to deceive. Even today, it is common Euro-Christian theological teaching, and therefore Christian thinking, that the Old Testament has been fulfilled. The teachers of darkness are afraid of the law and the prophecies, for they are the light; they are the essence of what is required to set man on the path and show him the way back to his Maker.

The Europeans have destroyed the ancient wisdom of African theology and the vision of African people. They have plotted this through religion, television, movies, pictures, and by presenting positive images of themselves (men landing on the moon, flying airplanes, space adventure, etc.), and presenting negative images of African people (cannibalistic, uncivilized, cowardly, etc.).

Africa was a powerful land whose people had tremendous faith in God prior to 1555 (when the first slaves from Africa reached America) for it was Black African brothers — Moses, Jesus and Mohammed — who set the tone for the basis of the three major religions of the world today: Judaism, Christianity and Islam. The truth concerning this matter cannot be found in the history and religious books of Europe or America. These Black men's intentions were to save first their people and afterwards they would evince a Holy people unto the world, in accordance with the will of God and prophecy. Their attempt to establish a righteous nation coincides with the Plan of God.

Even today, higher ideals and a better way of life cannot properly be defined unless one has a contrasting, flourishing manifestation of the progress achieved outside of the confines of what is termed "a society based on higher ideals." It is the same with moral values and principles. One can never define or censor the effects of homosexuality in the community or nation until one finds a community free of it and its corruption. One cannot speak authoritatively on the issue of establishing a nation, founded upon the principles of the laws of God, and emphasizing the intrinsic moral values and obligations, unless one has found an example of a people redeemed, progressively expanding, and excelling through the adherence to the laws and statutes of God, who is the spiritual ruler of that nation.

This plan began with Moses bringing the Children of Israel out of Egypt to make them a Holy nation which would be a light unto the gentiles. The objective was to establish a nation governed by the laws of God that the world would see the benefits of righteous living. The gentile adherents to ancient Christianity understood the same opportunity existed for them that through the adherence to the teachings of Jesus, they could establish that nation which would *spiritually* be Israel and thus become the light of the world.

It was that same spirit that prompted Mohammed to inspire the Ishmaelites to be that chosen people. All of these men knew what had to be done; there had to be a standard of Godliness to be a light unto the nations. Mohammed, and the early gentile Christians, knew that the Spiritual Magna Carta had passed from the hands of ancient Israel and that they were given a historical season to assume the role of the Chosen People of God. Needless to say, they all have failed to produce a righteous people who were Moses-like, Christ-like or Mohammed-like.

Mohammed is referred to in some religious circles as the last prophet. Whether he was or not is of little significance, but one fact does stand, and that is that he was the last of the great African scholars to understand this ancient wisdom and attempt to apply it to a nation for fulfillment. After Mohammed came the Dark Age, the age when the power of the Word of God lay quiescent. The Holy writings were making their way into Europe where they would undergo the great transformation. Men of evil purpose took possession of these High, Holy and Sacred writings and changed the Truth of God into a lie as the Era of the Great Deception began. This era ended only with the coming of the Kingdom of God.

Now in these, the days of the Kingdom of God, success has come and nations without God will be obsolete by comparison, and eventually extinct. In our quest for God, we are instructed in the prophecies to seek the old paths in order that we may find the right way. We must halt and remove ourselves from this path which is defined as progress by this world, for progress in this world is regress unto God.

Therefore, when the world says we are regressing, then we are progressing unto God. It is the same when the world says you are foolish: unto God you become wise, or those classified as bad guys by satan are the good guys unto God. Do you think that you can be classified as a righteous soldier in the army of satan, and at the same time a righteous soldier in the army of the Lord? The friends of God are inimical to the world!

We have tasted what the world defines as wealth, but we have lost all of the former wealth which we possessed as a people. The inherent feeling of closeness is gone; to talk of helping your own is as if we are talking of complete strangers. All of our national wealth has been destroyed or stolen, even the mother, father, sister and little brother have been bargained away. Let us confess. We made a bad deal; it is time to regroup, take account of our losses, and cry out unto God...never again!

As we start the journey back, we will find our people clothed with ungodly lifestyles, symbols and perverted Euro-gentile wisdom. There has to be an undressing piece by piece until we arrive in Genesis naked (innocent) and pristine before God, that He may redress us in Holiness.

A primary area to begin with is our culture, specifically dance and music, for rhythm and movement are inherently in our soul. Do you recall reading in history books and sometimes viewing in movies how the African and American Indian danced — sometimes until they were totally exhausted? We could not comprehend what was taking place because for us, dance was the ego-tripping, all-night party.

Beyond that, the performing arts meant very little to us. An African that could not relate to dance was like a soul without spirit. (Dance was formerly synonymous with Africa). At its inception, it was a magnificent expression of African creative genius; it was first and foremost a form of prayer through Divine and Holy movement. The first dance was entitled "Praise ye the Lord" (Hallelujah). After this form of expression was accepted, there came the dance (prayer) for strength and understanding. There were prayer dances for the seasons of harvest, planting and the rains, for births and marriages, all a continuation of praise for God. Dancing in Holiness was a part of our soul expressions of thanks unto God.

How did we as a people get so far from the realization that the worship of God is an entire way of life, from the performance at your theatre to the painting on your wall? Everything that we do and create has to reflect the righteousness of God. There cannot be one entity that escapes, not the hair on your head nor the clothes on your back. The "I believe" and "just have faith" era has ended. Divine creative genius of the "God Mind" has to be seen throughout our land. Our dance has to once again become prayer and praises. Dance a prayer for strength for the warriors, understanding for the leaders, and love for the sisters. Let God see His image and mind lifted up among the people.

> *"Praise him with the sound of the trumpet; praise him with the psaltery and harp.*
>
> *Praise him with the timbrel and dance; praise him with stringed instruments and flutes.*
>
> *Praise him upon the loud cymbals; praise him upon the high sounding cymbals.*
>
> *Let every thing that hath breath praise the Lord. Praise ye the Lord."*

Psalms 150:3-6

Music is much more than a form of entertainment; music identifies races, nationalities and communities. It has far-reaching, hypnotic effects on the brain and soul, and can take complete control of the body and mind. Music can determine the mood of a person or a people. After comprehending its profound effects on the mind, it stands to reason that we must beware, for the effects can be good or evil. Music is like a series of thought waves that cause men to think and do right or wrong, wise things or foolish things. In addition to that, there are sounds that destroy ear drums, shatter light bulbs, and crack glass. We must also ask ourselves: is there a mode or musical sound that can destroy the mind? The answer is certainly yes. Furthermore, there is the mind of the musician whose thoughts are transmitted through his music. Let us examine this point more thoroughly, using "popular, club and rock" music as an example.

Many entertainers are admitted homosexuals. The performers use explicit references to sex, drugs, perversion and other wickedness. Popular music lovers have their own way of dress, language, food and life-style. It can be said that a new culture has been created. Now the question must be asked: if many entertainers are self-proclaimed homosexuals and fornicators, then how much of their homosexuality and fornication is transmitted in their music? The creation and proliferation of such dances as the "da' butt," "sperm," "freak," "dog," and the "snake," answer the question. A large amount! Now consider: all of the aforementioned were created and are controlled by a musical sound.

"In the beginning was the Word, and the Word was with God, and the Word was God."

St. John 1:1

"And the sons of Aaron, the priests, shall blow the trumpets; and they shall be to you for an ordinance forever throughout your generations.

And if ye go to war in your land against the enemy that oppresseth you, then ye shall blow an alarm with the trumpets; and ye shall be remembered before the Lord your God, and ye shall be saved from your enemies."

Numbers 10:8,9

"And Moses sent them to the war, a thousand of every tribe, them and Phinehas the son of Eleazar the priest, to the war, with the holy instruments, and the trumpets to blow in his hand."

Numbers 31:6

There was a sound with God in the beginning; all things were made by sound, and without sound nothing was made. From this we know there is creative power in sound, for in Genesis a right sound brought forth life. In order that the people know the importance of sound, God instructed our predecessors to make trumpets to play a certain mode of music for the assembling of the masses. There was also a special music played when it was time to go to war. God evolved the entire success over evil forces around a sound, as He commanded our fathers to play a certain sound if they were under oppression by their enemies. When this sound was heard, He would hear, strengthen and save. Will God not keep His word? Have our musicians considered the true spirituality of music? Have they all gone astray? Are there none that understand? Should we not at least apply this ancient wisdom in our struggle for freedom? There are those of evil intentions that are constantly searching the scriptures and manipulating the contents and using these same instructions against us. Let us reflect on the history of the U.S. Cavalry in their wars against the American Indians.

Do you recall (if not, review some of the history books on the subject, or view some of the old movies), there was always a trumpet (bugle) player in every company of soldiers? The bugler blew the trumpet (bugle) for calling assemblies, time to get up, time to lie down, meal time. He even had a tune for solemn moments (taps). But more significant than all of those was when it was time to go to war against their enemy. The sound of the trumpet preceded the battle. He blew a certain musical sound and they charged forth and fought with unexpected strength and skill; and they won. When the trumpet player fell, fear gripped the soldiers as if the victory would not come. Up to now, you no doubt thought that this tactic was their own clever invention, never understanding that they had read, believed and applied this ancient wisdom against their enemy exactly as it is written in the Law of God.

In our quest for God, we must bring forth a righteous sound upon the instruments; we must halt the onslaught of music that weakens and destroys. The musicians have forsaken God and the people. They no longer understand their responsibility is not only to entertain and uplift, but also to educate their audiences and our people. The music has to make demands on the people and give them vision. We cannot allow the present, nonsensical satan-worshipping trend to continue (as in Led Zeppelin's *Stairway to Heaven* that when played in reverse is "I Live for Satan"). There once was a time when you had to play a record backwards to discern many hidden satanic messages. But today one only has to go to the record bin and pull out the liner notes to see and read blatant references to satan worship.

When our fathers went out to war against the Midianites, they were accompanied by a group of musicians with Holy instruments, including the trumpet for the priest. They lifted up a special sound unto God and they were delivered. The African applied remnants of this ancient wisdom as he played music for the warriors, and the Chinese used a frightening sound as they attacked during the Korean War. With the social and political awareness movement that developed worldwide in the 1960's there was a mode of music which accompanied and complemented it (*Rivers of My Fathers* by Gil Scott-Heron). The music reflected our predicament and our demands. We now find ourselves in this the "Decade of Decision," clothed with a strange sound that causes our people to do strange things. Blacks have once more fallen victim to the deceitful use of words. There has been a conspiracy against Black people, perpetrated through a musical transformation. The message of Black music had to be destroyed because of its strength and vision. Music is a part of our very soul and spirit; therefore it would have to be utilized and manipulated by any enemy attempting to control our minds and guide our destinies. As we begin our search for the quintessence, let us consider some of the problems and changes that will have to be made.

One disturbing phenomenon occurring in today's music is the existence of what is known as "crossover" music. "Crossover" is a commercial term used to denote that music from one culture, (e.g. European-styled rock) has consumer appeal to another cultural group (e.g. Black teenagers). In the name of sales, African jazz and reggae artists "water down" their music so that it will have crossover appeal to the larger, more affluent European and American listening audiences. While the practice may be successful in generating broader popular acclaim, it ultimately results in the destruction of African cultural music. In the end we find that the African musician/artist has sold his soul!

We must correct the modern terminologies used to describe our forms of music, for in many instances the terms are very misleading. It is imperative that the original names be understood and revived. The original name for what we call the Blues was the music of Lamentations. The original name for church music was Gospels or the Songs of Zion. The original name for what is now called Jazz or Modern Jazz — you may be shocked to know — was Spirituals or the Spiritual. Soul music has held its original name but is completely foreign in its content. Music of unrighteousness is based upon creating mistrust, arousing wanton, sexual desire and making wickedness appear pleasant (*Sexual Healing, Part-time Lover, Thigh Ride*). Our once pure, creative musical expressions — full of healing power and spiritual strength — have become adulterated, been made ungodly and are therefore, in their present form, useless in the struggle for righteousness (quest for God).

First and foremost, we must ask, how did Soul, Gospel, Lamentations, and Spirituals get separated? That is to say, who separated Soul music from Spiritual music or Songs of Zion from Lamentations? Once they were all one in purpose and intent. Know ye not that a house divided against itself cannot stand? How can you separate the soul and spirit, which are both necessary for our life, and still expect to live? So now they have fallen victim to a strange spirit and are at war with each other. Furthermore, how did Soul music become *Who's Making Love To Your Old Lady*? How did Soul music get to be *What's Love Got to Do With It?*, *Between the Sheets*, *The Freak, Pull Up to My Bumper Baby*, and assorted sexual moans and groans set to music? How did the Blues become *Living Together in Sin, I*

*Was Checking Out While She Was Checking In, Back-stabbers, Cheatin'
In the Next Room?* Originally the musician was to be a priest unto his
people. His purpose was not for ego-tripping or gross commercialism, but
was to keep God's love and the magnificence of His creations in the minds
and deeds of the people. Instead, through his music he creates hate and
lust, suspicion and distrust. He has allowed himself to be used to sow the
seeds of discord among the people. He is today possessed with a foreign
spirit, the same spirit which has as its latest musical creation, "Punk Rock"!

Soul music, Spirituals, the Songs of Zion (the Gospel) and music of
Lamentations were, in their pure form, all the same, but with a distinguish-
ing rhythm and manner of deliverance. Soul music in its pure form was the
expression of our soul: music of God and His creation, without necessarily
using the words "Lord," "God," and "Saviour." Examples such as "When I
see the trees and feel the rain upon my face, it is assuring to me that I have
a place" and "Let us walk by the riverside hand in hand, talking about love
for our fellow man," or "For pure love, no price is too high to pay," come
into mind. It required a nice voice and good vocal harmony with a back-
ground group in many instances. It was the music of the lively parties and
social gatherings.

The Songs of Zion, the Gospel (church music), were those songs in
which we used the words "Lord," "God," or "Savior" and related directly
to the Holy places, Biblical characters and events. This continues to be
reflected in the very popular music form reggae, which has its roots in the
West Indies. In fact many of the lyrics of reggae music are taken from the
Bible. The Songs of Zion and reggae music are both the fulfillment of
prophecy as seen in the reggae group The Wailers' rendition of *By the
Rivers of Babylon* (Psalms 137: 1-6): *"By the rivers (people) of Babylon
(America and Europe) there we sat down, yea we wept, when we remembered (sang) of Zion (Israel). We hanged our harps upon the wil-
lows in the midst thereof. For they that carried us away captive required of us a song; and they that wasted us required of us mirth
(merriment) saying, sing us one of the Songs of Zion. How shall we
sing the Lord's songs (the Gospels) in a strange land? If I forget thee
oh Jerusalem (not sing about thee), let my right hand forget her cunning. If I do not remember (sing of) thee, let my tongue cleave to the
roof of my mouth; if I prefer not Jerusalem above my chief joy."*

Now, allow me to briefly explain the above verses. First of all, these
verses are talking about *singing, the songs, and manner of deliverance.*
The first verse states we wept when we sang the songs of remembrance.

It made us regret our former deeds, which had caused us to be enslaved in a strange land. Next, our captors loved to hear us sing these songs about our God and our land; even they enjoyed its uniqueness and moving connotations. Last, it was asked how we should sing in a strange land. And we answered, *"We'll sing about Jerusalem, Jericho, the Jordan, Zion, our Land!"* Now just consider the manner in which the gospel is sung. Is it not the music in which, more often than not, there is something that makes you cry, moan or shout? Up until now, no doubt you have wondered why. And is it not in a class of its own in uniqueness? Are not virtually all Gospel songs about Jericho, Jerusalem, Galilee, the Jordan, our Land **ISRAEL**?! The Gospel in its pure form was our collective plea for understanding, mercy and forgiveness. It was to keep our hearts and remembrance on our Land, Israel (...if I forget thee oh Jerusalem...) and to keep alive our hope to someday return there. And so we sang, "I want to walk in Jerusalem just like John," "On Jordan's stormy banks I stand and cast a wishful eye to Canaan's fair and pleasant land, where all my possessions lie." And if that is not enough, then just ask yourself, *who* is it that brought the Gospel (Songs of Zion) to the world? Father, how did we forget?

Music of Lamentations or "Blues" was the music relating to the struggle and our captivity. They were properly called "The Lamentations" because they spoke of the long, hard days in the fields, the pain and the suffering. They were unique in that, to sing the "Blues" one did not need to have an outstanding voice. The songs and their deliverance were truly a lament, but the slaves loved it because just about anyone could sing them. Often the song would only be accompanied by a harmonica and it was usually right to the point in its deliverance (lyrics). For example, "I'm so tired," "I done cried so long," "Mother, if I could just see you again," "I worked all day, then he don't gimme no pay."

What is presently called Jazz and Modern Jazz music is a poor attempt to negate and overshadow the original "Spirituals" which were created by the African Hebrew slaves. The use of the term "modern" (jazz) to describe this once highly spiritual form of music is to beguile us into thinking that whatever direction the music takes is "progressive" and that you are lagging behind or not progressing if you do not keep up with whatever trend is being set. The current products of Jazz and Modern Jazz have become ungodly. The so-called Jazz musician of today has become commercially motivated and is producing tunes with such titles as *Sitting On the Slop Jar* (by Donald Byrd), *Bitch's Brew* (by Miles Davis), *Filthy McNasty* (by Horace Silver), and *God Made Me Funky* (by the Headhunters) not to mention the host of other non-spiritual themes. Jazz was once considered

"Black classical music" relating in its original form to the universal sounds and natural rhythms found in our nature. Modern Jazz has merged with other forms of "popular" music, such as Rock, and Rhythm and Blues producing what has been termed "fusion" music. *Con*-fusion would be more exact. The Spirituals (Jazz-Modern Jazz) in its pure form, was music relating to the sounds found in God's creation using a minimum or no words to express these higher forms. It attempted to capture the sounds of nature and to keep us in the knowledge that we were a part of the universe and all living things. It made us feel and put rhythm into everything we did. When we worked, we would always find the rhythm, often chanting as we moved in time, making our task much easier. We cleared land, picked cotton, laid rails by the rhythm. We walked, danced, sang, spun tales by the rhythm. Then, as now, rhythm and music were a part of our soul, our spirit, our essence, our very existence. Spirituals were performed upon instruments made from various elements of nature. The term "Spiritual" was originally applied to this natural music based on the fact that it depicted the dynamic world of the ear — the unseen: no words, only sounds. What was being portrayed was all left to the minds and imaginations of the listeners.

Indeed, our music was likened unto the song of Moses; only he could sing it. No one could sing or play our music but us. It was a special soul communication. It was a special means of relating our feelings and experiences to one another. It formed a sacred bond between us — keeping us together as a people — through time and across distance.

Our history and the phases through which we have passed in our lives are in our music. The institutionalized history books about Black slavery mostly center around George Washington Carver and Booker T. Washington. It was like nobody else existed. We had no widely recognized folk heroes in any books or films, ever. Yet, in fact, our history is locked into our music, and passed down from generation to generation. A close, truthful examination of our musical history would prove that the slaves knew of and felt Jerusalem and the Holy places to be sacred and that one day they expected to return there (a return from exile). Howbeit, it was the cunning slave master, after realizing this relationship, who mythicized these places and put them in the sky. Furthermore, there are no people that plead and lament in their music like Black people, as if they had made some type of regretful mistake against God and were trying to find a way to make God know their pains and remove their burdens. Our music has kept our eyes and remembrance on our heritage — the Holy Land (Jerusalem, the Jordan, Jericho) Israel. It kept us in constant supplication before our God. It kept us continuously praising His name and His mighty works. During chattel slavery, music was our friend. It has now been made our enemy.

> *"After that thou shalt come to the hill of God,where is the garrison of the Philistines: and it shall come to pass, when thou art come thither to the city, that thou shalt meet a company of prophets coming down from the high place with a psaltery, and a taboret, and a pipe, and a harp, before them; and they shall prophesy:*
>
> *And the Spirit of the Lord will come upon thee, and thou shalt prophesy with them, and shalt be turned into another man."*

I Samuel 10:5,6

This company of prophets with musical instruments was a band of musicians. The mission of a prophet was to speak the Word of God. Thus these prophets, musicians, played the Word of God, the sound of God unto the people. The musicians must understand that there is a direct correlation between sound and the Black mind. Being led by the Word of God, we see that God used musical sound in governing and protecting our fathers. History is now calling for the prophet- musician to come forth and once again "play the Word of God." I know you recall that in Black folklore, the end of the captivity was signaled by Gabriel the angel "blowing his horn." He that has ears to hear, let him hear. Gabriel! Blow your horn, blow your horn, blow your horn!

The quest for God is of the utmost practical and temporal significance. It has nothing at all to do with fantasy or mysticism or the so-called "supernatural" world. The inability of societies today to reflect Godliness (righteousness) in their lifestyles and various cultural activities is evidence of the inability to discern the simple, common-sense essence of seeking God — and worshipping Him in "Spirit and in Truth." For, after all of the profound philosophizing has been done, "Truth" of a surety is merely the right knowledge of reality.

"Supernatural" is a Euro-gentile term and concept originating from the satanic spirit of error and deception. We note historically that original African (and other traditional) peoples held no force "superior" to nature. They knew by the spirit of truth that the works of God (nature) had not been overdone, could not be outdone, and need not be redone.

When we look back and critically examine almost any facet of today's modern society, we readily and plainly see how far off we have gotten in the quest for God. Common sense has been replaced by *uncommon nonsense* and we have been given a concept of God which has not made us Godly. Slave-oriented Christianity and its institutions have made us anything but Christ-like in our attitudes and actions. They have not strengthened our families, increased our brotherly love or inspired our honesty. Indeed, what we have been given has *destroyed and undermined* our sense of what is ethical, moral and "naturally" right.

Do we not surely need to go back to the very beginning, searching it out again, seeking the keys to true righteousness? If we no longer have righteous lifestyles and true culture, then we are set in a continuous cycle which excludes the instituting of Love, Truth, Justice, Mercy, Equity and Peace among men. All that can thus be left is the halting of human development and the *eternal damnation* of the race of man on earth. The process of human development is tied fast to the quest for God. When one ceases, the other must halt. We have come full cycle to the point where — if we are to go any further — we must begin again. For, due to the spiritual darkness of today, it is as it was in the beginning and, "...the earth is without form and void..."

The process of human development is another phase of the quest for God. It is the progression of man's upward evolution toward his higher (true God) spiritual nature and is based upon patterns set down in scriptural literature in the primary book of Genesis. The 26th verse of Chapter 1 of these sacred writings reads as follows:

> *"And God said, Let us make man in our own image, after our likeness; and let them have dominion over the fish of the sea, and over the fowl of the air, and over the cattle, and over all the earth and over every creeping thing that creepeth upon the earth."*
>
> **Genesis 1:26**

Thus we see how the God of Creation, during His establishment of Divine Universal Order, brings forth man into a unique and specifically defined relationship to the world — and to the Godhead. Upon further examination, the aforementioned scripture yields much understanding of the true intent of God concerning the true role of man. First, observe that the Creator did not deign to fashion man until the "sixth" day of the Divine creative cycle. Thus, man is not the primary creation. One might easily ask,

"...why, if man was to ultimately be God's highest creation, was he not made first...?"

The answer, through discernment of the scripture itself, becomes obvious. The Creator brings forth a world of *substance* from His unlimited, Universal Consciousness and man, to whom "dominion" over this realm of substance is given, must necessarily be fashioned of *this substance*. For the Godhead, being pure Consciousness, imposed "image" and "likeness" upon a formless void, then, proceeding in orderly fashion, orchestrated these forms into an ultimate expression — man. So that one sees in clear simplicity that the "dominion" given man is based upon *his relationship to* the substance, the physical world of which he is a part. By way of example, we recognize the shepherd as such primarily by his *relationship* to his flock; we recognize the king as such by his *relationship* to his kingdom.

Wisdom would also point out that the specified order of events should not be assumed to be coincidental. The unfolding of the Divine Plan of Creation contains, in the very order and sequence of its steps, keys to the proper (true) understanding of the process of human development (quest for God). For man is fashioned from and brought forth into a world and a universe upon which God has already imposed Divine order. It is not man's task to impose order upon the Creation, but to maintain, reflect and harmonize with this Divine order. "Dominion over" does not infer privilege; rather it confers responsibility upon man.

The understanding of the nature of man's stewardship — his "husbanding" of God's creation — is a fundamental principle governing the success (or failure) of the process of human development. This misunderstanding of the principle of "dominion" is undoubtedly the root cause of much of the dehumanizing behavior and misuse of God's Holy Creation so common among men today.

The important lesson from the scriptural account of man's genesis is this: the "earth" (all of God's Holy Creation) was not made for man, but man was made for the earth. For at his coming it was already in existence. He neither consented to nor advised in its creation.

Just this simple understanding alone can be the basis for a more ethical, more righteous life. In our quest for our true God, everything in our societies must be ethical and righteous. We must have ethical education, ethical music, ethical eating habits, ethical politics, ethical clothing, economics, etc. We must keep God living in the midst of us. He must be a God near at hand, in our every deed. This is our *responsibility* to His Creation. For God is the justice for injustice, the clarity for confusion, the light for darkness — the answer to every question.

As we continue to examine "culture" as the measure of our position in the quest for God, we see great danger for man. Even the way he eats has become ungodly. Let us view food preparation and consumption at the "highest level" at this stage of mankind's development. Certainly we cannot overlook such an important area of cultural expression as this. I must remind you that *your blood, tissues and all of your organs are made of what you eat.*

Now allow me to quote from *Time* magazine, February 21, 1978. The article is entitled "Cooks Tour: French Kitchen Diplomacy."

> "The tour was the idea of Claude Lebey, food critic for the French weekly *L'Express*. He took with him four of France's leading chefs: Alain Chapel, proprietor of an *esteemed* restaurant in Minnonay near Lyon; Pierre Troisgros, from the *famed* Freres Troisgros in Roanne; Alain Senderens of Paris' L'Orchestrate; and Michael Guerard of Eugenie- Les-Bains. [Emphasis by author]
>
> Lebey and his culinary gang of four began their tour in Hong Kong with a brief primer in pre-Maoist cuisine that included such wonders as bears' paws and snakes skinned live at the table and plunged into boiling water.
>
> Then the chefs moved on to China itself. There the touring chefs were also treated to some unusual delicacies. `You have arrived at the best part of the season for dog,' they were told by their eager host in Nanking,... `so that is what we have prepared for you.' What followed was an example of the Chinese practice of building special banquets out of sundry variations from one animal: dog soup followed by dog cutlets (which tasted said one chef, `like young lamb'). Although the dog banquet was a success — Guerard and Lebey both *asked for seconds*. [Emphasis by author]
>
> The climax came at an 112 year-old restaurant that prepares up to 500 ducks a day. They feasted on jellied duck tongue, deboned duck feet, flattened duck livers and duck hearts..."[3]

At this point I would remind you that French chefs are considered the world's best. Certainly there has to be a new form of "intelligence," for whomever made caviar (sturgeon's eggs), hog guts, brains, groins, veal (unborn calf), etc. "delicacies," truly needs to be *re-educated*!

To seek and serve a Living God, a man must maintain a living body and mind, fed with the life-giving "live" foods: the fresh fruit, green vegetables and "herbs of the field" diet which God gave to original man.

The blood and organs of the flesh of dead animals can only produce its counterpart. The calf livers, dog cutlets, and bear paws you eat today will also be your blood, organs and thoughts of tomorrow. This realization makes it easier to understand much of the madness and self-destruction of today's societies of death; the mention of which leads directly to an examination of today's political systems — which have as their motto, "Get it (power) any way you can and keep it at any price!" The past decade has seen a continuing parade of corrupt leaders, wicked plots and vicious schemes among the governments of the world. From the manipulated 1987 Stock Market Crash to the insider-trading on Wall Street by men like Ivan "the Terrible" Boesky, the Iran-contra rebel arms cover-up of Ronald "Irangate" Reagan, the murderous racism of P. W. Botha of South Africa, to the atrocities committed during the bloody dictatorships of Jean-Claude Duvalier of Haiti, Ferdinand Marcos of the Phillipines, and Jean-Bedel Bokassa of the Central African Republic, one could compose an ever- increasing list of vice, greed, corruption, lies and murders.

Leadership worldwide is mistrusted, disrespected, and ignored. Prominent figures fear for their very lives as terrorists stalk the world acting out the hatred, mistrust and doubt of the people with bullet-ridden dramas of death. In what land is there safety? Where can peace be found today? What system do *you* trust? One need not dwell on any one point in the politics of the world, lest the false impression be created that they are not *all* thoroughly corrupt.

There has to be a change, a personal change, a national change and a universal change; this quandary cannot continue. The urgency of our situation requires that we work diligently day and night; we can leave no stone unturned in our quest for God. Since our greatest obstacle on this path will be satan, the arch adversary of God, it stands to reason that we must recognize his character and know his presence.

> *"Now the serpent said unto the woman, Ye shall not surely die;*

*For God doth know that in the day ye eat thereof,
then your eyes shall be opened, and ye shall be as
God, knowing good and evil.*

*And when the woman saw that the tree was good for
food, and that it was pleasant to the eyes, and a tree
to be desired to make one wise, she took of the fruit
thereof, and did eat, and gave also unto her husband
with her; and he did eat."*

Genesis 3:4-6

When we consider carefully the attributes of the devil, we find that he was a liar and master of crafts. He was very convincing in his outward appearance and most of all, he had the ability to make evil or unrighteousness appear attractive.

This last characteristic, beyond a shadow of a doubt, is most profound. He has taken his wicked inventions and most unholy way of life, and made it sought after and desired by all nations. He has certainly deceived the whole world. Test tube babies, after his explanations, appear "progressive." Homosexuality appears as an expression of one's freedom. He has made tying of tubes, vasectomies, hysterectomies, and even uterus rentals (surrogate mothers) very fashionable under the beautiful title "family planning." He now boasts of extending the life-span of those afflicted with cancer ("ye shall not surely die").

The eating of caviar (sturgeon's eggs) is a "delicacy." The consumption of oysters, lobsters, frog legs, martinis, and Johnny Walker-labeled alcohol are signs of "wealth." He has convinced you to prepare early so that you can have an attractive funeral after you die, as if you were going to be able to see it. He has convinced you and your children that mind-destroying drugs will elevate you into the clouds, make you "high" or elevated; that you should enjoy your solar lamp for it is as good as the sun; that everyone will get a cancer anyway, so continue smoking; that the heart transplants and piggyback baboon hearts are possible now for those who continue to destroy their original hearts. Your bridge implants or false teeth are just as good as your originals, so don't be overly concerned about your sugar consumption.

You boast about the mineral-less, vitamin-less, lifeless abundance of food. You are like a drug addict. You are addicted to evil and you love it. Satan is a master at making evil appear attractive. He has made his wicked, decadent, degenerate societies the attraction of the world. Everyone —

from boat people to island people — is trying to get there. I recall a product named Oleomargarine. The advertisement stated "it spreads like butter; it looks like butter, it tastes like butter." In the imitation you have everything that you need, so why bother with the more expensive, real thing? You ate it, no longer concerned that it still was not butter.

You cannot deny the Biblical truth: he made it pleasant to the eyes, and a tree to be desired to make one wise. The educational institutions of the Babylonian (Euro-gentile) world are the standards of learning. No one has considered that these institutions have produced a continuous line of rulers that have overseen the creation of the worst societies, deadliest weapons and chemicals ever known to man, and have led the world on its path of damnation and destruction. The air is gone; the water is gone; the food is gone; love or care for neighbors is gone, and confidence in government is gone. They legislate laws to protect gays and prostitutes. The world's leaders that supply the arms instead of withholding them during a crisis, are the "cream of the crop" from Babylonian (Euro-gentile) educational institutions. These well-educated men represent the teachings and purpose of learning institutions. It is evident that since the chain is unbroken, these so-called academicians could not have proceeded so perfectly on the same path except that they have similar educational backgrounds. How is it possible that no one has escaped this dreadful fate? Do the curriculums of these institutions teach and prepare the way to salvation? Obviously not! Have we forgotten that the transformation of man and society comes through education? We can therefore conclude that the transformation of the world is a result of improper education: in the final analysis we all do what we are taught.

It was through education that you were taught to accept homosexuals as normal. As a matter of fact, it would not be overly exaggerated to say that you lost your children, your family, your history, your race and even your life in the classroom. I conclude with this acknowledgment: you are now top students in the schools of sin... "And the serpent said unto the woman, Ye shall not surely die..." **(Genesis 3:4)**

> *Wherefore do the wicked live, become old, yea, are*
> *mighty in power? Their seed is established in their*
> *sight with them, and their offspring before their eyes.*
> *Their houses are safe from fear, neither is the rod of*
> *God upon them. Their bull gendereth, and faileth*
> *not; their cow calveth, and casteth not her calf.*

> *They send forth their little ones like a flock, and*
> *their children dance. They take the timbrel and harp,*
> *and rejoice at the sound of the organ. They spend*
> *their days in wealth, and in a moment go down to the*
> *sheol.*
>
> *Therefore they say unto God, Depart from us; for we*
> *desire not the knowledge of thy ways. What is the*
> *Almighty, that we should serve him? and what profit*
> *should we have, if we pray unto him?*
>
> *Job 21:7-15*

The arch adversary of God has convinced men that you receive the benefits anyway, that is to say, without paying homage or worshipping God. Man has been deceived into believing that to abandon God's way of life makes no difference. This too has been a part of the plan. In America, the normal life expectancy of a Black man is sixty years; for a Black woman it's sixty-five. Everyone lives that long, whether he is pious or wicked. Mankind has cunningly made it seem as if they improved or extended man's life span, therefore they feel greatly blessed. Everyone gets cancer, diabetes, venereal disease, heart attacks and also share equally all other illnesses. The wicked have large homes, positions of power and authority; their children are honored. The wicked enjoy the good life and just like the supposedly pious, they die. Certainly to the natural eye, everyone is being treated the same. So by this he has shown, without necessarily saying it, that we are all the same; there are no benefits forthcoming from your service to God. They have not greatly erred, for until the resurrection of God and the establishing of a New World Order, the benefits shall not come forth. For prophetically, God hates this present world for satan is the prince of this world. To receive the blessings of God, you will have to come out of the present world, for it is a world without God.

> *"And in the days of these kings shall the God of*
> *heaven set up a kingdom which shall never be*
> *destroyed; and the kingdom shall not be left to other*
> *people, but it shall break in pieces and consume all*
> *these kingdoms, and it shall stand forever."*
>
> *Daniel 2:44*

God has established a Kingdom from which His blessings will go forth to present an alternative to the present-day wickedness. You must be partakers of the Kingdom of the Resurrected God in order to implement His laws and carry out His instructions, and thus find perfection and experience everlasting life. Men will begin to see with their own eyes the benefits of serving God. Cancer will disappear, and so will all other ailments. Life spans will first be comparable to those in the book of Genesis, then on to everlasting life. Love of neighbor, trust of brother, collective concern for one another and a host of other Godly attributes will make the New World a utopia. The things which you have been taught to accept as normal (sickness, death) are abnormal, but without the normal you have no way of knowing. So Lucifer told the woman, "Ye shall not surely die" — that is to say, not any sooner than anyone else.

Returning to the traditional pre-European educational roles of our grandfathers and grandmothers is not as outmoded an idea as we would imagine. To survive, we must mend the family structure. That is going to involve much more than we can imagine, considering the state of things today. The plight of the African American family is second only to the plight of the Black race. Whether we acknowledge it or not, most families are in serious trouble: mounting divorce, premarital sex, drugs and unwed motherhood. No family has escaped. The only question is how deep the pain; how much the suffering? The problem is already at the crisis stage; something has to be rethought. The price we have paid far supersedes the returns we have received. If we are to succeed in this awesome task, we must have a clear understanding of the problem. What is missing? The two missing elements are *authority* and *order*. Everything has to have order. Waste is the rule where disorder reigns. Where you have no order in your day, you waste your time; no order in your meals, you waste your food; and where there is no fiscal order, your money tends to get away from you. Everything seems to be negatively affected by disorder. In the family without order, the man has lost his woman, the woman has lost her man, and the children have lost their parents. The woman decided against being a helpmate to man; the man decided to stop providing for the family; the children decided to stop being little servants to their parents.

There is a proverb that says "the fear of the Lord is the beginning of wisdom." What is this fear of God? It certainly does not mean a continuous nervous state of existence where one stands and shakes all the day long, but it does have great significance when understood. What is actually meant is *the respect of God is the beginning of wisdom.* The respect of God is to give credence to the way He has established His order. The family today seems to be everyone doing what they want to do, when they desire to do it. Every child continuously hears and repeats "this is my life to do with as I please." The impression seems to be that order lessens the freedom. In truth, however, it only takes away that which you should not do and the times when you cannot do that which *is* permissible. Your quest for God is also your quest for the order of your all-important family unit.

God has established an order for the people He created in the world which He fashioned under His dominion. After all, being who He is gives Him the right. That order does not allow for women to be men, nor does it allow men to be women, and children must remain little servants unto their parents. The order of God does not permit children to rule their parents nor justify the existence of perverts. Without order a mentality develops which is in opposition to God and life.

In the beginning God created man from the soil of the earth; woman was fashioned from man, and children were given life by their parents. This order is not oppressive, nor regressive. All that has been required is that each give respect to the source from which its presence was derived. Man, keep your hand in the hand of God; woman, keep your hand in the hand of man; and children, "honor thy father and thy mother that thy days may be prolonged upon the land which the Lord thy God givest thee." To respect God's order is to live. To violate that order is to cause chaos. God, in giving the woman to man, was establishing an order. Woman was made the feminine part of man. There was no need of conflict, only understanding. As man was made a God, she was made a female God or Goddess. When man is made a king, she is made a queen. When man is made a prince, woman is made a princess. Every height, every place, she was always there, for she was him. But God knowing all things, established order to prevent confusion. Authority has always been shared with woman. God revealed His order because woman had to know that to destroy her man was to destroy herself, for she would lose the source of her being.

As we look to and fro now for comfort, we see no queen, for there is no king, for queen is a derivative of king. We see no princess for there is no prince, for she was deceived to believe that she existed without the prince; no Goddess, for there was no God. She knew not that spiritually she and her man were one. She was everything with him, but without him she also lost her glory.

> *"Beware of false prophets, which come to you in sheep's clothing, but inwardly they are ravening wolves. Ye shall know them by their fruits. Do men gather grapes of thorns, or figs of thistles?*

*Even so every good tree bringeth forth good fruit;
but a corrupt tree bringeth forth evil fruit.*

*A good tree cannot bring forth evil fruit, neither can
a corrupt tree bring forth good fruit.*

*Every tree that bringeth not forth good fruit is hewn
down, and cast into the fire.*

Wherefore by their fruits ye shall know them."

St. Matthew 7:15-20

Anyone with eyes can certainly see that the fruit from this modern technological, scientific way of doing things is rotten to the core. The Bible teaches that we will know if we are doing things right by the fruit, or results. How long before we acknowledge our iniquity? Can't you see that we have "bottomed out?" Our conditions are a result of the way we are living. Someone has very craftily substituted a *way of death and damnation* for God's "way of life." We must attribute the fruit to the tree. If the fruit is rotten, then the tree (order of life) is rotten. Undoubtedly, you are blind if you do not see the evil fruit of our race and people.

There has never been a time in history when we were weaker, sicker, and more fragmented. The men are in jail, the women are in lib, and the children are in confusion. We must *swiftly* reorder our lives, change our priorities and restructure our families. This process begins with a return to God. God the Father, once said that He was married unto our people, but we played the harlot by turning away from Him and His instructions. We married a new way of life (death), and it has beaten us to pieces and ground us to dust.

*"And I will not have mercy upon her children; for
they be the children of whoredoms. For their mother
hath played the harlot; she that conceived them hath
done shamefully: for she said, I will go after my
lovers, that give me my bread and my water, my wool
and my flax, my oil and my drink.*

*Therefore, behold, I will hedge up thy way with
thorns, and make a wall, that she shall not find her
paths.*

*And she shall follow after her lovers, but she shall
not overtake them; and she shall seek them, but shall*

not find them: then shall she say, I will go and return to my first husband, for then was it better with me than now.

For she did not know that I gave her corn, and wine, and oil, and multiplied her silver and gold, which they prepared for Ba-al."

Hosea 2:4-8

If there was ever a time when we needed God, it is now. If there was ever a time when we needed to plead unto God, it is certainly now. I can leave no stone unturned; it is doubtful if you, with your head so high in nowhere, even know how to plead.

Let us journey back into our childhood. When you erred in your actions, and your father first entered the room with the belt, you began to talk, trying to get the matter straightened out by confessing very sincerely. But as the blows began to come, you changed from talking to pleading; as the pain increased, you began a wailing, hollering plea; you jumped, sometimes ran in fear. But you kept pleading: "Father, I'm sorry; I know I made a mistake; I was wrong"!! And you always said, "If you just give me one more chance, I'll never, never do that again"! You kept that up until the whipping ended. I repeat: we need to *plead* unto God, our Father, using the aforementioned instructions, and not cease until this terrible whipping has ended.

Once we have made reconciliation with God, then authority has to be reestablished. Authority begins with the African American male. African American men are the number one victim of American wickedness, because it has always been the man who is singled out as the head of the family and nation. To succeed in suppressing us as a people, America had to cut off Black men economically, socially, and spiritually in order to suppress all authority.

According to census reports, there are nearly a million more Black females than males in the 24-44 year-old age bracket, or seven percent more Black women than men. Much of the imbalance can be attributed to the high rate of Black male homicides (the leading cause of death for ages 15 to 35); male infant deaths, which are the highest the first month of life than among other infants; the vast number of Black males who are incarcerated; and the Black accidental death rate which is America's highest. Finally, Black male life expectancy is the lowest of all groups, at age 60.

The first charge of the enemy has been to destroy the authority and stature of the Sons of God in the land of the Great Captivity. The self-destructive war between man and woman has frightened the woman away from returning the authority of the family unto the man. This fear has been the catalyst for the national disunity that permeates the race and which has prevented the establishment of a centralized authority for Black America. All over the world people have a tendency to respect authority. We have no respect, because we as a people have no authority.

Have you ever considered from whence comes the warring and striving between the brethren? Why do you lust and fight one another? Why are you so blind? Is it not that the lusts of the world have possessed you? Remember, when we had so little, we fought less. When we were considered poor, we shared more. When we were considered illiterate, we understood our predicament and the evil master.

The Power to Define

Are men really following their own minds today, or are they following trends and patterns defined by others as *chic, in the know, in style* or *out of style*? Have we always liked to eat hog guts (chitterlings), hog brains and eggs, mountain oysters (hog testicles), neck bones, chicken gizzards (chicken waste sacks) or did these things become an integral part of our diet because some defined them as "soul food?" Have we always felt that the best place for us was a land governed by those who hate us and are guilty of murdering, maiming, lynching, torturing and committing genocide against no less than 40 million of our men, women and children? Or did our patriotism grow because someone continued to define America as a just society that believes all men are created equal? Who defined the land of horrors for Black people as "the best place to be?" Were we born hating Africa, or did we turn aside from Africa after she was defined as a land of cannibalism, poverty, ignorance and backwardness?

To today's rulers, truth is only what and when they officially confirm it to be. All of those who are influenced by these wicked-minded men and who only accept those things which they confirm as true, are foolish puppets. Accordingly, "the powers that be" decide who is a good negro, a loyal negro, and who is qualified to be a leader in the Black community. In other words, the measuring rod used to determine a "good negro" is based on the negro's relationship to the plan and purpose of those who are defining — certainly not his relationship to God, but rather his relationship to the definer's objective.

Therefore, a good negro is good for what today's rulers are doing, and a loyal negro is one loyal in the war against God and God's people. We who have freed ourselves from the Euro-gentile's power to define, define for ourselves, speak for ourselves and name ourselves and thereby control our destiny. History has proven that the good which is relevant to white America is evil unto the Sons of God.

The Power to Define in the hands of evil men is a weapon of oppression and a satanic control method. However, the Power to Define in the hands of *righteous* men will bring forth Godliness, Holiness and Peace. The problem in the world today is that wicked men are being defined as righteous, evil societies as progressive, and the rulership of satan is defined as rewarding. The whole world has been blinded by the Spirit of Err, and does not see evil, nor the source from which it comes. Therefore, satan has sat on the throne until these days of the return of the Sons of God. Evil will be exposed, satan will be revealed, and the plot to destroy all flesh uncovered.

What is the true spiritual significance of the return of the Sons of God? The return of the Children of Israel and the subsequent establishing of the Kingdom of God signaled the end of Euro-gentile dominion over God's creation and people. The Euro-gentile societies or world is off of its axis, reeling to and fro under the mighty hand of God's judgement. There will never be a return to the former prosperity of what was called the "good ole days." The Word of God and the entire planetary force have combined forces to bring about instability, hostility, anxiety and fear in all countries of the world.

The Word of God is the major destabilizer, bringing all evil doctrine into judgement. Nature and the elements are again coming under the rule of the Sons of God. The authority is first meted out in small portions in the season of the test; whereas after showing themselves to be steadfast in Truth and dedication to God, all things will be given back into the hands of the Sons as it was in the beginning. As it is with all things, in these the days of the Kingdom, it will be the spirit that quickens. The blind will not just have their eyes opened to give a sign, neither will the deaf receive vain ears, or the lame be made whole. All things will be tied into their relationship with God. Eyes to see what? Ears to hear what? And a body to do what? Those that come now unto God must believe that He exists and dedicate their lives, after their new birth, unto Him.

All of the major elements are now actively playing a major role in the process of overturning. The volcanic (Mt. St. Helens) eruptions, the cold, the wind, the rain (or lack of it), the heat, earthquakes, economic recession and depression are but a few of the things working against the Euro-gentile world. These are the forces in the army of the Universal Corrective Force. Their presence at this juncture should be seen as a warning to those seeking God, to come out of this world and unite under the banner of the Kingdom of God. Not many will have the vision to recognize the greatness and the significance of this decade that is before us. Then there are those who may recognize it, but will not possess the strength, devotion and dedication toward a righteous cause to stand for the Kingdom of God. There are many who have had the opportunity to receive the truth about God's kingdom and righteousness, but they have chosen to turn away because they did not want to sacrifice and struggle to perpetuate this Truth in God.

> "Enter ye in at the strait gate: for wide is the gate, and broad is the way that leadeth to destruction, and many there be which go in there at:
>
> Because strait is the gate, and narrow is the way, which leadeth unto life, and few there be that find it."
>
> St. Matthew 7:13,14

In this spiritual war there is a creed that says if freedom is ever to be realized, those freedom fighters who dare to challenge a powerful enemy must be equipped with Divine skill and understanding: skill to know how to confront such an enemy, the understanding to know when and where, and the blessings of God Almighty to undertake the task Divinely. The Power to Define — the ability to discern and the will to interpret and implement ideas and philosophies in order to be totally victorious in battle against one's enemy — is the essentiality of spiritual warfare. Those who would be champions of the battle must comprehend spiritual warfare and be prepared to face it and overcome any hurdles. Therefore, in this work I have attempted to convey unto the righteous, God's plan to confront His enemy. Essentially, the righteous, the Saints of God, must be serious about freedom. Moreover, they must understand the network of impediments which hedge up the way to freedom. They must be aware and beware of the many obstacles placed before the Saints of God. For this reason special emphasis is given to the writers and the educators of the Kingdom of God concerning the Power to Define: *the power to direct minds and conditions that will cause specific results in a struggle.* The Power to Define is as important as the power to control. In fact, the Power to Define is one of the greatest weapons that can be used to control men and nations.

The power to define freedom through the doctrines of the writers and the interpreters of the Kingdom of God cannot be placed in the hands of any people other than those Divinely inspired by God. God- inspired men must now seize and control the Power to Define. Prior to the emergence of the Kingdom of God, our enemies monopolized and manipulated our struggle and determined those results they deemed desirable for us. They defined God, salvation, religion, how to be saved, where we were going and how to get there. Your adversary defined the problem and the solution. Yet with the coming of Godly men, a new course has been charted to establish the

New World Order. When we say "New World Order," we mean simply a new arrangement of life-style and purpose, being cycled back unto God and a life wherein Godly principles will rule supreme. You must restructure your mind in order that you may reorder your day, your purpose in God's kingdom, and feelings toward your fellow man.

The order in which things are done may be playing havoc with your emotions, family, pleasures and health; for the order adhered to today was established by men of evil purpose, who had no intentions of working in harmony with the Creator or the created. They have disdained His cycles, rules and guidelines, and have not only cast them aside, but have attempted to destroy them altogether. These men were established by satan to carry out his devilish plot against the Creator, while attempting to supplant God as the supreme authority over the earth and its inhabitants.

The adversaries of God have convinced the world that only they have the answers and solutions, and that without them nothing can be done or accomplished, and if it is, it receives no credibility. It is rebuked, and the individual is scorned and mocked. Consequently, everything based upon truth and righteousness is rejected by the present order of things. This is why the righteous are ridiculed and blasphemed. Therefore, every thesis, invention, discovery or creation must first be submitted to the establishment for approval, and if it is based upon justice, truth, nature or the existence of another authority (God), it is immediately rejected. Not that it is not good, but it is not in accordance with the established order, which satan dictates as the supreme authority. So when we say "New World Order," we call into question the present order in which you do things and value things — from yourself to your friends, even your enemies; from your work hours, play hours, drinking hours, study hours, eating hours and rest hours. Everything in the present order of things must be called into question.

How is it possible for you not to have noticed that the present order is not conducive for the creation of family stability, harmony, mutual trust, love, dedication, good health, and certainly not peace of mind, body, society, neighborhood or home? We must conclude that this world's order is not ideal for perpetuating these principles, virtues or effects.

A new man with a new mind has been created — one who will not bow to the dictates of the system nor fear the threats of the adversary, but one who fears his God and loves his people enough to give his all to save them. It is time now for the righteous scribes who have been reborn and redeemed from the pits of hell to declare the good news that the Kingdom of God has come. It is time for them to take their rightful place as the New World definers, designers and interpreters of ideas and conditions that will be used to teach, govern and guide the New World to salvation, destroying the lies, distortions and influence of the old one. The New World definers are empowered with the ability to chart the course for a New World Order, because they have the sovereign right to name, rename, surname, even nickname every living thing. This right is encompassed in the Power to Define.

In the beginning of time, God bestowed this power upon the Sons of God but because of their distinct violations of His laws or instructions, they forfeited the right to the dominion and authority over God's creation, wherefore the Power to Define descended to the adversaries of the Sons of God.

Reflecting to my childhood and early adulthood, I now see that I was totally oblivious to the wickedness around me. Darkness (ignorance) covered me like a cloud. I was taught to believe that God was something other than a spirit and that He dwelled in some far away place, remote from earth and man, sitting on a throne, observing the works of man on earth. Surrounding Him were angels — women in nightgowns with wings — who descended and ascended between heaven and earth doing God's work. I never contested the authenticity of the Anglo-Saxon characteristics of the angels, or the idea that these flying creatures were a part of God's empire. I never inquired by whose authority God and His angels were defined. It was much later that the realization of the colossal effects these fabrications have had on the world dawned on me.

The Power to Define invested in the hands of the ungodly is terrifying. The defining of right as wrong and wrong as right is *spiritual tyranny.* I recall not too long ago an incident which serves to illustrate my point. A youthful-looking mother strolled into the dentist's office with her son to have his tooth extracted, a tooth which had caused much havoc with his activities at home and studies at school. Moments after his tooth was extracted, she breathed a sigh of relief. Yet, as the mother prepared to leave the dentist's office, she attempted to relieve some of her son's discomfort by giving him a large peppermint stick, adding quickly, "you can't eat this now, you'll have to wait a while."

There is no doubt that this mother desires excellent oral hygiene for her son, but someone had defined for her the "nice things" to give her child. This is a clear case of simply treating the effect while ignoring the cause. As a matter of fact, all her responsibilities as a mother have been defined by the adversaries who desire that her child experience numerous trips to the doctor, dentist, psychiatrist and finally the grave. She, attuned to fitting properly into the world of evil, meticulously follows these instructions and destroys her son's teeth, thereby destroying his ability to masticate his food properly, causing poor digestion, poor elimination, sickness and death — the effects of awful things defined as "nice things" by the "powers that be."

We have now arrived at a time in history when men who stand for God and Truth must manifest the spiritual courage to reexamine and redefine all things according to their relevant place and purpose in God's plan. We must question every facet of existence under Euro-gentile dominion. All things must be brought to the Sons of God as they were brought to Adam, for naming and renaming.

Who defined God as being European? Who defined angels as being women wearing nightgowns? Who defined heaven as a far-off place for the dead and hell as being beneath the ground? Who defined satan as a body-less spirit? Are they not the same ones that sit in the seats of authority and government and say daily that they want peace as they manufacture all of the weapons to "protect the peace?" Are their ways the ways of peace or the ways of war?

> *"Their feet run to evil, and they make haste to shed innocent blood: their thoughts are thoughts of iniquity; wasting and destruction are in their paths.*
>
> *The way of peace they know not; and there is no judgement in their goings: they have made them crooked paths: whosoever goeth herein shall not know peace."*

Isaiah 59:7,8

Have not these men yielded themselves to be servants of satanic principles of selfishness, greed, resentment, envy, competition, jealousy and hatred? These men, the warmongers, manufacture the weapons to feed the disordered systems, while continuing to rule the nations of the world. Those with the Power to Define have made God unreal. They have taken the people far from God and His ways of peace. Even the educational institutions reflect a commitment to adverse standards and principles. They instill attitudes in the minds of the people that perpetuate evil and godlessness.

In the redefining of life under God and justice, men will clearly see that the arms race is an obstruction to peace and that armaments are a prelude to war. There has to be an end to the production of weapons of mass destruction. Man has to be taught the ways of peace, the most important of which will be the total disarming of nations. The educational systems must be developed according to the "God Mind" to enhance life and truth. There has to be a return to lifestyles characterized by simplicity and righteousness, not militarism and destruction.

Modern spiritual worship — religion — is also a fitting illustration of the ruse perpetuated on the world in which right is actually wrong, heaven actually hell. We have been taught that slave-oriented Christianity is the only correct vehicle to explain God. All other religions are false and paganistic, according to European definition. The last word on God, Christian theology, now comes from the Vatican or England's Canterbury, contrary to the prophetic truth that the Laws of God shall go forth from Zion and the Word of God from Jerusalem. As a result of the influence of the Catholic Church, men are worshipping idols — crosses, figurines of Mary and Jesus. Ironically, an African who bows before a fetish idol is defined as profane and unholy. Paradoxically, innumerable Africans abandoned their traditional manner of worship for western religions, exemplifying the forcefulness endowed in the Power to Define. The worshipping of a chalk figure as right and holy, and the worship of a fetish idol as wrong and unholy denotes the confusion brought about by those in power. The promulgation of the belief that a fat man (Santa Claus) delivers toys every December 25th by descending through hot chimneys in every home in the world overnight, clearly illustrates the fabrications taught to us through Christianity. Rabbits that lay eggs during the Christian celebration of Easter is yet another.

The whole world has been deceived. We have been persuaded to believe lies to the extent that our every breath promulgates these falsehoods. Contemporary Christianity has contrarily designated heaven as a mystical, remote place to which one, if he is righteous, ascends after death, when in fact, as it is written in St. Luke 17:20,21, Jesus proclaimed heaven to be a thought within you; a righteous thought or plan that is perceived in the mind first. That is to say that first a picture is formed in the mind and in the final stage is made manifest or brought into existence by works or deeds. Thus, heaven is the reality of the righteous as they live, not a place for spirits after death. A change of consciousness can and will bring about a change of environment. Hell came into existence only after evil possessed the minds of men. Hell today is depicted as a fiery lake of burning flesh, the punishing grounds for the evils committed on earth. As ridiculous as it sounds this is the picture millions have of hell, based on the distorted theology of slave and missionary-oriented Christianity, in order that they not take into consideration that the earth, ruled by the wicked (U.S.A.), unrighteous (Europe), evil (South Africa) and ungodly (Soviet Union), is hell.

Heaven, though, is the manifestation of the Kingdom of God, where life is perpetual. Heaven is the love of one man for his neighbor, the actuality of family as God ordained it and peace for all peoples, harmony between nations. These are the attributes of a heavenly world as opposed to the hellish one in which we now live.

One must be audacious and holy bold to step out into the path of a world that is bent on a course of destruction and proclaim oneself a pioneer for its salvation. It takes even more nerve to say you are the definers, designers, and prophesied governors of God's kingdom and further to say you are God-commissioned to have the wisdom and vision to be its instructors, guides, and saviors. Men of God are not appointed by men to be saviors, prophets, and holy men. Saviors become saviors when they, being God-inspired, realize the need of those crying out to be saved from those who have an unholy command of their soul and future.

One of the first steps in freeing an abused people is to understand what has blocked them from attaining freedom, and crush that obstruction. Six thousand years of experience with the adversaries of God has taught us who the adversary is, and what has been his wicked plan to perpetually enslave the minds and bodies of our people. The adversaries of God used the Power to Define fraudulently, for they feared truth. The revelation of Truth spells their end. Moreover, the adversaries are aware of the reactions of the Saints if they are made aware of the plot surrounding their enslavement. Time and prophecy have run their course and the prophetic enslavement — physical and spiritual — of the Children of God by the enemies of God has ended. The power invested by God into the hands of our enemies, to command and control has now been returned to those anointed and appointed by God. They, by using the true Power to Define, will instruct and guide those of the world who will hear the Word of God. However, as long as our people continue to believe the distorted definitions of the adversary and believe that his motives are beneficial for gaining freedom, then they will remain slaves and dead men.

Thanks and praises to God Almighty for the revelation that the Power to Define must never fall back into the hands of the enemy again. If so, our destiny will also fall into his hands. Now that we again have control of our minds, control of the Power to Define and the foresight to attain the right objectives necessary for our Divine destiny, then the salvation of the world is assured.

The perfect illustration of the deception of the adversary of God is seen in the turbulent revolution of the 1960's. What started out as a revolution *against the oppression of Black people* in America ended up being a revolution *against Black people.* The cries of a people for freedom were cries for true freedom, not an imaginary superficial freedom that the villains would devise. Initially, the adversary was uncertain of what Blacks meant by freedom, because our people were not clearly defining what they expected their freedom to be. Consequently, before they specified their goals, the adversary quickly seized the opportunity to define what Blacks in America were struggling for and when he did, he also determined the means: non-violence. In addition, there was no unity, no objective and no established order or manner to teach the power elite. When the oppressor comprehended the division, he knew what to do. He used his old divide-and-conquer technique to keep the minds of the people void and ignorant concerning their leaders and purpose, until he was able to devise and establish a plan to give them tokens that would symbolize freedom. By keeping the minds of Black America divided and controlled, while simultaneously keeping their thoughts from their identity, Black Americans were lured into accepting the adversary's solution for pacifying them with cars, homes, and jobs — a small return for such a large investment: a car for a man's soul, a home for his heritage, and a job for his freedom.

Since the African American leaders at that time were void of the vision and the Plan of God, they were easily duped by the enemies' scheme to keep African Americans off balance. Therefore, African Americans could not wisely define their objectives and their goals, and were not properly equipped with the know-how to reach the power elite. Every time a positive move developed in the midst of our people, the adversary of God, through his press, his religions and educational institutions, determined how and what was going on, even when it would go on. Immediately he began to declare unto the freedom seekers, as well as the world, the definitions of what the Black struggle was all about. By so doing, the adversary manipulated and took control of the struggle, and determined where it was going and how it was going to get there.

Whenever we begin to formulate anything for ourselves, the world media then labels us Communist, cultish, weird, perverse and criminal. The media creates and controls all images. No matter how many times you deny it or how you fight it, the media controls your minds. The standing order of these villains is scare them, chastise them or kill them. Therefore, the earth's afflicted people must now look to the Kingdom of God for their salvation.

The Kingdom of God has not come in the time of peace; it has come at a time of trouble. The Kingdom of God is the vehicle which will bring deliverance, hope and redemption unto all men. Moreover, it shall break in pieces the Euro-gentile's power to define and through wisdom and determination, will lead the people of God to freedom.

Generally speaking, our people were unaware that there are various forms of freedom within the framework of the Constitution of the United States; for example, freedom of press, freedom of speech, freedom of religion, etc. But freedom not practiced is worthless. What type of freedom were Black Americans striving to obtain? They insisted "We want to be free!" yet there was no clear-cut definition. The adversary, capitalizing on this, cunningly and craftily fashioned a freedom suitable to himself. Thus, he began to delude the masses into thinking that "integration" was synonymous with freedom.

His craftiness worked. Suddenly, everyone began talking about integration. Black people began to think that integration was going to bring them equal opportunity to fulfill their needs and that they would eventually achieve integration into the educational system, the neighborhoods, and the power structure in America, even though in the beginning this was not the purpose of the struggle, nor the objective.

Initially, the masses were not speaking of a materialistic revolution. They were deceived by their own political and civic leaders who deluded the people because they had been misled by their rulers. They fed the lies and deception to the masses. Subsequently, the Black masses, because they had not soundly evaluated what was being told to them by Black leaders, were confused. Thus, the adversary took complete control of their minds and their struggle by using the Power to Define, and consequently derailed the objectives of Black America. At that time Malcolm X proclaimed the struggle to no longer be a struggle for freedom because it had become a circus. Malcolm further stated that the "March on Washington" was a *three-ring circus*. The leaders had sold their people out. Not only did the power structure con us into seeking integration, but also jobs and housing; thus we forgot about freedom. Soon after, one did not hear the talk of freedom but instead "rights": right to live, right to work, right to eat, etc. Suddenly, Blacks were talking about integrating the schools, jobs, busing and money. Thus, the power structure made them believe that freedom, as they defined it, made the "system" their friend and savior.

During the revolution of the 1960's and 1970's, the disorder and division that resulted from not having the defining power caused the true meaning of freedom to be lost. Also lost, early in the struggle, was the desire and willingness to fight. The 1960's revolutionaries thought they were beyond ever becoming slaves again. They were unaware that they were pacified; they were still slaves, but only this time wearing a white shirt and collecting a paycheck. Thus, despite the shackles of slavery having been broken from their bodies, the chains of oppression remained securely in place on their minds. Despite the advancements and gains of a visible few, most of our people were and still are worse off than ever before. This new freedom promised independence but demanded submissiveness.

From that time, the adversary began to make plans and take steps to inhibit any future coordinated activity by the Black masses. Using his Power to Define, he developed the course for future development of the Black mind. As a result, we see no national movement and no national issues of any significance to unite the people. Social and economic issues have supplanted nationalistic aims; nationhood is no longer a goal of Black America. Social stratification has fragmented the move toward the realization of the dream to be free.

Every successful plan is always preceded by a dream or thought, but, unlike those who dream that the answer is in the system, you must learn to be a Divine dreamer and dream Divine dreams. Divine means after the manner of God. He who dreams worldly dreams only dreams conclusions. He never dreams the plan, so consequently when the plan is brought unto him, or tribulation arises because of the plan, by- and-by he becomes offended.

Dreamers of the world dream of when they will live in big, beautiful homes, but they never dream of the days when they have to dig ditches and use the picks and make the bricks and the mortar. Dreamers of the world always see their children running and playing free, but they never see the blood, sweat and tears that are on the path which leads to that freedom. Consequently, when something adverse arises, they become offended and cease the struggle for freedom, and cease to build the house.

Divine dreamers dream beautiful conclusions, but they also dream beginnings so that it is clear to them what must take place in order to arrive at that conclusion. Unlike dreamers of the world, Divine dreamers know the plan, anticipate the obstacles, overcome them by any means necessary and thereby arrive at beautiful conclusions.

Black people in America were so blinded with their inadequate plans and worldly dreams that they did not really know where the non-violent philosophy or any of the other essentialities of their struggle came from early in the 1960's. Blacks were burning and destroying everything because they had no sense of what revolution was or how to achieve freedom. Let us define "revolution." Revolution is to destroy through change. Revolution is an overthrowing; it is the tearing down of evil forces. Revolution is the power to change, lead and determine ways to influence the mind and control the man. When have you ever seen revolutionaries who, after determining who and what the adversary and his system is, fight against it to destroy that system, and after the victory go out and integrate into it? Then they ask, "Why are we not yet free"? Our people are lost for lack of knowledge. They were deceived!

Now is the time to reverse the deception and refuse to partake of ungodly systems which are being destroyed. This is the purpose of revolting in righteousness. The revolution of God is the destruction of everything that is in opposition to God's Master Plan. We, who are revolutionaries on the battlefield of God, must be prepared to pay the price for whatever must be faced or suffered on the pathway to freedom.

Let it be clear that we have taken the Power to Define into our own hands, and the results will be freedom for all men; but we must bear in mind that the road to freedom is like the desert terrain: rough and uncharted, sometimes even to those who know the way.

When the "establishment" began to open certain neighborhoods, jobs and positions, and allow Blacks to integrate, the true flames of freedom were smothered — snuffed out! How did our adversaries determine what we wanted and how we should get it? It is evident that the news media, the educational institutions and the religions were unleashed upon our people to divide their minds and objectives. When they did, the inevitable results came. Our people got snared in the trap of a materialistic revolution which at its conclusion gave them bigger houses, bigger cars and more color televisions, but certainly *less* soul, *no* land and *more* enslavement than ever — only satisfied deception. And still, no freedom.

For this reason there is less participation in the struggle today for freedom. Our people have no interest in the struggle because they have made materialistic gains their freedom. The so-called Black "middle class" work good jobs, receive good paychecks, own big cars, have big television sets in every room, and generally exhibit all the showy manifestations of their so-called new wealth. They see no need to continue to struggle because the adversary has determined and defined for them what these determinations and definitions are, and they are well satisfied. Actually, they are in a trap, spiritually and morally. The spirit of brotherhood, struggle, participation and even the need for your fellow Black brothers has been destroyed. With his newly-defined freedom the middle-class African American is culturally dead, a tool to be used any way the system dictates. His new freedom allows the slave to exist and make a living...but not to live. No one has explained to African Americans what true freedom is or has stirred up the desire in them to be free in God. The 1960's started off as a *reforming* revolution, an overturning, a tearing down of systems, ways and means, yet ended up being a struggle for integration — a materialistic *conforming* revolution that allowed them the privilege to join those who were responsible for their grief and sorrow.

Black America, you, in no uncertain terms, are not free! Allow me to define some of your so-called freedoms. There is something called Freedom of Religion — which really means free to keep as much confusion as possible about God in the minds of the people, to make God abstract. Freedom of Choice — you are free to vote for any of the corrupt officials that are competing, who have all pledged their dedication to the perpetuation of your captivity. You are free to make your choice of which one you prefer to be your own personal tyrant. You are free to participate in politics. You can achieve status in some of the high offices of slave management for "good boys." As a matter of fact, you are free to be anything or anybody you choose — except yourself!

Now it is time to redefine the objectives of the struggle in terms that are clear to all. The New World definers must learn, explain and define clearly to our people what it is that we who are struggling for true freedom are seeking, so they can see clearly that they have not yet achieved it. As long as Blacks think they are free, they see no need to struggle again for it.

The Power to Define: how did it all begin? It began with the prophecy written in the book of **Daniel 7:25:**

"And he shall speak great words against the Most

High, and shall wear out the Saints of the Most
High, and think to change times and laws: and they
shall be given into his hand until a time and times
and the dividing of time."

"He" in verse 25, spiritually and prophetically engulfs the entire structure of Euro-gentile authority, the power which speaks against God. As a
matter of fact, they represent the coming of the anti-God dominion over
God's creation and people. The entire purpose of European authority has
been to challenge God, destroy His people and earth. To accomplish their
portion of this mission, the Power to Define was given into the hands of the
adversaries of God. ("...think to change times and laws: and they shall be
given into his hand.")

In evaluating European dominion, let us look for one non-European
country that is a true friend of Europe. After 400 years of rule, they have
not earned the true friendship of even one country or established one country whose works pay homage to the God of creation. Let the Black slave in
America be the measuring rod. Consider his relationship with white America.
Has white America earned his friendship or have they bought it? Check
the record: his loyalty, servitude, and stewardship is constantly being paid
for, not merited. After 400 years, America is still buying Black talent, not
making Black friends. I pray that you are taking notice that as the money
supply dwindles, there will be less demand for Black "commodities." To
what do we attribute the "friendless" European? The truth is that he is
cunningly making war with God, His creation and people, as evidenced by
the fact that any nation dealing with Europe feels an ulterior, evil motive
behind everything she does. The entire non-European race, whether listed
as friend or foe, feels a need to defend themselves against her presence;
that she is inherently up to something evil! As the great captivity of the
Children of Israel draws to a close, the suspicion and distrust is the absolute
same as in the beginning or more so.

The problems of Black America are defined as the most complex in
the world; so complex that, not one of the major problems touching the lives
of the captives has been solved. Today we still see the social problem,
economic problem, educational problem, political problem, and race problem as acute as they ever were. Therefore, either America *cannot* solve
these problems, or *will not* solve these problems. Either way, it leaves us
no choice. We must take our destiny into our own hands and solve the
problems ourselves. After centuries of allowing others to define for us the

solutions, we have not left a stone unturned in our pursuit of justice and equity.

We changed our nationality, our soul, the way we talked, the way we walked and the way we dressed. The adversary then defined the problem as being our poor Black minds, so we even cast that aside for a white one. As a matter of fact, we have done all that was required; we changed everything! Now as I deeply ponder this matter, I see one thing which has not been changed over the entire period of our domination that remains to be changed: we have the same "master." I define that to mean that the "master" is the problem and even if you do not really believe that to be true, it is worth considering since we have tried everything else. Let us make the daring final change; let us seek "a new master." He that has ears to hear, let him hear!

One must wonder how the Euro-gentiles, being motivated by the Spirit of Err, greed, and self-assertion, have accomplished their mission. First and foremost, God no longer had any opposition to the enslavement of the Sons of God. Second, the Euro-gentile very meticulously lulled the captives to sleep, in order that his hoax, joke and scheme might be pulled off on an unsuspecting world. He then proceeded to remove the influence of the law and prophecies, (the Old Testament of the Bible), on the manner of worship of the Sons of God. In doing so, the Euro-gentile removed the standard and the measuring rod; the principles of life were taken away along with the source of the Sons' strength and wisdom. Without the Old Testament writings, you cannot understand your past, evaluate your present plight, or understand the evil of the Euro-gentile systems. The Euro-gentile statesmen and speechmakers were continually promulgating "all men are created equal." This doctrine had the effects of a powerful narcotic. Everyone began quoting the beautiful things the Euro-gentile said, but no one noticed the ugly things they were doing. If all men were created equal, it certainly ended immediately thereafter, because from that day until the African meets his grave, everything is inequitable. Every land governed by Euro-gentile persons or principles is sustained by hate and division. Every political system, economic system, social system, building code, industrial code, quality code (poor quality, poor people; rich quality, rich people), and war code breeds inequality. Without the "God Mind," no one knew that all men are neither mentally nor physically created equal. But men governed by God and by righteous systems make men equal. Without true understanding, you have a tendency to feel that the defect is within you personally, that *you* are the cause of your condition and not the evil government of men under the influence of the spirit of err.

Who are these men of crafts? Certainly they had to be master magicians to pull off this hoax!

> *"And in the second year of the reign of Nebuchad-*
> *nezzar, Nebuchadnezzar dreamed dreams, and his*
> *spirit was troubled, and his sleep broke from him.*
>
> *Then the king commanded to call the magicians, and*
> *the astrologers, and the sorcerers, and the*
> *Chaldeans, for to shew the king his dreams. So they*
> *came and stood before the king."*
>
> **Daniel 2:1,2**

> *"As for these four youths, God gave them knowledge*
> *and skill in all learning and wisdom; and Daniel had*
> *understanding in all visions and dreams.*
>
> *And in all matters of wisdom and understanding that*
> *the king inquired of them, he found them ten times*
> *better than all the magicians and astrologers that*
> *were in all his realm."*
>
> **Daniel 1:17,20**

Here in Daniel we find our answer. During the reign of Nebuchadnezzar, after dreaming a dream which greatly troubled him, Nebuchadnezzar summoned the wise men of Babylon, at that time called magicians, astrologers, sorcerers, the Chaldeans. Updating this situation to modern Babylon (America) with the understanding of today, we know that Nebuchadnezzar summoned his cabinet or politburo. Today they have changed their titles for reasons of deception, but their functions are still the same. Today they are referred to as Secretary of State, Attorney General, Secretary of Defense, and National Security Advisor. Whenever the President is troubled, he summons these men and places the problem before them. They must know all things taking place in the firmament above and on the earth beneath. These men are the wise men of Babylon: the magicians, astrologers, sorcerers and Chaldeans of yesteryear.

No one can surpass these men in wisdom except the Sons of God who have sanctioned themselves to carry out God's will. The Sons of God were by Nebuchadnezzar's conservative estimate, ten times wiser than the members of his cabinet. No one can exert the wisdom to surpass these men except the Sons of God who have been purposely blinded and covered with darkness (wisdom of this world) in order that the wise men of Babylon reign supreme. Only after the resurrection and return of God through His Sons will that reign of wickedness be challenged, broken and ground to dust by the Divine presence of the "God Mind." Then will come the utopia as the creative genius of the Sons of God comes into its own, shattering the influence of the insidiously evil mind of satan upon man, and thus allowing the Spirit of God Almighty to flow freely unto all men.

In the days of Jesus of Nazareth 2,000 years ago, the power of the day was invested in three segments of the society who had the power to control and guide the masses. Who were they? The Scribes (the writers), the Pharisees (the educators), and the Sadducees (the religious institutions). Today, whenever the system wants to control the destiny of the people, the rulers call on the Scribes (the news media), the Pharisees (the educational institutions), and the Sadducees (the religious institutions). The press, as well as educational and religious institutions, define and design every direction of the lives of our people.

The enemy has not changed. They use the same tactics today that they used 2,000 years ago. The same tactics against the same people, bringing forth the same results. Two thousand years ago Pontius Pilate, the Roman procurator, invested power in the press, the educational and religious institutions to control the masses of the people. Who was there every step of the way when Jesus was teaching? Who was it that always confronted him? The Scribes, the Pharisees and the Sadducees. Everywhere Jesus went he was confronted by these three segments of that society. He could not escape them. They were on his trail, blaspheming him, downgrading him, lying about him. The same three segments of society today dominate the Power to Define. Everywhere the Sons of God go today, they are confronted with these three segments who have been invested with the Power to Define.

> "Then gathered the chief priest and the Pharisees a council, and said, What do we? For this man doeth many miracles.
>
> If we let him thus alone, all men will believe on him: and the Romans shall come and take away both our place and nation."
>
> **St. John 11:47,48**

At first thought it would seem that these Black Israelite leaders would have been filled with joy at the great works of Jesus, and that they should have collaborated to determine how they could help expand his ministry. It does not seem logical that these Black leaders came to plot against the Deliverer and the Deliverance. Why is it that the betrayal was carried out by men professing to be religious, professing to believe in God? Is this not something of utmost importance? A historical perspective of this great mystery and phenomenon will shed light.

It was the priest Aaron whom the people approached to desecrate God in the Wilderness of Sin. They wanted him to lead the procession of evil by building the golden calf. It was the Levites, Korah, Dathan and Aviram, that led the rebellion against Moses in the wilderness. Even with Jesus, those who were supposedly God's representatives were his chief adversaries. Even now, it appears that the oppressive authorities always have confidence in the Black clergy.

Let us consider this oddity. During Jesus' time, those African-Hebrew leaders were primarily concerned with their positions of authority and good standing with the Romans, not with God or salvation. Why didn't they feel that the success of Jesus' teachings would have been good also for them? Why didn't they want the salvation which he offered? What were they doing that Jesus threatened, when he, too, came in God's name? Why did Jesus' simple doctrine sound so strange to those Biblical scholars?

One day the Scribes, Pharisees and Sadducees asked Jesus, "Why have you allowed your apostles (students or disciples) to eat without washing their hands?" He was accused of breaking the traditional law of the elders, (African-Hebrews), by teaching the use of unorthodox methods to supply the needs of the people.

They made it appear that Jesus and his apostles were the "bad guys" and were ignoring and breaking the law while the Pharisees and the Sadducees were keeping it. The Scribes, Pharisees and Sadducees were always complaining because it appeared that the apostles were not feeding (teaching) the people in the manner which the elders (entrenched leadership) prescribed. These religionists complained to Jesus, "You are breaking the traditions of the elders by using `dirty hands' in supplying the needs of the people." He answered them and said, "But why do you by your traditions keep my people in captivity?" But Jesus knew them and he said to them," Ye hypocrites, well did the prophecy of Isaiah describe you. You hypocrites draw nigh unto God with your lips; you pay lip-service to God. But your heart is far from him."

I command you to hear and to understand the true Power to Define. The results justify the means which you use, for the portion of Jacob is not like unto them. We are the former of all things.

> *The portion of Jacob is not like them; for he is the former of all things: and Israel is the rod of his inheritance: the Lord of hosts is his name. [20] Thou art my battle axe and weapons of war: for with thee will I break in pieces the nations, and with thee will I destroy kingdoms;* ***(The Authority to Define)***
>
> ***Jeremiah 51:19-20***

How dare they accuse the Sons of God of feeding (supplying the needs of) the people with unwashed hands? It is better to feed the people with dirty hands than to not feed them at all. The instruments used to turn the minds of the people against the deliverers are still the same: the Sanhedrin, Scribes, Pharisees and Sadducees — the African Israelite leadership established by Herod and Pilate, to maintain order among the masses and keep them abreast of the mood of the people. They were loyal to Herod, even as most leaders today are loyal to the establishment. They are the same ones who in former times coaxed the people to allow the thief and murderer (Barabbas) to go free, while crucifying the righteous. He that has ears to hear, let him hear.

Their traditions have made the Word of God of non-effect. They have gotten the supposed-righteous to think that you can follow the Word of God and not accomplish anything. This is not true. The Word of God, when you understand it, causes a revolution against the world. Revolution is not to build up the systems of the world; revolution comes with a two-edged sword, using the Power to Define and any other means necessary.

When you were growing up, you thought that in order to "get smart," you had to get an education, not understanding that educational institutions all over the world today reflect a commitment to Euro-gentile standards and values. They instill white attitudes in African people, as well as a mentality that perpetuates white superiority and the cultural oppression of Africans. When the Euro-gentile heard us say that we were poor and oppressed, he immediately set out to imprison our thoughts by defining what we did not have and what it was that we needed. The media began to focus upon the slums, where we lived, reprogramming us to think "we need bigger and better houses." They used the inferior school system to determine that we needed "better" education.

The adversary heard us moaning and groaning that we were poor and oppressed, yet, having no ways and means to define our plight, he took the liberty to define what we were seeking and what it would take to make us rich (or as we thought — free)."We shall overcome" and "I am somebody" were popular slogans and cries of African Americans in the 1960's. When the souls of our people began to cry out that they were poor, needy and destitute, they were not referring to the need for bigger houses and paychecks or more education. They were desirous of spiritual things. However, the Euro-gentile defined the need not as spiritual, but as material and social. The materialistic gains made African Americans feel like "somebody" for a moment, as material substance usually does. After that it is placed on the shelf. Then the search begins for your true gains — the soul-pleasing treasure of a people, and the moral gains which are enjoyed by one another through one another. These are the things that give eternal joy and wealth.

We were poor and needy of things we once received and felt from one another. We were poor and in need of our Black African soul. We were reaching out to feel one another again. We were poor and in need of direction back to God and one another. The pleasures of materialism last but a moment, as we now realize.

The prophetic poor and needy were those that were poor and in need of the knowledge and forgiveness of God. It had nothing to do with the materialism of the world; they were poor in wisdom and comprehension of the Plan of God. For at least 300 of the last 400 years our people's objective was not to be free to join the society of the slavemaster who has been their enemy, but to escape and return to their motherland (Africa) where they could hope for love, righteousness, justice, truth and most of all, freedom.

There is a distinct difference between the poor and needy of the world and the poor and needy of God. The wealth of the world is for the people of the world. Our people, under the rulership of the Euro-gentile oppressor are poor in God. The intention of the European is to destroy forever our minds and our desire to unify and achieve the freedom we are destined to receive. He almost succeeded in his plan to destroy the past and the future; to destroy man. But there was a small trickling, a mustard seed portion who ignored the threats of prison, death and deprivation. They turned their eyes and ears to their God and His prophecies for their help and deliverance. He heard them and they heard Him.

The Euro-gentile deceived the majority by imprisoning their thoughts. He altered their original feelings so that the true meanings were all lost, leaving the people in total confusion. There has been a master plan of wickedness, and in order to combat the plan of this cruel adversary, it requires a Master Plan of God. His struggle is with us, but his war is with God.

Remember as a child when you would go into the stores and get what you thought was a penny's worth of candy? You thought you were really getting a good buy, and you continued to buy the candy. Then one day you were grabbing your cheek because you had a toothache. All of a sudden your gums were bothering you, and then you finally realized that the penny candy was not such a good buy after all! You had been deceived into thinking it was cheap and good, but in the final analysis you found that the price was too high. The penny candy was too expensive for the results you received.

The adversary took away your ability to think; took away your ability to eat; took away your ability to live; and took away your health. And, you thought you were getting a good buy for a penny. You were cheated. They convinced us to eat cakes, pies and white sugar — three and four table-spoons in coffee — and told us we were eating a "rich" diet.

Eating "rich" food ate up our lungs, our kidneys, our minds. This rich diet was in actuality a poor diet. The devil, the adversary of God, is a deceiver, a master deceiver. He designed poor diets to create a people poor in mind and comprehension. You were purposely raised on nutritionally poor diets rather than nutritionally potent diets. Things such as "soul food" were not deceiving until the adversary defined it. "Soul" used to mean all things that were good about "the good ole days" for the African slave in America. But somewhere around the end of the Second World War, the mass media seized the power to define "soul," and the spirit of African people in America was lost. "Soul" started to mean food detrimental to your health instead of grandma's good cookin'. "Soul" became obscene musical lyrics instead of the soothing harmony and jazz that typified the past. "Soul" became clown clothes instead of the smooth styles African Americans were known to sport. "Soul" became an abandonment of God instead of a search for God. "Soul" became a rejection of our past and the death of our future.

The adversary has continually lied and has caused you to unconsciously perpetuate the same. You have given children what they wanted instead of determining and giving them what they need: justifying the wicked and condemning the innocent.

Truth has been lost. All the original meanings have been lost, lost in the deceptions of the adversary. This is the epitome of the Power to Define. There is no way to make it sound good. You ought to hate the captivity.

In the early days of the captivity in America, Blacks were always trying to steal away from the slavemaster. Even in their songs their cries rang out for their God and their land. They sang songs like *Steal Away, Over Jordan,* and *Jerusalem, My Home.* Centuries later we no longer understand the significance of those songs. African Americans are out of tune with God. They are without the instructions of God.

When you understand our struggle, you will understand that it is a struggle to free the souls of our people to think as God would have us think, to do as God would have us do, and be the mighty people God has destined us to be. Anything else would be a disgrace to humanity. Up until now the adversary has defined his objectives as if they were ours. We that stand for God can no longer accept America and Europe, defined as rich when we are poor; mighty, when we are weak; lands of the free, when we are slaves. Hereafter, we shall define our objectives and the ways and means of achieving them.

We seek the blessings of our God to allow us to return to Him and to live for Him for the salvation of our people and all men. We are seeking the things *which we determine* will make us wealthy: our God and our people.

Blessed are ye that hear and understand these words; that hunger and thirst after righteousness. Verily, ye shall be filled. If people of African descent are to be persecuted by the Euro-gentile, then Abba (Father), let us not be persecuted trying to get an education in his school system, nor trying to be accepted in his societies. But rather let us be persecuted, with his batons and police dogs placed upon us, (as they were during the civil rights protests of the 1960's), in search of Heaven, and trying to acquire the wealth of God. Father, if we are to be persecuted, (and we understand that persecuted we must be), then we want to be persecuted for the sake of righteousness. Let us be persecuted at the doors of the Kingdom of Heaven. Let them blaspheme us for trying to educate our people in truth and not for trying to integrate into a system of evil. If we must fight, let us fight for our people. If we must perish in the fight, let us perish trying to get them free. Let us not perish as in Viet Nam, Grenada or Panama.

For these, little children, are the reasons they smote the prophets before you. Did they smite the prophets for trying to integrate into Babylon? Did they smite Moses for trying to integrate into Egypt? I said if we are the Children of God let them smite us for trying to fulfill the will of our God. They persecuted the prophets because the prophets prophesied *against* their systems and *against* them. Jesus was persecuted because they had made his Father's house a den of thieves. Jesus was persecuted because he was found teaching the Truth. He was not persecuted because he was trying to get into the courts of Pontius Pilate. He was persecuted because he was against the council of the Sanhedrin and because his message was against Herod and a threat to the Roman tyrants.

There are some prophecies that make you laugh, and there are some prophecies that make you cry, but one thing is for certain: that Justice determines that we shall not cry forever. It will not be a struggle which will end except that it ends with us once again in possession of our own land.

The freedom which we are talking about is to live according to the Plan of God and to live in harmony with the creations of God. When we have achieved that — verily, let all the voices ring out and let them declare: **FREE AT LAST! FREE AT LAST! THANK GOD ALMIGHTY, WE ARE FREE AT LAST!!!**

The Resurrection

The stages of the resurrection are to be read from the bottom up. This is to symbolize one's rise from a state of utter helplessness, hopelessness, despair and futility, to one of being revived, strengthened and fortified by a rebirth in the spirit of God.

RESURRECTION, according to the original, Biblical definition is:

תחיה (ti-kee-ah) — a quickening or revival (mental) of God's spirit.

⇧ ⇧ ⇧ ⇧ ⇧

קימה (key-mah) — to establish oneself: to rise to one's feet. To move from invisible (dead) to visible (live).

⇧ ⇧ ⇧ ⇧ ⇧

הקצה (hah-khah-tsah) — a dreadful, fearful awakening (seeing or being made aware of the state of the world).

⇧ ⇧ ⇧ ⇧ ⇧

ght now the whole world lies in a state of paramount ruin and confu- because of the numerous religions, sects and denominations which clude everything from devil worship to sex worship. For the past few years, the entire world has been beset by chaos and decadence because of the varied concepts and misinterpretations of God, the Holy Scriptures and the Children of Israel.

Today, we must reinterpret the scriptures to help those who are seeking an understanding of resurrection and Truth in these final "end-time" days of the rule and dominion of European civilization. We must wade through European religious doctrines, dogmas, traditions and cultures which are found under the banner of Christianity and Communism. The religious institutions of the world have defined and interpreted the Holy Scriptures in the light of their carnal understanding and not with the spiritual insight and understanding of prophetic revelations concealed in the Bible.

This chapter will clarify what is meant by "resurrection," as confirmed by the writings of the prophets, and also as mentioned in the gospels; and it will determine which meaning is most relevant to the African Americans freedom struggle and will serve as a catalyst for the redemption of all men. Although my writings are in English, the thought is in Hebrew because they are written according to the understanding revealed in the original Hebrew text.

In order to be saved from this inevitable destruction, man must now learn to think and act anew because he has existed in a world he created for himself without the laws or acknowledgment of the Almighty God. Thus, man has fallen victim to his own ways and understanding.

> *"There is a way that seemeth right unto man, but the end thereof is death."*
>
> ### *Proverbs 14:12*

The time is approximately two thousand years ago; the place, Israel, Northeastern Africa. Jesus of Nazareth has begun his preachment; the Kingdom of Heaven has come. He begins at a time when there is no strong leadership among the Children of Israel. The destiny of the people who had become religious, not righteous, is in the hands of the clergy and a few elders who were more accountable to the Romans than to the people. A great majority of Israelites belonged to or were active in the many sects that existed at that time. They did not love the Romans, but their leaders offered no alternatives, and deep within their souls the people yearned for a change. Although those in positions of authority and power, (the clergy and elders), had become complacent with the crumbs from the table of their enemies, Jesus knew that there would be fierce opposition from these enemies and that his immediate task would be to loosen their control over the people. It would not be an easy task, not so much because the people themselves believed in the Romans, but because the clergy and elders would stir up religious fervor, which was very emotional and reactionary against Jesus. In addition to that, the political risks, compounded by the warnings of the elders, set the stage for the great confrontation.

In the beginning Jesus tried to appease the sectarians by stating clearly his position:

> *"Think not that I am come to destroy the law, or the prophets; I am not come to destroy, but to fulfill.*
>
> *For verily I say unto you, Till heaven and earth pass, one jot or one tittle shall in no wise pass from the law, till all is fulfilled.*
>
> *Whosoever, therefore, shall break one of these commandments, and shall teach men so, he shall be called the least in the kingdom of heaven: but whosoever shall do and teach them, the same shall be called great in the kingdom of heaven.*
>
> *For I say unto you, that except your righteousness shall exceed <u>the righteousness</u> of the scribes and Pharisees, ye shall in no case enter into the kingdom of heaven."*
>
> **St. Matthew 5:17-20**

Yet, at the same time he could not leave the impression that he was in agreement with the clergy, or that he was one of them. Wherefore, he closed by admonishing "except your righteousness exceed the righteousness of the scribes and Pharisees, you shall in no case enter into the kingdom of heaven". This attempt at appeasement did not last long, for soon he stated "ye have heard that it was said by them of old time," or, as he would have stated were he talking today, "you have been taught that..." At that point he began wholeheartedly tearing into what was being taught by the clergy and the elders. The teachings were all wrong he said, and except they were changed, the people would most definitely not enter the "Kingdom of God."

The clergy and the elders pondered: how could it be that what we have been teaching for so long is all wrong? They reacted, satisfying their egos by saying "if it is, we will only believe it when the Messiah comes, for this is just Jesus the carpenter from Nazareth." Consequently, they never changed; the clergy and the elders held fast to their religious beliefs and traditions until the end.

The laymen were also in amazement. "How could it be," they wondered, "that the doctrine we have been following for so long is wrong?" One can certainly understand their predicament. Here we have a situation where people had been going to church for generations, feeling in earnest that they were worshipping and honoring God. Certainly, they had called upon and used His name innumerable times. They recalled the times wherein the fervor was great, the emotions had been stirred, the many occasions when they had burst forth with tears, and that what they felt were praises unto God. How could it be that these teachers who had moved them so many times, preaching and teaching about God, be now revealed as wolves in sheep's clothing? These certainly had to be some very trying times for both segments — the clergy and elders, as well as the laymen.

How could they face their families? What would they say to those whom they loved? Would they appear to have been hypocrites to their friends?

There were so many confusing doctrines. There was even confusion about the relationship of parents and children. The different oppressors had greatly influenced their thinking, for children were considered the blessing in a manner which made the parents the curse. Parents were afraid of children; there was no order or discipline. Jesus knew that this was a reversal of God's commandment. Their new traditions had made the commandments of non-effect. The servant does not surpass the master; neither is the gold in the temple greater than the temple. The parents were to be the gift to the children, to be revered and honored, for parents give the children life, not the other way around.

> *"But he answered and said unto them, Why do ye also transgress the commandment of God by your tradition?*
>
> *For God commanded, saying, Honour thy father and mother: and, He that curseth father or mother, let him die the death.*

> *But ye say, Whosoever shall say to his father or his*
> *mother, it is a gift, by whatsoever thou mightest be*
> *profited by me;*
>
> *And honour not his father or his mother, he shall be*
> *free. Thus have ye made the commandment of God of*
> *none effect by your tradition."*
>
> *St. Matthew 15:3-6*

Jesus also talked about freedom. He said that if they allowed him to guide them, his teachings would set them free from both spiritual and physical bondage. But the Sons of God had made themselves very proud under foreign rulers; they had actually forgotten the many phases of their captivity. Consequently, they replied, "we be Abraham's seed and were never in bondage to any man. How sayest thou, ye shall be free?" How could they be so proud until the truth offended them? They were offended by the revelation that they were still slaves, and not free. Why couldn't they understand him? Why did his doctrine sound so strange to a people that professed to know Godliness? No doubt, they outwardly appeared close unto God, but in truth they were far away. They thus became more afraid of him than they were of the Romans.

It was a time of great decision, and no doubt many times they felt that Jesus of Nazareth should have come in someone else's lifetime instead of theirs. Nevertheless, a decision had to be made, for Jesus had made it clear: "if the blind lead the blind, both shall fall into the pit."

So the decision was made. The clergy and elders decided to reject Jesus, but the laymen decided to listen and see. They would not choose sides...yet. Their initial fears were somewhat justified, for no doubt they felt that Jesus and his apostles were just another sect in this already complex situation. How could they actually have known that he was any different? There were but two sure ways to know: by his words and his works. The promise is he that is of God can hear God's teachings and know God's work. He that is seeking Truth can hear Truth. This is the impregnable Word of God. When one cannot hear Truth, he is not seeking Truth. For my sheep can hear my voice and know that I am no stranger. Finally, Jesus had no choice but to declare: **"I AM THE RESURRECTION!"**

This declaration, when interpreted in light of circumstances today means that at the time of the resurrection of African Americans, they could be likened unto Lazarus (the brother of Martha and Mary). Their condition would be similar to that of the Children of Israel in the days of Jesus of Nazareth. With the coming of the resurrection, there would be a defining of and return to the true substance of Jesus' teachings.

The resurrection is really the day of triumph for the Word of God; the day when God's word will suddenly come alive and instill in men the desire to live again under the simple rulership of God. It will come again through a body of men who will invoke the presence of God on earth and give the people a plan of redemption and show them in truth and through works the way back to God. The people in turn would, as a reward from God for obedience, be given the keys to everlasting life outside the realms and literal bounds of society (hell on earth). We will experience paradise — a world without end, a world of the original creation, a world wherein men live together as brethren without fear. For us, as it is written, hearing is the first means of salvation.* You must hear the trumpet: the trumpet is the Word of God. The Word will come forth first. First was the Word and the Word was God. The Word will be spoken, written and sung. The Word will have a message — a message of deliverance from hell. You are in hell now. You must be delivered.

The scriptures say the Word will come from the East; that salvation shall come forth from Zion. Zion is located in the East — at Jerusalem. The Word will come testifying of the works of the Most High God among His cast-off people. The Word will be made flesh, (Messengers of God), and the flesh shall declare the good tidings of the Lord: that He has returned unto His people to call them home. The Word shall come forth from Zion unto the cast-off people of God on the shores of their captivity — America.

Our people have always looked forward to the presence of a literal savior to deliver them from the oppressor and to "carry them home". Proponents of western ideologies and doctrines hate and fear these concepts. What would be more damnable for western society, with its corrupt doctrines, institutions and delusions that trap the minds and souls of the ignorant, than for a people with a Divine culture to be established outside of the

---

*Salvation, in this Age of the Resurrection, is to be rescued from the alien doctrines, adverse concepts, world ideologies, philosophies, opinions, religious decrees and dogmas, and to be reconciled back unto God. Salvation is to be saved (by the instruction of God) from open heart surgery, the dialysis machine, the lost children, the broken families, the cancers, the tumors, the division of race, that hate for one another and the innumerous ills of the wicked, degenerate and decadent world.

confines of the western world and define themselves as "the Kingdom of God?"

How will the Children of God know for sure this time that salvation awaits them and that the Kingdom of God has come? It is easy to be judgmental as we read of our ancestors' error of not accepting Jesus. Perhaps, if we turn back the clock and reexamine Jesus' works, we will shed light upon the present day decision of accepting the resurrection.

At the very same time when Jesus said "I am the resurrection," he was faced with a family in mourning for their brother Lazarus, who had been dead four days. The meaning of these things today is symbolic: the mourning family is the family of nations reeling to and fro under Euro-gentile rule. Lazarus exemplifies the Children of Israel buried in the dark pits and graves of America. To be defined as dead in the spiritual context means: having no knowledge of God; being in a helpless predicament, wherein one no longer hears, sees, discerns or moves. The African American community today is lying helpless in its grave, covered with the dirt of false gods, false doctrines, false worship, false history, envy, strife, disunity, disrespect, hate of one another, and a diet fit for the dead.

We can see the parallel of Noah's contemporaries to Black America. "As in the days of Noah they shall be eating, drinking, marrying and giving in marriage." Just like our people today, under foreign dominion and religious sectarian confusion, Noah's contemporaries were not the least bit concerned about God nor His judgement.

Jesus realized that the key to reviving Lazarus was found in certain words being spoken — a resurrecting doctrine. The revival or quickening of Lazarus' spirit, or his resurrection, can be likened to the situation affecting African Americans today.

There Jesus stood, before the tomb of death. He then proceeded to speak the Word of God, causing a movement in the tomb from which Lazarus came forth. He prayed and cried out unto Lazarus to break the bonds of death. Even now, Black America (Lazarus) is lying in the grave. The Word has come forth to quicken God in the minds of His people. After God is revived in the minds of the Children of God, there will be a great shaking in the graveyards of the world; the dirt of false doctrines will begin to crumble and shake loose, then will come forth the command.

"Arise, shine; for thy light is come, and the glory of the Lord is risen upon thee.

*For behold, the darkness shall cover the earth, and
gross darkness the people; but the Lord shall arise
upon thee, and his glory shall be seen upon thee.*

*And the gentiles shall come to thy light, and kings to
the brightness of thy rising."*

Isaiah 60:1-3

To further illustrate the predicament of African Americans, especially
the leaders and those well-learned, let us recall the incident of Nicodemus,
a leader of the people, a scribe in the temple, and a teacher. First and
foremost, when Nicodemus sought out Jesus, he came by night because he
was afraid to be openly associated with Jesus or his teachings. Even now,
African American leaders are afraid of the doctrine of the Kingdom, for the
Sons of God are portrayed as lawbreakers, those not following the traditions of the elders.

When Nicodemus finally did steal away to present himself to Jesus, he
was no doubt greatly shocked when Jesus told him that he was a dead man,
who needed to be reborn and retaught all things, with another concept of
God in mind. I have no doubt that Nicodemus, a teacher and leader in his
own right, could put forth a good argument on his own behalf, utilizing his
writings, scrolls and other books which he cherished. Nevertheless, all his
knowledge still rendered him dead in God, a very disturbing revelation for
one of such high stature.

The irony is that Nicodemus, like African American leaders today, did
not know that he was dead, because he looked just like Jesus. He could
breathe, think and do everything as any other person physically alive could
do. Yet, he was told by Jesus that he would have to be "born again," (reborn
in righteousness and possessing the purity of a child), in order to inherit the
Kingdom of God.

By what instrument does one gauge life and death? Is life determined
by one's intake of oxygen? By illustration, let us consider Lake Erie, one of
the Great Lakes in America that has been declared a "dead lake". How
does one determine that a lake is dead? What could possibly kill an entire
lake? The destroying of a great lake, like the destroying of a great people,
(ironically, water in prophecy is symbolically linked to people), begins with
pollution and unnatural filth being cast into the waters. These pollutants,
mostly synthetics, work against the nature of the lake because they are
foreign and cannot be absorbed, recycled or dissolved. As these pollutants

continue to flow into the lake they accumulate, overpower and destroy the algae and oxygen. When these two components are destroyed, the great lake can no longer breathe nor function according to the Plan of God. Subsequently, it is pronounced dead. However, from a distance, the lake still looks like water, and when you touch it, it feels like water. You may even see a fish every now and then. But, beware, because the great lake, without its life-giving substances, will cause disease and death.

So, likewise was Nicodemus. He had all of the characteristics of one that was alive, yet he was dead.

> *"For as the body without the spirit is dead, so faith without works is dead also."*
>
> ### St. James 2:26

Even as the life of that great body of water is algae and oxygen, so the life of the body is the Spirit of God. I can hear Nicodemus saying: "I am somebody," and Jesus defining, "Right, a *dead* somebody."

Thus, a return to the basic message of Jesus will cause the stirring in the graves of Black America, and ultimately the resurrection of the entire African world. The stage is set; the time is now. The doctrine or message of Jesus could be summed up as being a call for a fundamental change in contemporary teachings about God and worship, which are now under heavy foreign influence. We must seek the old paths; we must turn around.

Ezekiel, the prophet, further substantiates the death (spiritual) and resurrection of African Americans (the Children of Israel). With the Spirit of God, African Americans will rise to their former glory in God. They will reestablish themselves, moving from invisible to visible. Their wise men will come forth; they shall lift up their voices with the authority of God. The resurrection of Black America will be a very frightening occurrence to the inhabitants of this evil, degenerate, satanic world. As Black America is resurrected, those that take hold to the hem of their garment shall live; those that refuse and rebel shall die. This is the time when the great vision of freedom shall defeat weakness of spirit, flesh and will.

> *"The hand of the Lord was upon me, and carried me out in the spirit of the Lord, and set me down in the midst of the valley which was full of bones, And caused me to pass by them round about: and, behold, there were very many in the open valley; and, lo, they were very dry.*

*And he said unto me, Son of man, can these bones
live? And I answered O Lord God, thou knowest.*

*Again he said unto me, Prophesy upon these bones,
and say unto them, O ye dry bones, hear the word of
the Lord.*

*Thus saith the Lord God unto these bones; Behold, I
will cause breath to enter into you, and ye shall live.*

*Then he said unto me, Son of man, these bones are
the whole house of Israel; behold, they say, Our
bones are dried, and our hope is lost: we are cut off
from our parts.*

*Therefore prophesy and say unto them, Thus saith the
Lord God; Behold, O my people, I will open your
graves, and cause you to come up out of your grave,
and bring you into the land of Israel.*

*And ye shall know that I am the Lord, when I have
opened your graves, O my people, and brought you
up out of your graves,*

*And I shall put my spirit in you, and ye shall live, I
shall place you in your own land: then shall ye know
that I the Lord have spoken it, and performed it, saith
the Lord."*

Ezekiel 37:1-5; 11-14

If you had to relate these verses to a particular race or ethnic group,
whom would you select as the people most suited to fit the aforementioned
words of Ezekiel?

You need not be a Biblical scholar to give the right answer. There simply
are no other people that come even close to the description given. It
could only be the African Hebrew captives, stolen from the shores of East
and West Africa.

The prophet Ezekiel was taken by the Spirit of God to foresee the
condition of African Americans (the Children of Israel) during the North
American captivity. Their predicament was such that even the great prophet
Ezekiel was afraid to answer positively to the question "Can these bones
live?"

Immediately after this question was posed to Ezekiel, we find the all-important key to the resurrection. Before God would give a positive answer, in the fourth verse He gives the requirement: "O ye dry bones, hear the Word of the Lord." The resurrection will come in the Word, by the Word, and with the Word. The Word will be a doctrine, a living doctrine so it will give life. The Word will have life within itself, and when you hear it and follow its instructions, you will pass from death into life. It will cause great works to be done, so great until you will know that it is God.

> *"The wind bloweth where it willeth, and thou hearest*
> *the sound of it, but canst not tell from where it*
> *cometh, and where it goeth; so is every one that is*
> *born of the Spirit."*
>
> **St. John 3:8**

Spoken words are like the wind; they cannot be seen. They have no image or form. You hear the sound, but you cannot tell where it comes from or where it goes. Words are so alive until they penetrate your heart and mind, sometimes making you wise, and sometimes making you a fool; sometimes causing much joy, and too often — much pain. It is with words that you honor or deny. With a Word, God came, and without that Word, the Sons of God died.

> *"But the hour cometh, and now is, when the true*
> *worshippers shall worship the Father in spirit and in*
> *truth: for the Father seeketh such to worship him.*
>
> *God is a Spirit: and they that worship him must*
> *worship him in spirit and in truth.*
>
> *It is the spirit that quickeneth; the flesh profiteth*
> *nothing; the words that I speak unto you, they are*
> *spirit, and they are life."*
>
> **St. John 4:23,24; 6:63**

Since that time man has regressed into an abyss. He has boastfully forgotten that it is God who changeth times and the seasons; who removeth kings and setteth up kings. *He needs no man, but all men need Him.*

Prior to the resurrection, God was no longer feared or acknowledged to any great extent in the religious and academic institutions of the Euro-gentile societies. Thus, there was no desire in the youth or the elders to be Holy or Godly. Neither is there, at this time, an urge among the elders to advocate a way of life conducive to the things pleasing unto God. There is no true knowledge of God, and God is "dead" because He is not known. So there is no desire to seek out His ways or implement any program for the dissemination of Divine knowledge based upon His laws and commands.

As Ezekiel talked to the dry bones (African Americans) they began to shake and come together bone to bone. This coming together is reminiscent of one of the songs of Zion: "Them bones gon' rise again". If there is any doubt about whom the prophet is referring to, it would only take a moment to quickly consider the words heard and felt daily among the dry bones of Black America: "our hope is lost; we are cut off from our parts." Blacks certainly are cut off from their parts; there is no unity and no strength.

Finally, after "the bones" have been resurrected, they will be brought to their own land, Israel, as an ensign and a light unto the nations. The salvation of the world begins with the resurrection of the Children of Israel. All through the Holy Scriptures, the recurring theme is that there will be a Great Resurrection of a God that is supposedly dead, of a people that are certainly dead. Salvation would come in the revival of the values and moral codes established by God Almighty, the Creator of the Heavens and the Earth.

Yet now, all of these concepts are casualties of the spirit of error (satan). "Clones" have been made and given the same ancient names. A false god has been created, along with false moral codes and a false "land of the promise" (America). These things could only be created and perpetuated if the true ones were inactive or ineffective. Who would benefit from this great deception and moral misguidance except the arch enemy of God, Lucifer, the ancient dragon, also known as the devil.

The prophet Amos foretold of a period in history when there would be a famine of hearing the Word of God; a time when the Sons of God would search for God and not find Him. The crucifixion of Jesus of Nazareth represented the ushering in of that time, although the complete ramifications would not be felt for another 1,500 years. The crucifixion of Jesus was a sign of the sealing of the way, the truth and the light, attributes which Jesus used to describe himself. The crucifixion was actually the attempt to crucify the Word of God, to remove its presence from among the falling Sons of God, and to spiritually destroy God Himself. The carpenter from Nazareth was the instrument used to convey this prophetic message to the Children of Israel and thus, to the world. Jesus was to be the manifestation of the entire prophetic Plan of God; his coming symbolized truth before the people, whose rejection, caused darkness or death to befall them. God's chosen servant, Israel, and the Romans (the world), united to betray Jesus in the Passover plot, and by doing so killed the active, living Word of God.

Was it the man or his teachings that had to be stopped? It should certainly be understood that it was not their objective to destroy a body, for the flesh profits nothing. Thusly we can conclude that they had to destroy the force that was greater, the living doctrine or the Word, which was God. God's truth has been killed, His doctrine destroyed; His instructions are not honored or greatly esteemed. Having succeeded in destroying the way of God, the devil then, through craft, beguiled the world.

> *"For such are false apostles, deceitful workers, transforming themselves into the apostles of Christ.*
>
> *And no marvel; for satan himself is transformed into an angel of light.*
>
> *Therefore it is no great thing if his ministers also be transformed as the ministers of righteousness, whose end shall be according to their works."*
>
> ### *II Corinthians 11:13-15*

After having totally convinced the world that righteousness brings no reward or honor, the devil brought forth his materialistic gods in abundance and caused men to dedicate their lives and energies to acquiring them by any means necessary. Men engaged in the ruthless schemes of crime, deception and exploitation, as their minds dictated "get it at any cost, if necessary destroy your neighbor, your family, your friends, even your health and life". Nothing was too precious to sacrifice for these new, modern, sophisticated gods. The adversary of God was now riding high, portraying himself as an "angel of light" and his followers as the New World teachers of righteousness.

The world, now totally deceived, lusted to follow and pay homage to the new commander-in-chief. Its people had been convinced that they could not survive, nor succeed unless they "toed the line." The "Almighty Dollar" became supreme. Honor it and everything came within reach. Without it, no other god could improve or help your cause. To be pious or seek piety was out of style; its achievements were negligible. The pious were the failures, the iniquitous were the standards of excellence. Riding the crest of his glory, the adversary announced on the cover of *Time* magazine that God was dead, and it went unnoticed.

The devil was now in his glory. Prayer was banned from the schools.

The Biblical account of the creation was not taught. The righteous man, or man of God, was portrayed as never having fun, laughing, playing or even enjoying life. He was hard-faced and just sat around reading the Bible. He was always someone who you did not want to emulate, because it would prevent you from having fun. Everyone wanted to be like the devil. God's great works had long been forgotten. The great prophets were asleep and their teachings were sealed. No one talked any more of the great God of Abraham, Isaac and Jacob. The children were not taught about His great works in Egypt, or at the Red Sea, or at the Jordan River, or at Jericho. Elijah, Elisha, Joshua, Moses, David, Samson were almost totally forgotten, and when mentioned, it was without great honor. In their place we all were given a long list of what were called religions. Select the one of your choice. There was one for whatever you wanted to do, yet none existed for what God wanted you to do. Nevertheless, we selected, never considering. We began learning but never knowing the truth. Thinking we were being made wise, we became fools.

> *"Professing themselves to be wise, they became fools..."*
>
> ### *Romans 1:22*

> *"My people are destroyed for a lack of knowledge; because thou hast rejected knowledge, I will also reject thee, that thou shalt be no priest to me; seeing thou hast forgotten the law of thy God, I will also forget thy children."*
>
> ### *Hosea 4:6*

Contemporary history will record that we now live in a world without God, consequently today all men are beset with problems. They are frustrated, confused and confounded, mainly because they refuse to acknowledge their iniquity. As a result, the Euro-gentile is trapped in adversity. He has a woman, a child and a society that he cannot control because he has no "God Mind." He has continued to talk so extensively about computers and robots until, unknowingly, he has made himself into a robot locked into a computer.

> *"Enter in at the narrow gate, for wide is the gate, and broad is the way, that leadeth to destruction and many there be who go in that way;*

Because strait is the gate, and narrow is the way,
which leadeth unto life, and few there be that find it."

St. Matthew 7:13,14

Nearly all of the five billion inhabitants on earth today are adherents to one of the major religions of the world, i.e., Judaism, Christianity, Islam, Hinduism, Buddhism or Zoroastrianism, etc. Their theological institutions, which the world thinks represent God, (Creator of heaven and earth, the sun, moon, and stars), in reality are far from knowing Him, truly worshipping Him, having any knowledge of His Divine Plan of Redemption for humanity, or possessing any true spiritual foundation on which such a plan could be laid. These institutions will all have to undergo a fundamental change in order to be brought back to the path.

"Having a form of godliness, but denying the power
of it, from such turn away."

II Timothy 3:5

The problem with the masses is that they are ignorant of the fact that religion does not mean righteousness, (fear of God), as stated in the Holy Scriptures. Religion represents the concepts, ideologies and traditions of men, while righteousness represents a moral responsibility to God. The two are not the same!

Let us critically consider the religion of men. American and European societies, or so-called civilizations, were established under the leadership of Christian or religious men. When has a confessed atheist ruled America or a European nation? The various bodies of government throughout the western world and other symbols of authority and power are in the hands of Christians or Jews.

What greater opportunity has there been to build a righteous system of government? What, then, are the objectives of these men in government?: to establish righteousness on earth, or does the thought prevail that the establishment of righteousness is someone else's job? If so, does that not sound like a confession? They readily admit that someone else, and not them, will have to deal with bringing righteousness, or dedication to God. Then what is their mission to man? Let us take the simple opposites of their statements, or better still, confessions. If they are not the deliverers, we must know they are the oppressors. If they are not the bringers of good tidings, then certainly, they are the bringers of evil.

Why, then, do we continue to follow those who confess that someone else is coming to establish right if we are sincerely in search of that right ourselves? Why do we accept his standards as anything other than what they are? (Evil!) We must not be naive, but see and understand in his confession that he has not come to bring righteousness, but unrighteousness. Has Christianity then, as it has been handed down out of Europe, had the opportunity to establish righteousness on earth? Have they succeeded in one country? No! Not one! Furthermore, not in one state, city or village!

According to the record, after having the power and authority, we conclude that beyond a shadow of a doubt, righteousness is not their business. We have a tendency to put their works far from their beliefs instead of equating their works with what they believe. The President, the Congress, the West German Bundestag, the French Assembly, the British Parliament, etc., are all doing what they believe is their mission, and as a result these devout, Christian men have produced sick, degenerate, lawless societies. Their's is a world without God. In this new contemporary society we possess their religion and it has not made us Godly. We have a religion that has not made us righteous. It has not made our family unity strong; it has not brought us respect from our children; and it has certainly not made us healthy. As a matter of fact, when we weigh it in truth, we were better off and much closer to God before we adopted these strange religions manufactured in Europe and America.

When the Word has been resurrected and taken on flesh, the presence of God will be known by the works of those who come in His name. No one can declare the possession of the keys of heaven as long as they are seen building and amassing material wealth and the modern comforts of hell with no apparent signs of "entering the door that leads out of hell," whether it be spiritual or physical. To be in a heavenly state of mind while living in hell will just not work. First of all, a heavenly state of mind in hell is either drug-induced or out of cycle with the natural state of being. In order for one to be in a heavenly state of mind, one has to first be in an environment that causes one's mind to reflect on the things of God. God is not a myth — God is real.

The systems of hell are not geared toward causing your mind to reflect on the things of God. Rather, hell is set in a cycle to cause you to hate God, believe Him to be dead, or question the order in which He has placed things — all without you having knowledge of who God is and how He works. The reason why our people do not know their heritage is because they do not know who their God is. If He walked up to you and said, "I am God", what would you say? If you wanted Him to prove Himself, what would you ask

Him to do? Something stupid, no doubt. Fly? Disappear? Make you rich? Walk through a wall? Give you material needs? Give you back a loved one lost? More than likely, any one of these. You would not ask Him who you are, who were your people, where is your land, what is your past culture or why you suffered the indignations and degradations of being cut off from Him. You would not ask, generally, for a working, permanent solution to your people's problems, because the truth and reality of being in hell has not really hit you in your search for peace of mind and "heaven."

Encompassed in the Great Resurrection is the resurrection of the church. The word church means a gathering or called-out assembly. The first church was the congregation of Israelites in the wilderness after the Exodus from Egypt. The first direct use of the word church is recorded in the Book of Matthew:

> *"And I say also unto thee, that thou art Peter, and*
> *upon this rock I will build my church; and the gates*
> *of hell shall not prevail against it."*
>
> ### St. Matthew 16:18

The most controversial portion of this statement is the reply to Peter: "upon this rock I will build my church," or in other words, my congregation. As with most of Jesus' *teachings*, this statement has been taken completely out of context. When we see how erroneous the explanation has been concerning this "rock," it is no small wonder that Jesus instructed the people to search the books of the prophets, for only through them could his teachings be understood and substantiated.

The church, (congregation), certainly, was not established upon Peter. This is not to say that someone has not established a church based on Peter's teachings, but it certainly is not the "church" nor the "rock" alluded to by Jesus of Nazareth. In addition, it would require a considerable stretch of the imagination to imagine Jesus being so ambiguous, saying "this rock" and meaning that he was building the church upon *himself*. If we take into consideration that the gospels were written in Greek long after the death of Jesus, possibly "this rock" could have been a grammatical error. But rather than cast doubt on the literary skills of the author, we should seek clarity from the words of the prophets.

It is essential that we investigate and clearly understand what the original church consisted of or was to consist of in order that we may know and bring forth the resurrection. The word "church" is translated from the Greek word "ecclesia" which literally means "a called-out assembly". The church today is certainly not called out of the world. As a matter of fact, it is worldly-oriented and was established to pacify the masses that suffer under wicked rulers who promise them something better in the hereafter. This apostate church offers no strong opposition to the evils of the world. Where there is resistance to inequality and injustice, it is mostly symbolic. The church today belongs to the world and not to God. The church of today is merely a government agency used for the pacification of the masses.

There has never been a general church uprising against American racism nor South African apartheid. As a matter of fact, the rulers of these countries are staunch supporters of *their* church. This is certainly understandable. Have you ever wondered how all of those evil people can attend *their* churches and never be influenced to change injustice to justice, racism to equality and their evil societies to *worship* God? As we continue to study the statement about the "church" and "rock" we will find, in the preceding verse (St. Matthew 6:17), Jesus thanking God for revealing His presence to Peter; which, no doubt, is why in turn, he promised to establish his assembly (church) on the Rock of God. In following the instructions of Jesus and through searching the books of the prophets, we find that God Almighty is the Rock, and there has never been another Rock of Truth!

> *"Because I will publish the name of the Lord; ascribe ye greatness unto our God.*
>
> *He is the Rock, his work is perfect; for all his ways are judgement: a God of truth and without iniquity, just and right is he."*
>
> *"But Jeshurun waxed fat, and kicked; thou art waxen fat, thou art grown thick, thou art covered with fatness; then he forsook God which made him, and lightly esteemed the* <u>*Rock of his salvation.*</u>
>
> *They provoked him to jealousy with strange gods, with abominations provoked they him to anger,*
>
> *They sacrificed unto devils, not to God; to gods whom they knew not, to new gods that came newly up, whom your fathers feared not.*
>
> <u>*Of the rock that begat thee thou art unmindful,*</u> *and hast forgotten God that formed thee."*
>
> **Deuteronomy 32:3,4; 15-18**

Who is this rock that the church has become unmindful of; that is lightly esteemed in their minds? At the turn of the century, a body of men began to move in the southern United States, attempting to resurrect the church upon the rock of Truth: God Almighty. These men, Bishop Charles Mason of Mississippi, William S. Crowdy of Virginia, Bishop William Boone of Tennessee, Bishop C.P. Jones of Mississippi and Elder Saint Samuel of Tennessee initially included in their teachings that Africans in America were descendants of the Biblical Israelites. Their theological instructions encompassed the law (instruction) of God and the teachings of Jesus. They understood that the resurrected church had to keep the commandments of God and have the testimony of Jesus. They gave their churches the proper name, "The Church of God in Christ" which I interpret to mean the church of God with the testimony of Jesus. The original beliefs of these men were soon polluted with a strange doctrine which caused these churches to slowly turn away to a more acceptable preachment in order to receive the stamp of approval.

Likewise, did the knowledge of African peoples' sacred heritage survive among numerous tribes and peoples the length and breadth of Africa and the Diaspora. The Hebrewisms of the Ashanti, Yoruba, Ibo and Vai tribes of West Africa are extensively documented. Less well-known, but nonetheless prevalent, are other Hebrew cultural traces and teachings present in the Lembas of South Africa, the Sons of Judah in Zimbabwe and the Tamils of Sri Lanka and southern India. Recently freed South African nationalist Nelson Mandela, relates how in 1921, the South African Prime Minister, General Smuts massacred a village of 163 men, women and children at Bulhoek. According to Mandela's testimony, they were members of an "Israelite sect."

These very heroic attempts to resurrect the Sons of God were destined to fail, but the memory of these valiant efforts still lingers and shall become a legacy for the Children of Israel. These all-important signs were to assure us that someone in the midst of us always knew this sacred truth concerning the African world. Now that you have paid your dues to the Euro-gentile world, it is time to start the journey back to the rock which begat you: the Rock of your salvation. Let us ascribe greatness unto our God.

The church (assembly) which Jesus talked of and established, died or disappeared shortly after the consummation of his ministry. Although his apostles attempted to maintain a semblance of his teachings, division and confusion soon set in, destroying the last remnant of his congregation. After the Dark Ages, (the period of time when the world lost all understanding of and contact with the Great God of Heaven and Earth, called in the prophecies, the God of Israel), we find another church, a foreign apostate church being established by the Euro-gentiles. This church is prophetically called "The Great Whore (false church) which sitteth upon many waters," (meaning sitting or ruling over the masses of the people) wherein the deification of the papacy, idols and images is required. This church, using the name of Jesus, was sanctioned by the Euro-gentiles as a control mechanism for the masses and had nothing to do with the ancient church of salvation. As this complicity between Europe and the Vatican developed, the seat of authority for the church was moved from Jerusalem to Rome and England. Under no circumstance could someone know Jesus and not know his love of God, His Law and Jerusalem. No church established by Jesus or the Sons of God could have its seat of authority anywhere but Jerusalem, for this is forbidden by the Law and the prophecies.

As Jesus surveyed the social and political situation among the Children of Israel, what were some of his observations which preceded the establishing of his church (called-out assembly)? The situation was very complex, as it is today among African Americans (the Children of Israel). He initially thought to just teach and clean up the existing institutions, but he soon realized that the clergy saw any call for change as offensive. Instead of being the life of the people, they had made the people their source of income and livelihood. Their network of sects were interwoven with so many other evil vices until an internal cleansing bordered on impossible. Jesus departed from this confusion for meditation. He prayed and concluded, "Let the dead bury the dead." Instead of cleansing the establishment, he would call out an assembly of those who believed to start a new church. He would have to call out the believers from within those existing communities in order to establish the ensign of righteous worship. Whereby, he said,"Those of Truth will hear Truth" also "My sheep shall hear my voice and a stranger they shall not follow." It was a call for the separation sanctioned by God. This church was considered dead in Jesus' eyes.

> *"For the Lord himself shall descend from heaven with a shout, with the voice of the archangel, and with the trump of God: and the dead in Christ shall rise first:*
>
> *Then we which are alive and remain shall be caught up together with them in the clouds, to meet the Lord in the air: and so shall we ever be with the Lord."*
>
> *I Thessalonians 4:16,17*

We have now come to the time of the resurrection of the church, (the called-out assembly). The resurrected church will make Jerusalem its seat of authority and will be founded upon the Rock of Truth, God Almighty. The called-out assembly (church), will keep the Commandments of God and have the testimony of Jesus.

The message of the resurrected church will be to fear God and give glory to Him, for the hour of judgement is come; and, worship Him that made Heaven and Earth, the sea and the fountain of waters. The resurrection of the church will coincide with the resurrection of the Sons of God. The Sons will feed the Children of God the Spirit of Truth, which will cause their minds to comprehend their predicament and how to eliminate it. Today, there will not be an internal cleansing of the apostate church. There will only be a calling out; first, of the believers of the *true church*. Afterwards, all others hearing this truth will be caught up in the Spirit of the Sons of God, under the authority of the One God. This signifies the season in which all religions and denominations will dissolve and flow in one order of worship, becoming one again with God, the Father. Then, all men will become brothers. Those that overcome and heareth these words shall do the works of God until the end and will receive power over the nations, even over death. The time has come that judgement must begin at the House of God. We must begin restoring, building, growing and undoing the incredible damage left in the wake of Euro-gentile dominion.

The True Worship of God

We have all heard the statements "one man's success is another man's defeat" or "one man's medicine is another man's poison." Did you ever stop to consider why such statements are in prevalent use in this society? The answer is simple. When you live in a society where dichotomy is normal, you will find a schizophrenic approach to understanding certain realities.

How should the works or acts of man be defined? Should they qualify as just good or bad? If so, then the bombing of Nagasaki and Hiroshima was an act of good as far as the American government was concerned, but the reverse for the Japanese people.

The morning after President Harry Truman gave the order to drop the atomic bomb upon those Japanese cities, he went to church. What did he hope to accomplish by going to church? Did he pray that the bomb fall on target or did he ask forgiveness for that hellish act? No matter what, the inventing of, as well as the dropping of the bomb were both acts of devil worship. By attending church service after ordering the bomb to be dropped, Truman was prostrating and humbling himself before his maker, the devil.

First of all, the men who created that abominable instrument of war as well as those responsible for exploding it upon man and earth, and all of those engaged in adverse (ungodly) behavior, are chief worshippers of the devil.

Worshipping the devil is further exemplified by the behavior of the racist South African apartheid government. To show their unswerving devotion to the devil, they cowardly oppress, murder, imprison and torture African men, women and children in their own land.

Another illustration of devil worship can be seen in the world's economic system, which guarantees a surplus for the rich minority and financial woes for the masses. Rich landlords and property owners exude devil worshipping traits when, in their selfish and greedy attempts to hoard the wealth of the world, they publicize the lie that the world is overcrowded, causing men to panic unnecessarily, and to fear that the world will soon be overflowing beyond its capacity to support. As a result, men permit themselves to be sexually altered and at the same time women consume birth control concoctions in order that they may enjoy the sexual act without the risk of becoming pregnant. Furthermore, women allow gynecologists to probe their bodies, indiscriminately cutting and tying their inner organs.

Worst still, society's dichotomy has led to such schizophrenic behavioral patterns as homosexuality where demented and weak-minded men forsake women to cohabitate with other men, and likewise women, in their zealous pursuit to be men, seek out other women to release their morbid passions.

The manner in which people define these atrocious, devilish acts against man and the earth characterizes the state of the world. However, the Kingdom of God has come to denounce these dreadful acts and to set the world in order. Therefore, let us understand that no act of man during this point in time can be isolated for forgiveness because salvation is now more complex. Salvation now is not being forgiven for a certain ungodly work; that forgiveness alone will not save you. Instead, your complete life-style has to change. A truly new birth has to occur.

The adversary of God has deceived the whole world and has made everyone believe that correcting a wrong work or deed assures salvation. Hence it is no longer an act but a complete life-style and allegiance that is involved. Unfortunately, man has allowed himself to become a prey to the craftiness of satan by not understanding the authentic worship of God.

There has to be a total re-creation of man. He has to be given a new mind and soul. If dropping the atomic bomb had been an isolated act, then Truman needed only to have acknowledged his mistake and, thus, would have been back in good grace with the Creator. But all of his other acts are no less important, although less publicized, because a devil worshipper works for, labors for, toils for, worships the devil twenty-four hours a day. If the acts of the white Afrikaners and the invention of fiery weapons of war are not the worship of the devil, then what are they?

To whom should these damnable and deplorable acts against God and His Holy creations be attributed, if not the devil? What should they be termed, if not the worship of the devil? Who is the chief benefactor of these ignoble and despicable works of evil? Is it not the devil? Have not these wicked men strived to create his hell on earth? Have they not labored strenuously to destroy what is good? Then for whom or for what have they toiled? Have their actions been useful and advantageous, or useless and disadvantageous unto humanity? Regardless, justice shall render an equal reward for every act of man, justly, whether for good or evil. Likewise, positive or negative, *every deed of man is accountable unto man as worship.*

The objective of this work is to explain to the reader the correct manner in which to worship God. Through serious deliberation and study of the Bible, (in its original Hebrew form, not the English version), the correct interpretation of the scriptures have been uncovered and will be revealed to the reader. A clear interpretation of the Bible, as given by the people of the Bible or the Sons of the Prophets themselves, makes a vast difference in the understanding of the scriptures.

Throughout our generations, as the layman has attempted to read the Bible, he would always hesitate and say, "I don't read the Bible because it makes no sense to me" or "I can't understand the Bible." The reason that one does not understand the Bible in most instances is because through the many translations of the Bible from its original text — Hebrew — to Greek, Latin and English, the original thought, (Hebrew thought), has been lost. The interpreting of the Hebrew scriptures by European scholars is one thing, however, the uncovering of those same scriptures by an African Hebrew scholar is another. The present day interpretation of the Biblical writings has a strong western influence that is biased, discriminative and racist, due to the prejudiced natures of the western world against anyone of African origin. Yet, after more than 2,000 years of exile, the African Hebrew has returned to Jerusalem, Northeastern Africa, and is accurately interpreting the Word of the God of Israel, the God of our forefathers, Abraham, Isaac and Jacob. Moreover, the advent of the African Hebrew scholar at Jerusalem signals another, or new, understanding of the wisdom of God, an understanding that challenges Euro-gentile interpretation of the Bible, bringing into judgment the understanding of their world.

The Bible was written by African men, who because of their disobedience and violations of the Laws (instructions), lost favor with God. Consequently, they yielded the rule or dominion of the world to the Euro-gentiles for an appointed period of time. During the gentile reign, the African Hebrews (Children of Israel) underwent a chastisement (oppression) that caused them to descend to the lowest ebb of existence ever witnessed by the people of the world. However, the spirit of Jacob (the African Hebrew) is now resurrected and is contesting the spirit of Esau (Euro-gentile). The return of Jacob denotes the downfall of Esau. Moreover, with the truthful interpretations of the Holy Scriptures and its prophecies, the season of salvation is set in motion.

In order that the truth be made manifest, diligent study of the Hebrew Biblical text is required. Even the Euro-gentile translators of the Bible admitted that they were unable to give an "adequate rendering" of the Bible as it was originally written. For those who cannot undertake the study of Hebrew, which is the original language in which the Bible was written, this work will explain the true meaning of worshipping God. Every effort in the following writings will be made to simplify and broaden the understanding of the true worship of God. We will endeavor to convey the exact translation of the verb עבד (ah-vah-d). עבד, (the name of the letters in Hebrew are ah-yen, vayt, dah-let, and are read from right to left), is the Hebrew root of the word which means to work for, labor for, toil for, to work as a slave, to *worship*. עבד (eh-vehd) is the noun form of עבד and means *worshipper* of God. Therefore, it can be seen from the definitions, that according to Hebrew thought, work and worship are synonymous. Thus, the worship of God is one's every good and righteous work, deed or act. The word עבד is used throughout the Holy Scriptures to explain the worship of God, as shown in the Book of Exodus 20:3-5:

> *"Thou shalt have no other gods before me. Thou shalt not make unto thee any graven image, or any likeness of any thing that is in heaven above, or that is in the earth beneath, or that is in the water under the earth; Thou shalt not bow down thyself to them, nor serve them..."*

The Euro-gentile interpreters of the Bible translated עבד in the above scripture as serve. *Serve* is a feeble interpretation from the Hebrew language to English. The correct translation of עבד is *worship,* not serve. *Serve* suggests another thought, which reduces the understanding of the Biblical text.

In the Hebrew language, when one gets down on his knees and prays, or pauses for a Jewish Sabbatical, Christian Sunday or Muslim Friday rest break from the normal six days of work, toil, labor, or worship, then the word עבד which expresses the action of work, toil, labor or worship ceases. On the seventh day (Saturday), first day (Sunday), and sixth day (Friday), an entirely different action is activated inasmuch as people break from their normal routine to go to church, synagogue, mosque, etc. The action performed on these holy days can be expressed in English as to bow down oneself, humble oneself, prostrate oneself, pray, etc. which in Hebrew is השתחווה (pronounced heesh-tah-khah-vah), and which comes from the verb שחה (these letters are sheen, khet, hay). Attending a holy service at a church, a mosque, or temple, in the Hebrew sense does not mean worship, but rather, means to pray, supplicate, plead, or receive inspiration and direction from God as the verb שׁחה translates to. Therefore, in the Hebrew understanding, worshipping does not translate as שׁחה. The two acts (worship עבד and supplicate שׁחה) are not the same.

In the original Hebrew scriptures, there never has been the understanding nor could there be derived the interpretation of a separate day of worship. It is deceptive and misleading to make worship a temporary action, in place of a continuous and everlasting action. This fabrication (special day of worship), Friday — Islam, Saturday — Judaism, Sunday — Christianity, was instituted by the devil in order that man would not relate the activities which he performs the other six days in the week as the worship of God. Therefore, it is evident that the devil has deceived the whole world into worshipping him. He has been successful in his craftiness by causing man to disassociate his job, business, eating habits, shopping habits and recreational habits, from the worship of God.

Yet, in truth, all of these actions denote worship; it is only a matter of who is being worshipped — God or the devil. Thus, the people are not aware that they are worshipping the devil and his idols (money, cars, televisions, etc.), before which they prostrate themselves daily, and in fact, are perpetuating the corrupt systems and wicked societies that protect the devil, while producing his evil products (the idols), all in deviation from the Plan of God.

One has to understand that everything matters with God, for God is total and perfect. Anytime that the spirit of "well that doesn't matter" enters in where God's worship is concerned, you've stepped a foot into hell, and if it's not corrected, the whole body will soon follow. The true worship of God is an entire way of life, a continuous action, from the meal you eat in the morning to the job you work on. It encompasses your every deed and thought pattern.

Only when we understand the connection between work and worship will we totally comprehend how to build and live in a world where all of the people love and worship God. This is what inspired John the Apostle of Christ to state: "The prince of this world is the devil." Also, this is why the entire fiber of this world has to be destroyed. It is a world of devil worship; a world against God; a world of sin, madness, sickness, disease, ignorance, poverty and death.

No country, state, or city has escaped the wrath of God, yet most people continue to ride on the merry-go-round of false idol worship and moral corruption. From moral corruption there is no cure except to be born again; dead to society — born to God. You can't put new wine in old bottles, nor new cloth on an old garment. The prophecy says: "Come out of her my people, and be not partakers of her sins." One cannot be a part of a society of idol worshippers or pagans without being considered as the same.

> *"Ye adulterers and adulteresses, know ye not that the friendship of the world is enmity with God? Whosoever therefore, will be a friend of the world is the enemy of God."*
>
> **James 4:4**

A good example of one who had to separate himself from a pagan society was Lot, who dwelled in Sodom and Gomorrah. He had to come out. You, too, must come out. You must totally denounce this world and dedicate yourself to the building of a New World Order, where men, who are governed by God, govern the world; wherein we will live according to the Will of God, and live in harmony with His creation.

You may sometimes feel that you can be devoted to God, while you support, condone and perpetuate this world but you can only believe that when you don't comprehend true worship. You will continue to see nonbelievers only as Communists, when the truth of the matter is the entire world today is ruled by nonbelievers and supported by a pagan constituency. Therefore, to condone this world of sin and not partake of it in some fashion is utterly impossible. Have you failed to notice that the more involved we are in this world, the more ungodly we become?

Today, you, Black America, have interwoven yourselves into the fabric of Euro-American society, much to your own distress. While at the same time, as you view the state of our race, realize that you have fallen so far away from God. Therefore, the deceptions and fantasies of being a part of the "white man's world" must cease to be the vision of our people, who have been culturally robbed, and trapped on the shores of immorality, under the yoke of material and economic persecution by the pagan oppressors. Black people must stop fantasizing about Gabriel's horn blowing on Judgement Day and chariots of fire coming to carry them home (after they have partaken and enjoyed all of this world to the last drop). Black people must hear the trumpet of Truth. You must return to the God of creation; you must worship Him and Him only, and love Him with all your heart, soul and might. Black people taught and preached the Bible from ancient times. As long as you remained outside of the gates of American and European societies and their doctrines and ideologies, you remained closer to God than what you are today. You left the search for your identity, the Holy Scriptures and God when you were lured into tasting the "good life" (as defined by Euro-gentiles). Consequently, God has set you on an endless path of damnation and condemnation, because you lacked the knowledge of the true worship of God. The worship of God is the very essence of man's life. In other words, regardless of the sentiment of man, he has only two choices: worship God and live, or worship the devil and die. There is no neutrality.

Man today is making the same mistakes as his forefathers: bowing down to idols, prostrating before statues. In the days of his fathers the idols were made of wood, stone, clay, etc. Today man worships and prostrates before steel, concrete and aluminum. A prime example of the worship of inanimate, insensitive objects is the way men of today bow down to their automobiles. They even build temples (garages) especially for them to protect the cars from the elements. They sanctify their cars by washing and polishing them to keep them shining and bright. They buy the most expensive fuel for the vehicles, yet purchase junk food (fuel) for their bodies at discount stores. Man labors tirelessly to purchase his car, and often has to make grave sacrifices to keep it running. He has even been known to kill in disputes arising over his automobile. He brags about his car's appearance and performance and there have been cases of men requesting to be buried in their cars.

Naturally, his reward is equivalent to his works, for his swift chariot maims and kills man and beast alike, if they venture into its path. He even kills his own foolish self in it! His god, the automobile, fills the environment with pollution, and man, in turn, is affected by it. Yet, he refuses to put away his deadly idol. He is unable to function without his wicked inventions, for they have become a part of his life and he has certainly paid a tremendous price.

Another of man's favorite idols is the telephone. This small god isolates him from his surroundings, keeps him inside, and causes him to lose the personal relationship one acquires with interaction with neighbors. His wife spreads malicious gossip on it, and his children create much devilment with it.

Still another idol before which he prostrates himself is the television, which transmits the wicked values of a depraved society. Robbers and thieves covet this transmitter of foolishness, and much time, concern and energy (work) must be expended to protect it from their greedy hands. People have been known to brave the fiery flames of a burning house to protect this graven image. These "gods" also reward man for his ignorant worship of them, blinding his children and introducing them to perversion, crime and violence. They are subtly transformed into the monsters they view on the screen. Thus, children kidnap, kill and steal like the images they view on the television screen. It is estimated in America that by the time a child is 14 years old, he has seen 11,000 murders on television.

My consistent ridicule of materialistic devices such as televisions, telephones and cars, does not mean that it will be forbidden to possess these articles in the days of the Kingdom of God. The basic problem is the lustful emphasis that is instilled into the owners of these inanimate objects. The covetousness and lust for these gadgets far supersedes the spiritual love for one's neighbor and relatives. There are very few beings on this earth who toil, labor, or struggle harder for their neighbor, brother, sister, or mother than for their carnal possessions. We must cast aside the foolish, materialistic mentality and turn our minds to one another wherein humanity — people — will again become the wealth of the world and one another.

These are only a few examples of the countless idols worshipped by man. It is difficult to believe that scholars intelligent enough to translate the Hebrew language into foreign languages were not intelligent enough to differentiate between the verb שחה meaning to bow down or prostrate, and the verb עבד, meaning to work or worship. Two consecutive illustrations of inaccurate translations by the English translators are revealed in the scriptural passages from the Book of Psalms:

> "O come, let us worship and bow down: let us kneel before the Lord our maker."

> **Psalms 95:6**

> "Confounded be all those who serve graven images, that boast themselves of idols: worship him, all ye gods."

> **Psalms 97:7**

The verb root שחה or נשתחוה (neesh-tah-khah-veh) in the first person plural is what is written in Psalms 95:6 of the Hebrew text, and if accurately translated it means to prostrate oneself, to humble oneself, to bow down oneself or to pay homage. Nevertheless, the English translators in both verses translate the verb שחה as worship, which is definitely and indisputably incorrect. The interpreters define worship as a periodic or alternate action in place of man's every action. Thus, the verb   , which when translated means work or worship, is omitted altogether in the original Hebrew version of Psalms 95:6. Furthermore, in this case the Hebrew scribes did not intend to convey unto the reader the thought of worship. They were well aware of the fact that עבד (worship) expresses a continuous, incessant flow of action, whereas the verb שחה which they used, expressed a temporary or transitory action. The intent of the devil in concealing the truth regarding what King David meant in Psalms 95:6 and 97:7, was to convince the world that worship is something that is done at one's convenience. Thus, obviously, as evidenced by man's strict adherence to foolishness and wickedness, the devil has been successful in his efforts to separate man from his everlasting duty and obligation, — that is to worship his Maker every day, night, hour, and minute throughout his life.

In addition, Psalms 97:7 also states: "Confounded be all *those who serve* graven images, that boast themselves of idols, *worship* him all ye gods." Here, *those who serve* is denoted by the noun עבדים (ah-vah-deem), which means workers of, worshippers of, servants of, or slaves of. Once again the correct definition of King David's plea is translated erroneously. The verb השתחווה means to prostrate oneself, bow down oneself, or humble oneself, not worship. The true definition for worship is always and unvaryingly defined in the Hebrew scriptures by the verb עבד.

An accurate translation of Psalms 95:6 and 97:7 would read:

> *"Come we shall bow down and surrender ourselves,*
> *we shall bend the knee before God our Maker."*
>
> **Psalms 95:6**

> *"Confused be those who worship [work for, labor*
> *for] graven images [vain materialism] and praise*
> *themselves of their idols [materialistic gods]. Bow*
> *down to him all gods."*
>
> **Psalms 97:7**

After studying the true translation, we can easily comprehend and feel the spirit of King David's words. Psalms 97:7 is a complaint against vain worship or labor. While Psalms 95:6 is a prerequisite which could lead to the worship of God, it in itself is not worship.

In the book of Zephaniah 1:5 it reads:

> *"And them who worship the host of heaven upon the housetops; and them who worship and that swear by the Lord, and that swear by Malcam;"*

Again, שחה is defined by English translators as worship in place of to prostrate oneself or bow down oneself, in a temporary or transient manner. For certainly, it seems the translators should have known that if one were to bow down upon a housetop, it would surely be transitory, as opposed to a permanent situation, as worship is an everlasting and perpetual action.

St. Matthew 4:9, 10 states:

> *"And saith unto him, all these things will I give thee, if thou wilt fall down and <u>worship</u> me." (verse 9)*

Again, the שחה verb is used in the future tense תשתחוה (teesh-tah-kah-veh) to express bow down or prostrate oneself, not עבד (worship) which is written in the English version of the King James Bible.

> *"Then Jesus saith unto him, Begone, satan, for it is written, thou shalt <u>worship</u> the Lord thy God and Him only shalt thou <u>serve</u>." (verse 10)*

תשתחוה is again erroneously translated "worship" rather than its true definition, to prostrate oneself, to bow down oneself, or to humble oneself. The English verb *serve* is used by the translators in place of the more accurate verb *worship*. The Hebrew verb written in the Hebrew scripture is תעבוד (tah-ah-vohd), but in this case the English translation is distorted by the use of the word *serve*, when in fact the verb worship should be used as the proper and correct translation for the verb.

The English translators purposely inserted *serve* in place of worship, in order to mislead and deceive the reader. Further substantiation of the many Euro-American deceptions is illustrated by the fraudulous interpretation of the lineage of Noah. Ham was one of Noah's three sons (Ham, Shem and Japheth). Ham was the one son of Noah who was purportedly cursed black, according to Euro-American scholars, but in actuality Canaan was the one cursed by Noah and there is nothing written in the scriptures to suggest that he was cursed black. Generally, anyone cursed (as was Miriam, sister of Moses), was cursed white. The sons of Ham were Cush, Mizriam, Put and Canaan, or in the true translation of their names, Ham's sons were Ethiopia, Egypt, Libya and Canaan. In non-Hebrew Bibles these Hebrew names were written in phonetics. Whereas, the so-called Biblical scholars who translated and interpreted the Bible knew that Mizraim was translated as Egypt, Cush as Ethiopia, Put as Libya and Canaan, although given no English translation, was nevertheless changed to Israel.

Accordingly, the land of Israel was formerly inhabited by Ham's son's (Canaan) children. If Ham was Black, clearly so were his four sons. This fact substantiates that Israel was formerly composed of a Black race, just as the nations of Egypt, Libya, and Ethiopia are comprised of Blacks. Certainly, the translators were aware of the definition of Ham which means in Hebrew hot, burnt, black. Even today, in modern Israel, the Jewish people refer to all Black inhabitants indiscriminately as "Cusheem" (Blacks), which is derived from the name Cush, the son of Ham.

Why were these particular names left untranslated? This was not an oversight. European historians, Biblical scholars and translators conspired to disassociate Israel and Egypt from Africa, once again contributing to the concealing of any positive historical achievements by African people.

These examples of the many wicked strategies used by the devil to deceive the Holy people, the Elect of God, and conceal their true identity and heritage from them to insure their perpetual worship of satan, makes it imperative that the English interpretation of the Holy writings be reevaluated by those inspired by the Living God.

"Search the scriptures, for in them ye think ye have eternal life, and they are they which testify of me."

St. John 5:39

These facts confirm our tenet that there was a deliberate scheme to conceal the truth that the ancient Hebrews were Black. The evidence of these purposeful mistranslations makes the identity of the worshippers of God and the worshippers of the devil explicit. Most people imagine that the worshipping of false gods means falling on one's knees before a carved wooden or stone statue or image such as the idol which the king of Babylon, Nebuchadnezzar, erected in the sixth century during his reign.

"At what time ye hear the sound of the cornet, flute, harp, sackbut, psaltery, dulcimer, and all kinds of music, ye fall down and worship the golden image that Nebuchadnezzar, the king, hath set up."

Daniel 3:5

Here, השתחוה is translated to express *worship* which is not the true meaning, because שחה means in a temporary sense, to prostrate, bow down or humble, and definitely not worship, in the Hebrew sense of the word. For worship, labor, work or toil for God is expressed by עבד. Moreover, from the day of one's birth until the soul returns to the Maker there is a perpetual obligation to worship God. "And no marvel; for satan himself is transformed into an angel of light. Therefore, it is no great thing if his ministers also be transformed as the ministers of righteousness, whose end shall be according to their works."

From the very instant that the new baby enters into the world and draws his first breath, it begins the Divine cycle of worship of the Living God. As the baby nurses its mother's breast, it is worshipping God. If the mother alters from this natural cycle and begins to nourish her baby in an artificial manner,(by giving the baby cow's milk, from plastic and glass bottles and rubber nipples), she is guilty of devil worship.

If a child is fed by artificial means he's inevitably attuned to artificial vibrations and out of tune with God Almighty. By deviating from the perfect order which God has placed him in, and since there is no neutral position for those who would prefer to worship neither God nor the devil, then the child automatically descends to the worship of the devil. The mother perpetrates the child's worship of the devil because she strays from the natural order by refusing to breast-feed her offspring. She generally dries her milk artificially as well as prematurely. Her just reward is cancerous breasts and unruly, unnatural children. The father of the child is also guilty of devil worship because he, being the Godhead ordained by God to keep His Laws (instructions), is responsible for every action of his entire family.

> *"Let us hear the conclusion of the whole matter;*
> *Fear God, and keep his commandments: for this is*
> *the whole duty of man."*

> ### *Ecclesiastes 12:13*

Moreover, the immediate backlash of devil worship is felt by all those guilty of blaspheming God's law. The child, filled with animal hormones, becomes more like the beast than the parent. The proof of the reward for violating God's law is evident in the present European world where children have no respect for God, parents or law.

This assertion that work, labor, toil and worship are synonymous is based upon Biblical facts about work and its actual connection with the prophecy.

*"And while I am speaking, and praying, and con-
fessing my sin and the sin of my people, Israel, and
presenting my supplication before the Lord, my God,
for the holy mountain of my God; Yea, while I was
speaking in prayer, even the man Gabriel, whom I
had seen in the vision at the beginning, being caused
to fly swiftly, touched me about the time of the
evening oblation, And he informed me, and talked
with me, and said, O Daniel, I am now come forth to
give thee skill and understanding."*

Daniel 9:20-22

As Daniel prayed and made supplications (requests) unto the God of
all living, the angel Gabriel came unto him and told him what he (Daniel)
had to do. Daniel no doubt expected some great miracle that he knew God
was able to perform. Instead, he learned from the angel Gabriel that if he
was sincere in his prayers that he would have to *do something* to bring the
things he prayed for to pass. For faith without works (worship) is dead.
God is a spirit who feeds righteous thoughts to the minds of men, so that
they will know that to achieve their visions they must work.

*"Surely the Lord God will do nothing, but he
revealeth his secret unto his servants, the prophets."*

Amos 3:7

*"Turn, O backsliding children, saith the Lord: for I
am married unto you; and I will take you one of a
city, and two of a family, and I will bring you to Zion;
and I will give you shepherds according to mine
heart, who shall feed you with <u>knowledge and
understanding.</u>"*

Jeremiah 3:14,15

There was no great mysticism about the prophecies, or about the angel
Gabriel in the time of Daniel. They are the same in our time and have not
changed. All that the prophets did in the past was to direct the Children of
Israel in the path which God desired that they go. The righteous of times
past were given, (as it is even today), *plain ole common sense*; nothing
mystical or spooky, just righteous doings, work or toil inspired by God, who
is a spirit. Thus it follows, that those who worship Him must do so in spirit
and in truth. To whom do we attribute the mystical mentality? Certainly the
devil, who is also a spirit, but a negative one.

*"For if he that cometh preacheth another Jesus,
whom we have not preached, or if ye receive another
spirit, which ye have not received, or another gospel,
which ye have not accepted, ye might well bear with
him."*

II Corinthians 11:4

Consequently, every man, woman and child is susceptible to the wiles
of the devil. The devil's spirit conveys evil thoughts to the brain. The brain,
in turn, transmits messages to every member of the body, which performs
or is activated accordingly.

What is the mind? The Grolier Webster International Dictionary defines the mind as the unconscious and conscious processes that perceive,
conceive, comprehend, evaluate and reason. Accepting this definition, we
can then compare the mind to a way-station that transmits the spirit of God
or the devil to the brain, which then forwards that spirit on to the body's
members for activation. Therefore those ideas, thoughts, views, etc., which
are manifested from the mind are heavenly or hellish. Thus, if there exists
in one's mind a heavenly state it is because the spirit of God reigns.

Contrarily, if a hellish state of existence is prevalent, it is because the
spirit of the devil reigns. In other words, the mind can be heaven or hell.
The mind is the highest elevation of man. The mind is the place where the
great battle is fought.

*"And there was a war in heaven ("the mind");
Michael and his angels fought against the dragon
and the dragon fought and his angels and prevailed
not; neither was their place found anymore in
heaven."*

Revelation 12:7

It is further written in St. Luke 17:20, 21:

*"And when he was demanded of the Pharisees when
the Kingdom of God should come, he answered them
and said the Kingdom of God cometh not with
observation.*

*Neither shall they say, Lo here; Or, lo there! For,
behold, the Kingdom of God is within you."*

Man is the exemplifier of the spirit of God or the devil. Man's every action, deed or performance is the worship of God or the devil. Therefore a servant of God labors for, toils for, struggles for God. Jesus makes it very clear how to distinguish a worshipper of God from a worshipper of the devil.

"Ye shall know them by their fruits. Do men gather grapes of thorns, or figs of thistles?

Even so, every good tree bringeth forth good fruit, but a corrupt tree bringeth forth evil fruit.

A good tree cannot bring forth evil fruit, neither can a corrupt tree bring forth good fruit.

Every tree that bringeth not forth good fruit is hewn down, and cast into the fire.

Wherefore, by their fruits ye shall know them."

St. Matthew 7:16-20

The devil, as the evil spirit, has entered human vessels and subtly masqueraded himself as an angel of light. Thus, the devil has caused the masses of people today to accept the religious "pie in the sky" theory and the "sweet-bye-and-bye" mentality; wherein they are all looking for a reward of heavenly bliss after their physical death. The inhabitants of the world are bombarded daily by religious leaders advocating the doctrine that they only have to believe in God to be saved. However, these religious leaders never fully explain how this belief must be manifested. We can state with assurance that it can only be manifested by *doing something,* working or worshipping God in spirit and truth. Indeed, this wicked, devilish spirit has been instrumental in injecting idleness and slothfulness within the church layman and encouraging the vain worship of God. Surely, they have succeeded in transforming God into a fairy tale or myth.

In place of light, (knowledge and understanding), the devil has given darkness, (benightedness and ignorance). He has negated everything that he has touched. For example, his new day begins at midnight, in contrast to the new day sanctified and ordained by God in the Genesis which begins in the evening with the going down of the sun.

"And God called the light Day, and the darkness he called Night. And the evening and the morning were the first day."

Genesis 1:5

The visible change of day and night is evident, wise, and Godly, whereas the midnight-to-midnight day is contrary to the sensible cycle established by God. The masses of the earth have sat dumbfounded while the devil subtly and slyly instituted the midnight-to-midnight day into their lives, in exchange for the correct and sensible evening-to-evening day which was established by God.

Just as God established a way to distinguish day from night, He also commanded that six days of work, toil, labor, *worship* should be done, and that on the seventh day, the Sabbath, שבת (meaning stop, cease), man would rest. Therefore, He commanded that the usual activities performed during the first six days of the week come to an end. Thus, working, toiling, laboring, eating, playing, etc., stops on the Sabbath — seventh day.

> *"If thou turn away thy foot from the sabbath, from doing thy pleasure on my holy day, and call the sabbath a delight, the holy of the Lord, honorable, and shalt honor him, not doing thine own ways, nor finding thine own pleasure, nor speaking thine own words;*
>
> *Then shalt thou delight thyself in the Lord; and I will cause thee to ride upon the high places of the earth, and feed thee with the heritage of Jacob, thy father; for the mouth of the Lord hath spoken it."*
>
> **Isaiah 58:13,14**

The Sabbath day, שבת (sha-baht) in Hebrew, is a day of rest, a day when the general action was to cease that the individual might be refreshed. It was a day of inactivity, and in order that it may be sanctified from the activity of daily worship, it was called the Day of Cessation. The devil has deceived the whole world by changing the order of God wherein the Day of Cessation is called the day of worship, and the days of worship or of action are certainly not seen as the days on which you worship God.

The Day of Worship Conspiracy is an important part of the overall plan to inhibit the true worship of God. It is doubtful that you know anyone who relates his job at General Motors to his worship of God. Neither does the secretary, the engineer, nor anyone else understand the connection between work and worship. In actuality, every activity of your entire day is connected to the worship of God.

The verb שחה to bow down, humble oneself, or to prostrate oneself is the action activated on the Sabbath Day in order to refresh, revive, strengthen or renew oneself. In contrast, the devil completely reversed this law in the minds of men and instituted the six days of devil worship, prostration and bowing down unto idols. All of these blatant and apparent acts of the devil are unnoticed by the masses as they march onward into the pits of hell where the feast of the devil is going on.

Currently, as in times past, supposed devout worshippers of God reserve a special day in the week to worship or revere God, doing so in an unenlightened way, which is void of the spirit of Godliness, and ineffective as true worship. The worship of God is not just going to church on Friday, Saturday or Sunday, but working continuously to cast evil from the minds of men and to perpetually enhance and glorify the creations of God. For faith without works is dead. To say "I believe" and show no positive efforts to convert that belief into substance is worthless.

Thus, it is easily understood how a man who worshippeth not the Living God is equated to a dead man who, though he walks, talks, eats, sleeps and breathes, is still considered dead because his temple (body) houses not the progressive, positive, working spirit of God. Faith is based on works! You believe in who you work for (worship). Was not Abraham's faith justified by works when he offered Isaac, his only son, upon the altar? We see that his faith, joined by his works, was made perfect and the scriptures were fulfilled because "Abraham believed God, and was imputed unto him for righteousness; and he was called the Friend of God."

Understandably, the works of a man justify his existence. He cannot live by faith alone. For example, Solomon prayed to God, not for riches and vain materialisms; instead he prayed for wisdom and understanding. His request was answered and his reward was wisdom from God. According to the Biblical account, Solomon was proclaimed to be the wisest man who ever lived. As sober-minded men of God, we know that Solomon did not obtain his wisdom overnight in a dream, but he sought out wisdom diligently. He studied diligently and was amply rewarded for his faithfulness and hard work. The reward for working for God, (or worshipping God), is eternal life and happiness.

There are many Biblical examples of true faith. The Philistine, Goliath, had struck fear into the hearts of the entire army of Israelites, who had prepared themselves to surrender unto the enemies of God. However, faithful David, the little shepherd boy, was noted throughout the Holy writings as a devout and humble servant to God. Although his gallantry and bravery were great indeed he combined his tremendous faith with his works. David was an expert marksman with his small weapon, a slingshot; the stone from which had the force of a bullet when it entered the skull of Goliath. David's expert ability was not given to him by God in a thought.

Yet, all that David ever received from God or the angel Gabriel was skill and understanding. David became an expert marksman through toil, by his works. He believed that God would save him and he practiced diligently the use of his slingshot to substantiate that belief, making him a perfect servant of God. David became known as a man who touched the very heart of God. Therefore, one can readily see that the worship of God is work and *doing something*.

Indeed, work, toil, labor and worship are all used synonymously. Man must forever strive for perfection and even after reaching it, he must continue on that path forever. Every move made throughout the day and night, week or month is an act of worshipping God. For every good work (cause) there is a good result (effect) and vice versa.

If a man cultivates the soil in righteousness and sows good seed he will be blessed to reap a good harvest. And, after toiling the earth in ardent labor, he is rewarded with sweet sleep and peace of mind. Also, the healthy, wholesome food that he grows and ingests, nourishes his body and fortifies his health, giving him the strength to continue to work and fulfill the laws of God. The blessings are automatic; they don't come by chance. Tilling the soil and maintaining the ecological balance of nature complements the righteous worship of God. Keeping in harmony with and attuned to the natural cycles of God insures one's existence and confirms his oneness with the Creator.

This fact is confirmed on every level, as demonstrated by the fact that when one chews his food, works his mouth and grinds his teeth, the more masticated the food becomes, making it easier to digest. Easier digestion lessens the wear-and-tear on the inner organs, greatly reducing the chances of becoming ill. Good health means a healthy body, and a healthy body presents a strong foundation or temple, in which God may dwell. It is very important to know that the worship of God is so much more than just a mere word, as defined by the religions of the world. The worship of God is life-living, existence, breathing, acting.

Furthermore, it is impossible to go into seclusion, hiding in a monastery or seminary, closed off from the world, in an effort to please God. God did not create us to hide us, but rather to venerate His Holy name. If the members of the body are not used, then they will rebel against the working of the body, and often cause serious complications. Thus, the functioning of the members of our bodies, according to the spirit or Will of God, manifests the true worship of God.

Man cannot escape from his inevitable duty to his Maker. All of God's creations, including the celestial bodies, respond promptly and positively to the Will of God. To work in perfect harmony, complementing one another is the Plan of God. The sun, moon and stars continue their everlasting work (worship) obediently and dutifully unto the Creator. Woe be unto the inhabitants of the earth if the celestial bodies duplicated the ways of man and became disobedient, sluggish or rebellious. Everything created by God was created to perform perfectly. He set everything on the course in which it was to work or worship Him, including man. Not only did man stray from the eternal path, but he struggled to corrupt the incorruptible because it took tremendous pains, labor and toil for man to create wars and war machinery. He has toiled against great opposition to reverse the eternal cycles of life. He has labored endlessly and tirelessly to DIE! In his disobedience to his Maker, he has given honor and reverence unto the great adversary of God, the devil, and has received the everlasting reward for worshipping the devil, *death.*

Working harmoniously with the law of God means open communication with the Creator, insuring automatic protection against every type of evil invasion or attack, but a broken line of contact with God leaves one naked and vulnerable to attack by every vile and wicked force in the universe. Howbeit, many defy the Creator and manage to break the law, as exemplified by the breaking of the dietary law given our fathers in the wilderness, wherein, they were commanded by God to abstain from eating swine. The eating of hog was common practice in the lands of the Great Captivity (America). It must have been difficult to become accustomed to eating chitterlings, (hog guts), since one had to struggle to overcome the dreadful stench and rank taste of greasy pig intestines, which only a short time prior, had been filled with defecation. Man toiled to break the law, because it certainly had to be some endeavor to have to squeeze the stool out of the guts of a dead beast, then cook and eat them. It truly had to be a difficult ordeal! The instant reward for that violation of the law was a backlash of deadly diseases. Every part of the pig is equally dangerous to consume, and to do so is to assure yourself of having a diseased, sick and filthy temple (body). Surely you are able to discern whom you worship by the results received. To flagrantly sacrifice your health and well-being is quite an arduous and severe task to perform.

Consider how difficult it is for one to overcome the awful taste of strong drink, such as whiskey, brandy, gin or vodka. The latter two fluids look and taste like rubbing alcohol, and definitely have the same effect. Alcoholic beverages are identical in effect; they only differ in color. These strong fluids literally eat up the internal organs of those who diligently consume them. Thus, to consume them is a laborious task and continual intake insures the consumer the reward of death.

For every act there is a reward, regardless of triviality or minuteness. Contemplate the introduction of mind-deadening drugs to African Americans by the servants of satan. Drugs are used to entice an afflicted and frustrated people to take psychedelic trips from the reality of their wretched surroundings. The method used by the devil to trap his prey was to create situations of hopelessness, desperation and dejection throughout modern society, thus, causing man to seek an escape from such a fate. Naturally, the devil's panacea, or solution, to our overwhelming frustration was designed to lure us into his web of death.

Enslavement to these drugs, (which are also referred to as "dope," because they cause one to act dopey or stupid), is immediate. Certainly, anyone who would sniff hallucinatory, addictive drugs until the nasal membranes are destroyed, resulting in an uncontrollable flow of mucous from the nostrils, would have to be a dope! These same dopes are not content to simply destroy their noses; they also inject drugs into their veins until they abuse every inch of their bodies. They are covered with needle marks. No place on the defiled Holy Temple of man is safe from the probing needle held in the shaking hand of the drug addict.

If a victim survives, several years after his initiation he will find his body virtually veinless. However, his body would still crave narcotics desperately, causing him to inject drugs anywhere on his body: under his armpits, in his ears, under his fingernails and even into his sexual organs. Some women inject them into the vaginal tract. Let us not forget that men rob, cheat, kill, steal and lie in order to obtain the money to purchase drugs. They work, labor and toil day and night to keep their bodies filled with dope. Stopping the injections causes the helpless victim to writhe with unbearable pains. Very few escape this body-strewn path which invariably leads to death, for verily, the wages of sin are death.

It took great work for the Children of Israel to desecrate the law of

God and exist contrary to the cycles of life. God commanded that they have no other gods before Him, yet they willfully rejected His instructions and built graven images of wood and stone that had no saving power. Indeed, these idols had to be physically carried from place to place. Surely, it had to be a horrendous chore to sacrifice one's child unto these images of wood and stone. In fact, it was a very difficult mission. First of all, they broke the lifeline that safeguarded their lives — by disobeying the perfect laws of God. As a result of their blatant disobedience to the laws of God, the Children of Israel suffered enslavement and captivity in America.

Yet, satan wasn't satisfied just inflicting hardship upon the Blacks. He went on to bring tremendous suffering to the slave captors as well. They, too, experienced severe anguish and setbacks in their determination to enslave Africans. First of all, consider the amount of energy and work required to reach the continent of Africa. Months, and sometimes years would pass before the Euro-gentiles would see their families and loved ones again. Often, many of the slaves' captors were either drowned at sea or were killed by African warriors. Many died of the terrible sicknesses and diseases which ran rampant aboard the slave ships. Nevertheless, the slavers worked hard in order to afflict pain and misery upon the slaves. The insidiously evil minds of the captors, who beat, killed, or raped the slaves clearly demonstrate the kind of people involved in the slave-trade business. The work of the slave captors was a labor of hatred, a backbreaking, toiling, laborious endeavor to force a people into slavery. Yet on the other hand, it must be recognized that the suffering, endurance and perseverance of the slaves who withstood the long and furious ride at the bottom of slave ships, (not to mention what awaited them on the shores of America), was required because of their sins against the Living God.

> "Shake thyself from the dust; arise, and sit down, O Jerusalem: loose thyself from the bands of thy neck, O captive daughter of Zion.
>
> For thus saith the Lord, Ye have sold yourselves for nought; and ye shall be redeemed without money."
>
> **Isaiah 52:2,3**

However, they apparently preferred to accept bondage rather than humble themselves unto their Maker, because they worked even harder to remain in captivity. Yet if the turning away from the Living God has caused this vicious captivity, then the returning unto Him inevitably would free them.

"And it shall come to pass, when all these things are come upon thee, the blessing and the curse, which I have set before thee, and thou shalt call them to mind among all the nations, whither the Lord thy God hath driven thee,

And shalt return unto the Lord thy God, and shalt obey his voice according to all that I command thee this day, thou and thy children, with all thine heart, and with all thy soul;

That then the Lord thy God will turn thy captivity, and have compassion upon thee, and will return and gather thee from all the nations, whither the Lord thy God hath scattered thee.

If any of thine be driven out unto the outmost parts of heaven, from thence will the Lord thy God gather thee, and from thence will he fetch thee:

And the Lord thy God will bring thee into the land which thy fathers possessed and thou shalt possess it; and he will do thee good, and multiply thee above thy fathers.

And the Lord thy God will circumcise thine heart and the heart of thy seed, to love the Lord thy God with all thine heart, and with all thy soul, that thou mayest live.

And the Lord thy God will put all these curses upon thine enemies, and on them that hate thee, which persecuted thee.

And thou shalt return and obey the voice of the Lord and do all his commandments which I command thee this day."

Deuteronomy 30:1-8

Every work, deed or act, whether good or evil, receives its just recompense. Sin consists of every work, action or deed that is not done for the glorification and sanctification of the True and Living God of Israel. Every act, deed, and every movement of each member of man's body worships either God or the devil incessantly. Worship is inseparable from work, toil or labor and was instituted from the very beginning of the creation by the Creator of all things. However, that old serpent, satan, has disrupted the glorious cycles of God Almighty and deceived the entire world into worshipping him (satan). He has deceived and tricked man into performing his satanic and devilish deeds under false pretense.

Satan is an evil, wicked spirit and his entire existence is opposite God. His hate is perfect; he even hates himself, as well as all of those connected with him. He is unable to truly love, to be kind, happy, or gentle; he only knows sadness, hate, meanness, depression, and gloom. As forestated, the devil is a spirit; but the devil without a body (temple), "a tangible force," is dead. The devil needs a temple in which to dwell, in order to manifest himself and his evil deeds; for in actuality, the devil is a weakling and is nourished by the sins of men. Therefore, the devil can be destroyed and vanquished from the face of the earth simply by worshipping God or by doing those things which enhance God's every creation.

The advent of the Kingdom of God has caused men to come forth and dedicate their lives and the lives of their children to the vindication of the Holy name of God Almighty — today, tomorrow and even forever! Moreover, the mission will be accomplished by waging war against the devil, pursuing him into every corner and crevice of the earth and beyond, flushing him out of his hiding places, and exposing him unto the Children of the Light, who will annihilate his every thought from existence.

> *"And no marvel; for satan himself is transformed into an angel of light.*
>
> *Therefore it is no great thing if his ministers also be transformed as the ministers of righteousness; whose end shall be according to their works."*
>
> ### *II Corinthians 11:14,15*

The depiction of the devil as a red-clad figure of a man with horns, a tail and a pitchfork, which is the image accepted by most people as the "devil," is a "devilish" trick. The devil is a spirit manifested in men, women and children. If a man's job is machining instruments of war which are used by the adversaries of God, or the forces of evil, then that man works for the devil. He's a worshipper of the devil. Furthermore, every job that does not enhance God's creation is the worship of the devil. There is no neutral position. Either man worships God...or the devil.

> *"I know thy works, that thou art neither cold nor hot: I would thou wert cold or hot."*
>
> ### *Revelation 3:15*

The neutral spirit can be heard throughout every city, community and household: "you can worship God anywhere," "to each his own," "it doesn't matter what your religion is," "live and let live," "I'll do my thing and you do yours." These types of people—the worthless, weak fence-straddlers who change with every wind regardless of the direction—don't merit being characterized as worshippers of God or the devil. He that puts his hand to the plow and turns around is not worthy of God's kingdom. That is to say, that if you want a heavenly state of being or existence, then create it. If you set forth to create it and stop before or even after its completion, you are unworthy of it. Let us, henceforth and for evermore, differentiate the worship of God from the worship of the devil. Let's give a clear-cut understanding, describing the works or worship of God where each righteous entity and every good work is preceded by the word Divine. Divine—in a manner which is pleasing to God. A Divine scientist, for example, is one who creates works which enhance God's creations.

Likewise, the Divine banker, lawyer, judge, professor, clergyman, governor and politician, etc., are those whose actions please God. If a scientist or clergyman does not have Divine preceding his title or identity, he is of the devil. Furthermore, Divine education, agriculture, music, courtship, marriage, sports, etc., are best defined by the Hebrew verb (עבד) to labor, toil, struggle, worship.

Today the devil dresses in a business suit and carries a briefcase. He is a banker, a secretary, a lawyer, a musician, a professor, a writer, a clergyman, a politician, a factory worker, a clerk, a housewife, a president. The devil has incorporated himself into every dimension and facet of man's existence. The devil has caused all classes and levels of people to work, toil and labor to perpetuate his main objective, sin. The devil has become the economist, banker, and stockbroker, those responsible for the monetary systems that have placed man in an endless cycle of physical enslavement in the never ending struggle for materialism and power. The banker has caused man to lust greedily after materialistic wealth, stopping at nothing to obtain it. The banker is responsible for man having to work the best years of his life to pay for a house whose natural materials were taken freely from God's earth. Treasuries the world over have engraved pictures of "famous" dead men on their monetary notes, to perpetuate a feeling of dignity or honor about money. People are encouraged to hide and hoard money, placing it in secret vaults and steel safes surrounded by armed guards. People literally bow down to these paper gods, revering and honoring them. People foolishly sacrifice their lives and the lives of their family and friends for the love of these graven images. Influenced by the banker, men place more value on diamonds and gold than on the life and health of man. The deeds of the banker are a perfect example of the worship (עבד) of the devil.

Another example of a worker of satan is the lawyer. Years ago, the lawyer's purpose was to define the laws of the land for the layman. His occupation was considered menial and there was nothing outstanding in regards to it. In contrast — the lawyer of today is a professional liar and a defender of the guilty, as well as the innocent. He has become a viable force in the political systems of the world and is entrusted by the people to draft the very laws that he himself will eventually violate or circumvent for a price. His goal is to accumulate money by any means necessary. The best lawyer of today's modern world is one who is able to convince a jury or a judge that the guilty is innocent, especially when the guilty party is wealthy. He thus creates a respect for those who are affluent but disdain for the poor. He has the audacity to call himself a legal professional. This immoral practice has caused the entire judicial system of the world to be ineffective in eliminating crime, and has licensed criminals to perpetrate and impregnate the earth with evil and sin. The lawyer aids and abets the devil in his sinister work.

Why is today's world so imperfect? There has to be some underlying reason. Man is continuously projecting that he has good intentions, human-istic ideals and creative genius. Then why do things still tend to go wrong?

> *"There is a way which seemeth right unto a man, but the end thereof are the ways of death."*
>
> ### Proverbs 14:12

The answer is simple: it is satan that's behind the system. In this world without God, the way that *seems* right to man always ends in death. Man, under satan's system, has been convinced that he has the capacity to order his own steps. No matter what the intentions of the banker, lawyer, and judge, they all work for the system. We must confront more than just the physical enemy. We must also understand that there is an "enemy struc-ture" that has to be totally dismantled. The entire Euro-gentile political system is an enemy to both man and God. Man, in the genesis, was formed to evidence the creativity of the "God Mind," without which there would always be a lack of knowledge to bring forth what is right, because God is and always will be the Great Instructor.

"Trust in the Lord with all thine heart; and lean not unto thine own understanding.

In all thy ways acknowledge him, and he shall direct thy paths."

Proverbs 3:5,6

"O Lord, I know that the way of man is not in himself; it is not in man that walketh to direct his steps.

O Lord, correct me, but with judgement; not in thine anger, lest thou bring me to nothing."

Jeremiah 10:23,24

Mankind, cut off from God, descends into every imaginable immorality and sin; society has gone morally mad with injustice, greed, prejudice, war, famine, pollution and disease. Then, using his own mental resources to rationalize his evil, man justifies and explains it away.

Alongside the banker and the lawyer, is the contemptible professor, the educator of the aforementioned disciples of the devil. It is through him that the devil really boasts of himself. It is through him that the reprobate mind is propagated. A reprobate mind is one void of sound mental judgment. Such a mind negates the influence of God in favor of the system. He teaches man to begin *with himself* in the Creation, and if a substitute is needed, he makes available a gorilla or tadpole — *anything* but the dust of the earth of Genesis. It is upon the professor that the devil has rained down his evil thoughts, and through him that these evil thoughts are transformed into wicked substance. It is the professor who fills the minds of men with perverse "isms," devious ideologies and false doctrines which cause men to labor unceasingly to destroy the earth.

Through academics, men are trained to intellectually demolish the earth and exterminate every trace of life. He is responsible for war-mongering generals and admirals being seen as patriotic heroes. He has instructed the inventors of horrible weapons and instruments of war and trained men to kill millions of people with one touch of a button. He has taught men to create huge metropolises populated with barbaric inhabitants who hate one another. He labors incessantly for the devil, dedicating himself to the transmittal of his decadent educational system to the four corners of the earth.

He has a comrade in the clergyman (also known as a priest, nun, preacher, parson, pope, etc.). These aliases are used by the devil to subtly and craftily beguile men. Dressed in sheep's clothing, the clergyman, is in reality, one who feasts on the ignorance of the people. His job is to prevent the rebellion against evil; to destroy the simplicity of the worship of God through duplicity. The spirit which would make men stand for God is subtly destroyed. There is a distinct difference between those who say "I believe in God" and those who stand up for His principles. The world is full of the former. The clergyman, through his preachings, has alienated man from his Creator, woman from her man, and children from their parents. He has instilled, instead, a love of death and the "sweet-bye-and-bye" mentality into his followers. He has caused men to err in their conception of the worship of God Almighty. He is the blind shepherd who misleads his flock and causes them all to fall into the ditch. The clergyman portrays a perverted image of a man of God. Consequently, men of God are not looked upon as heroes or someone after whom all men should pattern themselves. Indeed, all men should be men of God. עבד, working, laboring, toiling, worshipping in righteousness, are the qualifications for being a man of God.

The false images and distorted teachings of the clergy have caused gross misinterpretations of the writings of the prophets and led men from God, instead of to God. He also teaches that prayer is answered by God in a mysterious and ambiguous sense, when, in fact, God instills skill and understanding. That simply means that if one prays that a huge mountain be moved, then, after praying, he rolls up his sleeves and takes a pick and shovel and begins moving the mountain. This is the true worship of God. The clergyman and his colleagues have promulgated multiple religious beliefs, dogmas and doctrines that further confuse and misguide men. Through him women are liberated from men, children are liberated from parents and promiscuity is the name of the game. The clergyman has been a chief instrument in causing the masses to submit to the devil's evil way. He can always be depended upon to find a way to justify the ways of the wicked, (especially if they are dues-paying members of his parish), while very seldom being qualified to renounce evil.

I have yet to hear a member of the clergy use the Law of God in the renunciation of homosexuality. He causes men to see through darkened glass; he gives no vision of God's Kingdom on earth. Instead, he instills false images into the minds of the children, causing them to believe the lies of the Christian holiday, Christmas, during which a fat white man, dressed in a red suit and driving a team of reindeer through the sky, delivers a sled full of gifts on December 25th. He delivers the gifts by descending into the smoky, hot chimneys and stove pipes of every house in the world in one night. Further, men mislead their children into believing that rabbits lay eggs and, consequently, have established a day of sanctification for egg-laying rabbits called Easter. In essence, man in many cases, initiates children in their pursuit of lies and fabrication, contributing to the deterioration of the moral fiber of the family.

Another chief ally of the devil is the scientist. He has broken natural cycles, profaned the natural elements that are conducive to the well-being of man and nature, split atoms and crossed the genes of man, beast and even the herbs of the field. He has exploited the earth of its natural re-sources and drained an enormous portion of the earth's natural blood (oil). Then he contaminated the earth, seas, atmosphere and stratosphere with toxic gases. He has even shattered the ozone layer (the earth's natural protection against the sun's deadly ultraviolet rays). He has, verily, created hideous weapons of war: atomic bombs, hydrogen bombs, neutron bombs, germicidal agents and poisonous gases made from matter which he is un-able to recycle back into the earth. He has made the Euro-gentiles the cruelest and most ruthless species to ever walk the earth.

> *"Their webs shall not become garments, neither shall*
> *they cover themselves with their works: their works*
> *are works of iniquity, and the act of violence is in*
> *their hands.*
>
> *Their feet run to evil, and they make haste to shed*
> *innocent blood: their thoughts are thoughts of*
> *iniquity; wasting and destruction are in their paths."*
>
> ### Isaiah 59:6-8

The scientist has blown gigantic holes in the earth which have in turn caused the natural weather cycles to change. Thus, normally cold places become hot and normally hot places get cold. He has thoroughly contami-nated the pure drinking waters of the earth. Naturally wholesome and nu-tritious foods have been made noxious and flaccid from the use of his innumerable pesticides, food additives, preservatives, colorings, etc. The scientist is easily identified as an obedient servant of his father, the devil, raising up the dead, putrefied image of decadence.

> *"Professing themselves to be wise, they became*
> *fools...Wherefore God also gave them up to unclean-*
> *ness through the lusts of their own hearts, to*
> *dishonour their own bodies between themselves.*

*Who changed the truth of God into a lie, and wor-
shipped and served the creature more than the
Creator, who is blessed for ever. Amen.*

*For this cause God gave them up unto vile affec-
tions: for even their women did change the natural
use into that which is against nature;*

*And likewise also the man, leaving the natural use of
the woman, burned in their lust toward one another;
men with men working that which is unseemly, and
receiving in themselves that recompense of their error
which was meet.*

*And even as they did not like to retain God in their
knowledge, God gave them over to a reprobate mind,
to do those things which are not convenient;...*

*Who knowing the judgment of God, that they which
commit such things are worthy of death, not only do
the same, but have pleasure in them that do them."*

Romans 1:22,24-28,32

Indeed, volumes could be compiled upon the aforementioned dedicated worshippers of the devil. There is neither sufficient time nor space to convey the magnitude or amount of havoc these workers of iniquity have caused upon the earth. Hopefully, the definition of worship has been clarified. Moreover, it should be perfectly understood that the reason that men throughout the ages abandoned their lands of origin is because they wanted a place where they could worship God properly. They understood that the mere act of living in a wicked environment caused them to be guilty by association. Enoch was transformed; Noah left the world; Abraham left his home in search of a city whose Maker and Builder was God; Jesus declared, "I am not of this world." This world has to be unsparingly renounced. You must come out of it and join hands with the Saints of the Kingdom, to build a New World Order where all men will work for, labor for, toil for — *worship* God.

Truly, God is exemplified by every positive action; to do good is the worship of God; helping your brother or sister is the worship of God. Divine dancing, singing, laughing or playing is of God and is indeed, the true worship of God. To plant and to harvest, to eat, and to be merry is the true worship of God. For truly, life is continued action — work and worship. They are inseparable.

The devil has deceived the entire world. While this work is only a minute portion of the testimony of God which condemns the entire world, hopefully it will revive the spirit of God in men and revive the will to truthfully worship God — that men may live!

The Making of a Slave
or Soul Transformation

PART I
New Names - New Gods

What is a name? A name is an individual's connection to his family or nation. It is the name, which distinguishes one person or race from another. Generally, through the name or nationality of a person, his language is extracted. For example, Hebrew people speak Hebrew; Germans speak German; French speak French; and Yoruba speak Yoruba. Languages transmit the knowledge of a nation's past heritage, present realities and future goals. Therefore, a name becomes the individual's tie to a nationalistic whole: the whole being a land, language and culture.

However, individuals who have been deracinated, (a condition of a people who have been severed from their nationalistic remembrance and forced to accept and function within the context of another's nationalistic remembrance), pay no credence to a name. A John Smith, descended from African slaves, who seeks the "American way," cares little about his name or its meaning. However, to be nameless is to be labeled illegitimate, obscure or unfit to be mentioned. John Smith, a former chattel slave, (or the descendant of one), is regarded by law and custom as the property of another, and is wholly subjected to the will of another. He is, essentially, nameless because in renaming slaves, the slave owners took caution not to give names of any positive spiritual prowess or significance. The slave owners made certain that the nicknames given to the slaves disconnected them from their land, language and culture. Throughout the African world, we witness the greater credibility and respect often given to "Christian" names versus family and tribal names.

The name "negro" fit into the scheme of the Euro-gentile slavers perfectly. It was also prophetic. The nickname "negro" is of Spanish origin and is an adjective describing the color black. When Spain entered into the slave trade, they addressed the Africans as "negro" which meant "the

Blacks." Consequently, this absurd title has remained as the European description of the Black race.

The paradox is not how the entire Black race became nicknamed "negro," but how and why they submitted to it. How is it that when a Black man is called "negro," he is not insulted? And why is it, even at this late date that Africans in America are still struggling with their obvious genetic, historical and cultural identity? For not until 1989, did the term "African American" gain prominence and popularity within our community.

As we reflect on our childhood, remember how angry we became when someone called us "out of our name"? We would be ready to fight if someone used a name of slander toward our mother or any other family members. We realized that there were good names and there were bad names. There were names we even called "curse names," which if related to us, made us feel as if another were "cursing" us. Are there names that carry a curse? If so, the converse should be that there are names that carry a blessing. Again, we find remnants of ancient wisdom not completely understood, because we have been concerned, yet unconcerned about our names. What do you imagine would be the end result of being called "Snake" or "Killer" all day every day? You were completely justified in your childhood fears of the negative connotations in a name. You needed only to understand the magnitude of the "curse" of an improper name.

It is evident that the name "negro" makes absolutely no spiritual or literal sense as it relates to a people or nation. If it was not the power and will of God Almighty that caused this gross ignorance to remain, then it is unexplainable. However, the reader can be assured that it was the will of God. Credit for such a deep wonder dare not be attributed to the European mind.

One of the most profound undertakings of the Euro-gentiles is what I term the Great Religious Conspiracy. The Euro-gentiles have deceived the whole world, causing it to honor and worship false gods and idols, while at the same time giving an impression of their superior intelligence and culture; wherein, no one would believe that they are pagans, still honoring the false gods of their fathers. No race of people has so negatively altered the laws, seasons and purpose of God's creation as have the Euro-gentiles, yet they are not seen as criminals that continuously violate the everlasting ordinances of God Almighty. The significance of Judgement Day is surely that the Sons of God will be awakened, to bring this criminal to trial, laying bare all of his evil deeds. We must always remember that satan is wise and a master of evil... a master deceiver.

Europeans rule the world today, and because of this rulership there is no justice, equity, peace, love of fellow man, love of God or true happiness. Instead of everyone accusing him and forcing him to relinquish the Spiritual Magna Carta (authority to rule), everyone continuously attends his conferences and forums, placing their hope in the cause of the calamity. This is a phenomenon if there ever was one!

Because words are interpreted as having a spirit, likewise, names have spirits and they too, convey life — positively or negatively. Generally, a person reacts to the sound of his or her name. The power of names, just like the power of the spoken word, must not be taken for granted or looked upon lightly. Names, as our forefathers knew, play a very significant role in the maintenance of a happy and harmonious life. The majority of African Americans do not realize the overt and obvious negativity attached to their American names, nor to the term "negro." As mentioned, the word "negro" is a Spanish adjective meaning black. During the era of slavery in the Americas, it did not matter to the slave master whether the slave was Hebrew, Ashanti, Watusi, or Mandingo; they were all labeled "negro" by him. It mattered not to the wicked enslavers that the Africans were of different cultures and nationalities and spoke different languages; they were collectively called "negro." What were the enslavers attempting to accomplish by renaming the captives (both personally and nationally)?

On a relentless pursuit of evil, the Europeans apparently were intent on destroying, negating and changing the spirit, and thus the lives of the Children of Israel, whom they had enslaved.

The captives had to be reduced to nothing in order to recreate them in the image sought by the slavers. How is it that, in a large proportion of the cases, the names given the African captives were rooted in European culture? Certainly, after affecting the lives of 100 million Africans, the Europeans were familiar with African names. However, in transforming the African soul, no Hausa, Yoruba, Ashanti, Vai or Hebrew names slipped through, an achievement so perfect that it could only have been sanctioned by God and planned meticulously by men of evil purpose. Certainly, these slaves were void of the Spirit of God, for they neither rejected their new names nor did they comprehend that they were being cunningly cut off from the Land of the Living. Had the Spirit of God been present it would have caused rebellion at this evil change, for the Spirit of Right rebels against wrong.

Even now, those possessing God's spirit cannot accept this world nor do they have a desire for the "king's meat" (materialism). The one bright spot which has baffled the slave masters are the lyrics of the Songs of Zion (gospels). Are these ancient hymns something we have just found or adopted along the way? (If so, then from whom?) Or, are they the oral tradition of our long-lost past? Euro-American historians have attempted to deny that there is a connection between the ancient Israelites and African Americans. Yet, we continuously find among our people all the ancient hymns relating to Jerusalem and Canaan's Land. These hymns, no doubt, were the prophetic "little light" which they sang about in the tune, "This little light of mine; I'm gonna let it shine."

> *"Therefore say, Thus saith the Lord God; Although I have cast them far off among the heathen, and although I have scattered them among the countries, yet will I be to them as a little sanctuary in the countries where they shall come."*
>
> ### Ezekiel 11:16

Everything connected with the color black, no matter whether it was race, religion, or culture was labeled base, backwards and uncivilized. A cardinal example is the definition of the word "black" in the Grolier International Dictionary* of the English language:

> "**black** — of the darkest possible color or hue, like soot or coal; absorbing all light or incapable of reflecting it; of an extremely dark color, noting or pertaining to a dark-skinned race, *especially* negro; soiled, or stained; dismal or gloomy; boding ill; sullen and forbidding; destitute of moral light or goodness; evil or wicked; causing or marked by ruin or desolation; calamitous or disastrous; deadly; malignant; indicating censure, disgrace or liability to punishment."

Whereas, everything associated with white was glorified, as exemplified in this definition:

> "**white** — of the color of pure snow; reflecting the rays of sunlight or similar light. Having a light-colored skin, as a Caucasian; noting, pertaining to, or controlled by the Caucasian race, as schools, housing and the like; free from spot or stain; pure or innocent; not intending harm; as, a white lie. Slang, honorable; fair; decent; dependable. Op-

---

The English-Language Institute of America, Inc. Copyright 1973, 1972, 1971.

posite to black; the condition or characteristic of being white."

This particular dictionary is usually found in the institutions, homes and offices of America's lawmakers, and is generally not available for sale to the layman. It is not surprising then, upon rereading the final offering of the definition for "black," to learn that U.S. prisons are overcrowded with African Americans. The definition of the word "black," given by the white lawmakers and the Grolier English language authorities, is exactly the manner in which the white race perceives the Black race.

Consequently, it is easy to comprehend how a people are nicknamed and misnamed "negro," "nigger," "colored" or Afro American according to the whims and desires of the oppressor. Acceptance of the absurd title "negro" or "nigger" by the slaves demonstrates the extent to which the spirit of Black people was subdued.

When the negro slave was African, (Ashanti, Hebrew, or from any of the other cultural communities), he was independent — the tradesman, artisan, builder, agriculturist, doctor, teacher, etc. As a matter of fact, the slaves were the brains and the manpower in the beginning stages of American industrial development. However, to obscure and undermine any possibility that their positive achievements could be attributed to Africa, their African names were changed to Anglo-Saxon names. In this manner, it thus appears as though the Anglo-Saxon culture and the land of the Americans were the root or source of their great understanding. It is very doubtful that you have ever seen a great "negro" whose positive characteristics were attributed to the past greatness of his African ancestry. Statements such as: "The Ashantis were very skillful carpenters, because most of the African American carpenters are of Ashanti origin" are not heard. Africa was not allowed to receive praise or to be the source of any great skills or attributes which the slaves may have possessed. At that time in history all learning and intelligence was to be seen as having its origins in Europe. Ironically, the European slavers were the murderers, rapists and maniacs who were expelled from Europe and sent to America. Helped and befriended by the Indians, these misfits later betrayed and annihilated the *real* Native Americans.

The process of renaming the slaves according to the particular whim or fancy of the master is just one illustration of the European's method of controlling the African. In the beginning, some slaves fought against this evil imposition. However, as prophesied, the Children of Israel, (the African in America), surrendered spiritually to their masters and oppressors, accepted their names, and as a result, became powerless and ineffective.

> *"And thou shalt become an astonishment, a proverb, and a byword, among all nations whither the Lord shall lead thee."*

> **Deuteronomy 28:37**

When the names of the master were instilled into the minds of the slave, his life-style took on the spirit of the master. All his habits mimicked his oppressor's. Essentially the slave became European in the spirit and remained African only in the flesh. Their spirits were dominated totally to the extent that Blacks hated their black skins. This negative spirit inevitably became active in every facet of their lives — their eating habits, emotions, culture, teachings, etc.

Sadly, the far-reaching ramifications which followed this capitulation are still evident in the present day plight of Black America. A people who walk in darkness, African Americans are nameless, landless, without a language or culture of their own. Today, they proudly sport names of Jackson (Jack's son), Coleman (coal man), Payne (pain), Taylor (tailor), Davis (Dave is), etc. Being slaves, they were given slave names of weakness, names which referred to another god; consequently, causing a "curse" word to be upon them all the day long. These names have played a very significant role in draining their strength and in transforming their souls. With titles such as these, it is no wonder why our people cannot prosper or overcome the simultaneous covert and subtle vices of their enemies.

Another illustration of the devious game played by satan's puppets can be seen in the manner in which those who seek to belittle the importance of this community refer to me by my "slave name" Carter, rather than by my Hebrew name Ben Israel. In the majority of the news articles or programs concerning the African Hebrew Israelite Community, I am referred to as Ben Ammi Carter, even though I have always made it clear that my last name is Ben Israel and not Carter. Still, writers and broadcasters are determined to call me Ben Ammi Carter.

There seems to be no problem for these same writers and broadcasters to remember to refer to Israel's first prime minister by his Hebrew name, David Ben Gurion, and not as David Green, the name given to him at birth. In the same newspapers, radio and television programs that refer to me as Ben Ammi Carter, Ben Gurion is never referred to as David Green.

Thus, I must conclude that if these newswriters and broadcasters are aware that it is a dishonor to write or speak of David Ben Gurion as David Green, surely they are also aware that it is disrespectful to write and refer to me as Ben Ammi Carter.

There was one segment of the European slavemaster college that understood the power of names and moved to take advantage of it. These men, the Goldbergs (gold prosperous, solid citizen), Wienbergs (wine prosperous, solid citizen), Silvermans (silver man), Diamonds (diamonds), Weismans (wise man), have profited monetarily, through their knowledge of the power of names. The spirit behind their names has manifested itself into a rewarding control of the world's economic systems. However, even their understanding has profited them only in a monetary or materialistic sense.

Failing to fulfill the spirituality or meaning of one's name is to be likened to a piece of fruit that never reaches maturity or the infant that succumbs in its embryonic state. Because of careful and methodical planning, the names of white heroes are a source of envy and emulation. For example, "Superman" is the idol of every Euro-gentile boy. Muscular and invincible, he is the epitome of power and strength. On the other hand, "Superfly," the Black pimp in the movie of the same name, is not only a man of negative qualities but his name suggests a symbol of one of the lowest species on God's earth — a fly. Yet this is the name and image after which Black youth pattern themselves. Where are the John Wayne, Charleton Heston, Arnold Schwarzeneger, "Sly" Stallone images of heroics and strength among the African American people?

The conspiracy dates back to ancient history when King Nebuchadnezzar of ancient Babylon took special caution to rename his slaves to fit his specifications. In other words, the spirit of the names given to the slaves complemented his kingdom and not the kingdom from which the slaves originated.

> *"And the king appointed them a daily provision of the king's meat, and of the wine which he drank: so nourishing them three years, that at the end thereof they might stand before the king.*
>
> *Now among these were of the children of Judah, Daniel, Hananiah, Mishael and Azariah:*
>
> *Unto whom the prince of the eunuchs gave names: for he gave unto Daniel the name Belteshazzar; and*

*to Hananiah, of Shadrach; and to Mishael, of
Meshach; and to Azariah, of Abednego.*

*But Daniel purposed in his heart that he would not
defile himself with the portion of the king's meat, nor
with the wine which he drank: therefore he requested
of the prince of the eunuchs that he might not defile
himself."*

Daniel 1:5-8

*"But at the last Daniel came in before me, whose
name was Belteshazzar, according to the name of my
god, and in whom is the spirit of the holy gods: and
before him I told the dream."*

Daniel 4:8

A careful study of Daniel 1:5-8 reveals three very significant points in
the making of a slave. (1) The significant role of improper diet in the preparing of one's mind to accept the necessary changes in his character. The
slaves were meticulously fed, like animals in hog troughs, a diet fit to keep
and nourish only evil. They were fed the scum of the earth. The mainstay
of their diet was a beast (swine), which God had commanded that they not
eat, or for that matter, not even touch its carcass. Clearly, an improper diet
will negatively affect the mind. Daniel, being wise, decided that he would
not "defile" himself by consuming the mind-destroying diet prepared by his
captors. (2) Names, like words, have meanings and all the names given to
the Hebrews by the prince of the eunuchs related to other gods. Every
society subtly forces its subjects to worship the god of that land through
laws, customs, names or seasons. (3) Those in power realize the power of
a name in the making of a slave. Gentiles have used this procedure in
grooming slaves for thousands of years and have not changed. King
Nebuchadnezzar's eunuch slave changed Daniel's name, meaning "God
has judged" to Bel-te-shazzar which means "favored of Bel," (the national
god of Babylon). With Daniel were Hananiah (God is kind), whose name
was changed to Shad-rach (circuit of the sun); Mishael (consulted or inquired of by God) to Me-shach (ram or sun-god of the Chaldeans); and
Azariah (God is my help) to A-bed-nego (servant of Nego, Mercury god of
the Chaldeans). Evidently, the Babylonians revered and acknowledged their
gods in their actions as seen in the names given their subjects, free or
bonded.

Had Daniel, Hananiah, Mishael, and Azariah been ignorant of the power of names and their spiritual significance, then their outstanding achievements in the land of their captivity would have not been manifested. They would have been physically and spiritually subjected to the modes of Babylonian society.

Nevertheless, the God of the Hebrews remained in the hearts of Daniel and the three Hebrew boys. Every other god was inferior to theirs. They remained steadfast to and strong for the God of gods. Consequently, they activated the positive spirit and power that emanated from their names. Their land remained imbued in their minds, even though they were chattel slaves, and they did not forget their own language because it bonded them to their God. Neither did they change their eating habits to please their captors. They were culturally uncompromising. This angered the subjects of King Nebuchadnezzar, because Daniel, Hananiah, Mishael and Azariah remained "The Hebrews," and not Chaldeans. Above all, their names continuously injected praise unto the God of Israel.

The adversary has always applied the standard of "no man can serve two masters." The changing of one's name directly leads to the praise and worship of another deity. The Black world is not conscious of the far-reaching consequences of Euro-American names because Blacks have been taught to believe that whatever Europeans give them is acceptable. Black scholars no longer study the events of the Old Testament, nor do they understand that Hebrew history is African history. Therefore, they do not attribute the disenfranchisement of Africans to the misunderstanding of the power of God.

Thus it was in the days of the ancients; so it is even today. The enemy has not changed his tactics. The power of names is as significant today as it was then. Each man's name has a profound spiritual effect on him because he hears his name over and over throughout his life. We need only to look into our communities to see the effects of nicknames like "Crazy," "Tough," "Killer," "Snooche," "Snake," "Spider," "Blood," "Hit Man," and others. Likewise, the constant repetition of a word by one person or a multitude of people has a very powerful effect, whether negative or positive. This is the basis of the science of brainwashing.

> *"Then said he unto me, Prophesy unto the wind, prophesy, son of man, and say to the wind, Thus saith the Lord God: Come from the four winds, O breath, and breathe upon these slain, that they may live."*
>
> ***Ezekiel 37:9***

In the Hebrew language the word "wind" is also interpreted as spirit. Thus, Ezekiel obeyed and by so doing he activated the Word of God. Just as the words of man are transmitted on radio waves, the higher spiritual order also transmits words and thoughts. Scientists refer to this higher order as metaphysics. I prefer to keep it in the simplest and most easy-to-understand terms: the power of the Word of God.

Let us consider the names of the days of the week. As written in the book of Genesis, God gave names to the days of the week by ordinal numbers. The original, God-given names were: First Day, Second Day, Third Day, Fourth Day, Fifth Day, Sixth Day, and Seventh Day (or Sabbath Day). The use of these names gives honor to the God of Creation by constantly using words or saying things that give pleasure to His ears. These words also keep us in harmony with all of the Creation, as we praise God, the Creator, by adhering to the order He has established. We no longer praise the God of Creation because the adversary has craftily changed the names of the days of the week as follows:

Sunday	Day of worship of the Sun God.
Monday	Moon day, day of worship of the moon.
Tuesday	Pagan day of worship of the planet Mars.
Wednesday	Heathen day of worship of the pagan god Mercury.
Thursday	Heathen day of worship of the planet or pagan god Jupiter (Thor).
Friday	Friggs, Scandinavian goddess; wife of Odin and goddess of marriage, love, and the heart.
Saturday	Heathen day of worship of the pagan god or planet Saturn.

Also, the adversary, in changing names, set in cycle a change of time and season. January, presently the first month of the year, was once the eleventh month of the year — a much more sensible order because in January there is no evidence of a new year. It is generally cold, rainy, or snowy at that time. There are definitely no signs of new life, and it is completely opposite to the new year that God ordained, which begins in the month of Aviv (between March and April), the time of Passover:

"And the Lord spoke unto Moses and Aaron in the land of Egypt, saying:

This month shall be unto you the beginning of months; it shall be the first month of the year to you."

Exodus 12:1,2

The month of Aviv was ordained by God as the first month of the year. The wisdom in this selection is perfect, for the evidence of new life is literally manifested for all to see: trees bud, birds migrate and many animals bring to an end their long winter hibernation. Julius Caesar changed January to the first month of the year and added two extra days. Moreover, he named the month after the Roman god Janus, whose name means "two-faced" or "double-faced." Janus was supposedly able to see in front of himself and behind himself at the same time.

"And in all things that I have said unto you be circumspect; and make no mention of the name of other gods, neither let it be heard out of thy mouth."

Exodus 23:13

Who gave mankind the right to change God's laws and standards? Has this been a diabolical, satanic plan or did this happen just by chance? We can vividly see one of the ways satan has deceived the whole world, as the people unknowingly give honor to no less than seven false pagan gods in the course of one week. Consequently, what could we expect of God because as the Commandment states, "I am a jealous God, and furthermore, be circumspect and give no honorable mention of any other gods"? Do not take these revelations lightly, for every word that you speak shall and is being brought for judgment before the throne of God. It is not the purpose of the Euro-American to bring all men unto God. You must accept this truth if you desire to live in God.

The apparent reason for the present world rulership to overtly violate the ordinances of God Almighty is that these violations are the vehicles used by the great adversary, (satan, the devil), to change the natural times, laws, ordinances and ways of God Almighty. Satan's obvious intent was and is to ensure that every name spoken on earth pays homage to him, not God. This is the only logical understanding to be gained after observing why the enemies of God have gone through so much stress and strain to alter the names of peoples, places and things.

PART II

History and Education

History should be treasured because it holds the key to the past and the hope for the future. Without a clear understanding of history, one cannot properly evaluate past mistakes and correct them. Where there is no clear historical experience, people are easily subjugated. This is true of the Black world. The history of Black people in America prior to slavery was not accidentally lost; it was purposely destroyed in order to teach Africans in America to be slaves. The first step in the training of a slave is to destroy everything connecting him with honor, glory, splendor or grandeur. The slave has to be made to feel that whatever he receives is better than what he had.

Before the coming of the European, Africans had cultural traditions far superior to that of the white slave masters. African builders, astrologers, artisans and engineers had already created wonders which would baffle the European mind for a thousand generations. Your West and North African educational institutions were turning out geniuses at a rate unimaginable to today's world. The children began their educational process at age three and by the time they had completed what would be termed elementary school today, they had an intelligence level beyond the highest degree attainable in today's institutions of learning. It was not uncommon to find professors in their early teens. There were kings ruling dynasties as young as eight years old. Do these things seem hard to imagine? If so, it is only because the adversary created for you a history of cannibalism and ignorance, and because African people are so far from God and from knowing themselves that their former greatness seems unfathomable.

The transfiguration of the African Hebrews (Sons of God) into a non-people (negroes) exemplifies the epitome of soul transformation. The people who once were rulers of advanced civilizations like Songhai, Egypt and Mali have descended into the pits of the most barbaric societies. The "apple of God's eye," the "light (Divine intelligence) of the world," the "select of God," have been transformed into base men, groping daily in darkness (ignorance) and chained to obscurity, their adversaries mocking and enslaving them — mentally and physically. Despite the apparent gains of the Black middle class, statistics show that, as a whole, African Americans continue to be treated as second-class citizens, despite having lived over 400 years in America. It is evident that the vast majority of African Americans have accepted this way of life for themselves because they continue to allow themselves to be victimized by the wicked hand of their oppressor: they are unemployed, under-educated, brutalized and condemned. The backlash caused by the soul transformation of these African Hebrews has made them the laughingstock of the world, disrespected by all people.

The former African, transformed into a negro, ardently endeavors to prove himself equal to Europeans. He is perplexed and filled with resentment when he is not respected. The negro must understand that no copy is as good as the original. His pursuit to become a full-fledged European will forever have an abortive end, because at his very best the negro is only an imitation, a carbon copy. Naturally, no one likes a copycat. As a matter of fact, carbon copies are eventually crumpled up and thrown into the waste basket.

For all their efforts to be like, and thus accepted by whites, Africans should take into consideration what life would be if the tables were turned. Allow me to give an illustration based on the situation of negroes living in the United States.

If negroes hated a race of people, and overtly and without reproach, exhibited that hate, how would be the negroes' feelings if that other race sought to be the negroes' equal: to integrate their neighborhoods, schools, jobs, recreation centers, private clubs, marry their daughters, etc.? Furthermore, if that other race envisioned, and aspired daily to be acclaimed, to speak and to be culturally endowed in negroism, how would the negroes react if those abominable beings appeared at each fork of the road and at every twist and turn, especially if the rejected race was a reminder of the negroes' hideous, scandalous, hellish past? If negroes were attempting to hoodwink the world into believing that they were a pious, God-fearing people and at the sight of that other group the memory of the vile past became vivid, how would negroes react? The presence of those whom they lynched, murdered, slandered, raped, and flagrantly imprisoned without cause, would cause negroes, at least, embarrassment and vexation. Certainly the undesirable presence of that group would cause the negroes' past to be forever an open book for all to see. Undoubtedly, the reactions of the negro, if the shoe was on the other foot, would be equivalent to that of Europeans. If the table was turned and the negro was a tyrant, a killer, a warmonger, a racist, a klansman, etc., he surely would not want his chief victim to be transformed into a super negro — a faultless, unblemished image of himself.

This is the case with the negro. He has become more European than the European. Therefore, everytime a European looks into the black face of a negro, the European sees himself, his work, his creation and he loathes it. How would it be conceived, in the eyes of the world, for an African to teach a classroom of Japanese students Japanese history and culture in the purest form of the Japanese language, in of all places, Japan? Would it not appear, at the least, unique or unusual? Yet, practices such as these are common in the U.S. and accepted as natural rather than peculiar. According to the deeds of Euro-gentiles and their evil sojourn on earth, it is evident that they hate the creations of God, the earth, its inhabitants and even each other; therefore, they surely would hate a carbon copy of themselves.

The irony of African Americans desiring to be white can best be termed ridiculous considering the agony they have undergone as a result. Everything brought to us from Europe divides us. It tears us apart. His religion divides us. His material wealth divides us. His standards of manhood and womanhood divide us. And, brothers and sisters, a house divided against itself cannot stand. Consequently, we are weak before the strong and foolish before the wise. Everything that they have given us is the fruit of dissension, the religion of discord, the wealth of chaos, the education of disagreement. They have torn us to pieces like a lion tearing at his prey. The more of his beliefs that we are fed, the farther we grow apart.

African Americans will never be united and will never taste freedom until we rise from the mental death, which has left us rootless. When the back doors of Euro-gentile education were opened, the plan was set in motion. The unseen title of the course was: "The Transforming of a Soul." We initially flocked to the educational institutions seeking the tools needed for our survival, but instead, we received the tools necessary for the survival of white superiority. Yet, it stands to reason, if you could deduce the process by which you could be free and you were given the necessary teachings in his institutions, you would have applied your training to the attainment of freedom long ago. Instead, after years of study in his institutions and the subsequent application of these teachings to the struggle for liberation, African Americans continuously fall far short of the mark.

A world that desires to keep us powerless and enslaved cannot afford to give the oppressed the teachings that will free us, nor a God that will save us. A tyrant that desires to keep you weak, cannot give you a history which will make you strong. The African American educator Carter G. Woodson put it accurately when he said, "No systematic effort toward change has been possible, for, taught the same economics, history, philosophy, literature and religion which have established the present code of morals, the negro's mind has been brought under the control of his oppressor.

The problem of holding the negro down therefore is easily solved. When you control a man's thinking, you do not have to tell him not to stand here or go yonder. He will find his 'proper place' and stay in it. You do not need to send him to the back door. He will go without being told. In fact, if there is no back door, he will cut one for his special benefit. His education makes it necessary."[4]

We were disconnected from our very soul. We became a non-people seeking to be every race except our own. We were totally de-Africanized. This was necessary for the survival of white America's superiority, because their superiority is established upon a weak foundation that cannot stand challenge or comparison. Certainly, they could not stand the competition of great African minds and institutions. Therefore, through their educational system, whites had to systematically destroy Africa. There could be no association or knowledge of past greatness.

As an African, the slave was forced into the back door; as a negro, he walked out of the front door, willingly giving credit unto his master. Unfortunately, he never saw the neon sign blinking overhead that read, "What has a man gaineth if he gaineth the whole world and loses his soul?" The oppressor listened to the playback of his product. It was a job well done, for now negroes spoke a strange language announcing "I ain't no African"; "I ain't lost nothing in Africa"; "Those people eat one another"; "I'm proud to be a negro." In the era of the negro, which brought with it the period of submission, self-alienation and self-contempt, the soul of the African was doomed.

The process of transforming a soul is a spiritual phenomenon. Executed properly, any species can be transformed. Remember in the movies when the soft-hearted European saved an Indian baby, then reared him as his own, educated him and exposed him to every facet of European culture? The Indian boy grew up thinking that he was European. His entire mental apparatus was driven by European thought. Though his physical characteristics were not that of his guardian, in essence, he was European in mind while remaining an Indian in body.

The spirit is the principle force that drives the body to execute its will. In the case of the Indian, his physical body was Indian, however, his thought was European. The subjugation of his Indian temple (body), to European thought, caused him to spiritually accomplish the will and desires of Europeans, and not Indians. Therefore, the control of one's mind, assures authority over the body.

Slaves are fashioned and formed in different ways: habit, fear, brain-washing, the destruction of images and education. Transformation of the soul results, causing the deracination of a people. The negro is the perfect illustration of a transformed soul. In the beginning, he was African in mind, soul and body. Today, like the Indian boy, he is only African in body.

As a result of over 400 years of subjugation, the African American has undergone a soul transformation. The process was so thorough, that he emerged legally defined as a mere fraction of a man. The United States' Supreme Court ruling of 1857, the infamous "Dred Scott Decision," upheld the U.S. Constitution's definition of the negro as three-fifths of a person. Ironically, the negro at his best is only three-fifths of a man because he is an exact replica and mimic of the European, whose deeds would deter anyone desiring to emulate him. What more could be the expectations of a world controlled by beings that possess, at the most, three-fifths the mental capacity of a real man? In such a case, destruction is imminent.

In the early days of chattel slavery, the African was not broken by the fierceness of his master. His sole thoughts were on freedom and Africa. He matched wits daily with his master and frequently outsmarted him. He hated his master and likewise his master hated him. He would even go so far as to injure himself to avoid work. He pretended to be stupid, feigned illness, poisoned livestock, set fire to the masters' quarters; he was African indeed. Yet any African slave that was not wholly transformed into a Euro-pean was constantly aware of the fact that his destiny was in the hands of others; that he was a piece of property that could be sold like anything else his master owned. The African was wise when he possessed his soul. In contrast, he became the most docile and tractable being on the planet when he lost it. After being thoroughly trained to be a slave, he would do all that was in his power to make his master proud of him. Each slave would attempt to outdo his fellow slave to win the award for being a slave "par excellence."

Gradually, as the African became more and more domesticated, more and more entangled in the web of European life-styles, he reflected the negative personality of his master as well as his own inferiority complex. (Inferiority is an intrinsic stigma ingrained in one that has undergone soul transformation).

If the soul transformation is positive and enhances God's creations, then an act of Godliness has been accomplished. However, if to the con-trary, it is negative, then the act is unholy and evil. Such is the case of the transformed African at home or abroad, especially the American negro. His demand for equality within white America's social structure is ludicrous. Is he totally without understanding or is he faking it? A lone sheep demanding equality in the midst of a pack of raving wolves is the correlative of the Black/white experience in America. How is it that negroes have forgotten the deeds of this damnable oppressor? Jewish people never allow the world to forget the atrocities of Hitler. They do not allow the guilt of western Europe to be expiated. However, negroes have forgotten and have allowed their children to forget the murder of over 100,000,000 Africans by Europeans! Not only have they forgotten, they detest those who attempt to reveal this truth unto them. Consequently, the negro is not respected and is thus, a prey to every existing desperado and bandit. Like honey is to the bee, so is the negro to his oppressors. They swarm around him like flies, and suck his blood like hungry leeches. The negro stands helplessly as a sheep prepared for the slaughter. He has no shield nor a protector. His strength fails him at the time of need. Fear engulfs him and anxiety is his lifelong companion. The Living God has turned His back on him.

Without God, the African Hebrew was easily made a victim of unprecedented brainwashing. To view the daily ritual of negroes in America is like watching a circus. Let me illustrate my point. Black women and girls parade through the streets wearing blonde, brunette or red wigs, their black faces painted and rouged. Because of the latest "jeri curl" or "wet look" hair fad, even Black men can be seen with curlers or plastic bags on their heads. No one is concerned about wearing African cultural garments, only styles befitting the Europeans. Spiritlessly, African Americans pass each other on the streets, with shunning eyes, careful not to speak to each other. Yet, when they do, the inflection of each word is meticulously pronounced. "Black English," uttered from the lesser-educated Blacks, is looked on as an absurdity and embarrassment by their professional or well-to-do brothers who emulate Europeans better and who have been thoroughly brainwashed.

The "super negroes," who shirk at the mention of the word Africa, are proud to be negroes. They would not be anything other than negroes. The arrogant and boastful negro-American, replete with patriotic energies, trembling with closed eyes as he recites the Pledge of Allegiance, is the one who sided with the establishment during the Black revolt of the sixties. He is the informer, the "Uncle Tom," the head-scratching, bowing and grinning negro.

In league with the negro is the partially transformed negro gone astray:

"the nigger." The spirit of his African past inherent within him does not allow him to tow the line as the conformist negro. His only similarity to the negro is his lack of vision. He is the renegade — the most hated, despised and feared of the race. He is the deserter, the criminal, the rebel; he hates to work for his oppressor. His thoughts are sporadic; his actions are impossible to monitor. Like a wild lion caged in a cell, he is constantly in search of an exit, a way out of his unnatural and evil abode. He does not adhere to the laws of the land. He is unstable and exacts his intellect to outwit his oppressors, as well as his prey. The nigger hates his oppressor and fights him physically and spiritually. The white establishment and its negro conformists are in collusion: the nigger must go; he must be eradicated from the society.

Just as in the Roman hierarchy (Pontias Pilate), the Hebrew "Toms" and their puppets (the Pharisees and Sadducees) agreed that Jesus was the problem and had to go, likewise are the sentiments of the white establishment and the negro "Toms." In order that the establishment continue freely in its exploitation of the race and to allow the negroes to receive their crumbs, the nigger has to go.

Therefore, the penal institutions are filled with niggers. The nigger prefers to risk being imprisoned than to obey the laws of the land.

The plan was to totally destroy your African heritage and former African mentality. Everything that was inherent to the African Hebrew slave was uprooted, and replaced with a foreign culture and nature. The African Hebrew was dead in God: genocide of the mind had been committed. After being taught to be a slave, he proceeded with his degrees and diplomas on a path of damnation and ignorance to become like Mao, Marx, Lenin, the British, the French, and on St. Patrick's Day, the Irish. These were the souls, which were given to the slave in place of his own. Why couldn't the Euro-American allow the slaves to continue to associate with the eastern and western African countries of their origins such as Ghana, Senegal, Liberia, Sierra Leone or Israel? Had this happened, African Americans would, at this time, be concerned and supportive of the internal politics of those countries as are the Irish-Americans in the struggle of the Irish Republican Army (IRA) and the internal politics of Ireland; as Jewish-Americans are about Israel; French-Americans about France; Polish-Americans about Poland; Lebanese-Americans about Lebanon.

The Europeans termed the slaves "negroes" so they would never form close political ties with African countries. The name negro was to prevent any association with Africa or Africans. Consequently, while Euro-gentile exploiters wallow in the wealth achieved at the expense of Africa, African Americans do not feel they owe any allegiance directly or indirectly to any African countries. They have become totally disenfranchised from their African heritage. The way back to God was plowed up; the way was lost.

Equipped with the deadly elements of individualism and a strange soul, it was not long before the full brunt of the transformation was felt. Africans became full-fledged American or European subjects. The trained slave put a picture of his oppressor on his wall, (the picture of the Last Supper showed the boss and twelve friends sitting around a table in Jerusalem), and deceived his children concerning Christ. The children, looking at the white Mary, the white Jesus (God), and his white Apostles, reflected on their Sunday school teachings. "God knows what is best for you," "Commit yourself to serve God," "God made all things, and God knows all things." Certainly, they had to feel inferior and helpless thinking that God was a European. The African American man looked into the mirror and hated the black skin and thick hair he saw, because it reminded him of his African heritage. He then purchased the bleaching creams, powder puffs, straightening combs, processing lyes, curlers, jeri curls and razors to proficiently attack these African defects.

On top of this, the role of the African American man and woman disintegrated. The firm, fearsome, masculine father we once knew disappeared, and a permissive, submissive one appeared, with hardly a trace of masculinity. The feminine, soft, lovable, submissive (to her husband) mother we once knew disappeared and a dominating, non-submissive, masculine, executive mother appeared. Often it seemed as if there were two men running the house, or two strange women. It became hard to separate or differentiate between "Mother" and "Father." Little, lovable brothers and sisters disappeared and so did the innocence of childhood. In their stead appeared hard, television-and-movie-trained little con men and exploiters who no longer shot marbles, but shot people. The neighborhood where we once knew everybody and found comfort after a long, hard day's work, disappeared. In its place came the Black ghetto filled with fear, anxiety, mistrust and hate, climaxing with Black-on-Black crime.

Euro-Americans have successfully transformed not only Blacks but the entire world. The present, degenerate state of the world is not something that just happened overnight. It did not become wicked, evil and corrupt by accident. The present decadent state of the world came about as a result of the demented image of those in control. A close look will reveal that today's Europeans, like yesteryears' corrupters of the earth — the Egyptians, Babylonians and Persians — have gradually influenced the world negatively until we are tottering at the brink of destruction. It is not difficult to see that present world policy originates in Europe. Every people, Black and white, are all influenced by that policy, whether one lives in Zaire, Cuba, Alaska or Japan. All fashions, mannerisms and institutions stem from some facet of European method or system. In every land, cities are modeled after Paris, London, New York and Moscow. Consequently, their citizens are actually cultured slaves, creations of an artificial medium.

It was like a scene from the movie "The Devil and Daniel Webster." The devil promised senatorships, mayorships and a taste of "The American Dream" in exchange for the soul of Daniel Webster (Black America). Daniel Webster agreed, much to his own distress, and by the time he realized he had been swindled, everything was gone. An unprecedented feat had taken place — a horrendous accomplishment, to say the least.

Like a magician, who fools his audience, the Euro-American had deceived the whole world and performed a stupendous and incredible feat never before accomplished — a soul transformation. No longer African, they even looked different, like a strange people, with a strange nature and desires. Inwardly the African American man had been made into an extension of the slave master, always waiting for the opportunity to prove to the boss that he knew how to handle Black folks. When he was allowed to perform before the master, he was at his cruel best; he was no longer a liberator of his people, only an oppressor. His evaluation of other Black people was the exact same as that of the white oppressor: a vessel prone for abuse and misuse. It was quite clear this strange creation possessed the soul of the adversary of God. He was the devil's representative. He traded his African glory for that which does not profit. He exchanged his God for a god that could not hear or redeem. Things that once touched his Black African soul had become strange to him.

> *"Wherefore I will yet plead with you, saith the Lord, and with your children's children will I plead.*
>
> *For pass over the isles of Chittim, and see; and send unto Kedar, and consider diligently, and see if there be such a thing.*
>
> *Hath a nation changed their gods, which are yet no gods? But my people have changed their glory for that which doth not profit.*

Be astonished, O ye heavens, at this, and be horribly afraid, be ye very desolate, saith the Lord.

For my people have committed two evils; they have forsaken me, the fountain of living waters, and hewed them out cisterns, broken cisterns, that can hold no water."

Jeremiah 2:9-13

Before the creation of the negro, there could not be found in the annals of history an enslaved people whose self-image was based upon the image of his oppressor. The negro cannot relate to things pertaining to himself because he is not himself. His soul is the soul of one that oppresses Blacks, so negroes oppress one another. They have no time for one another; they do not like to live around one another. They spend all of their time perpetuating the societies and systems of those that hate and despise them. Everyone has involved the negro in their struggle. The negro spends very little time being involved in the affairs of Black folks, for they have nothing to offer him. He has no desire to find himself or solutions to the problems of Black people because the problems of Black people are not his problems. He is afraid of truth, for truth keeps reminding him of his past, when he was merely an African slave. When the angels of God attempt to mobilize him in the struggle for total freedom and a land of his own, the American negro states very clearly, "I'm already free, and this (America) is my land."

Free!? Your land!? By virtue of what is that claim made? The more than 400 years spent in America does not automatically qualify Blacks to be one of the owners of America. Blacks are free, but the question is, free to do what? The Israelites spent 400 years in ancient Egypt, but it did not give them the right to be Egyptians, or even part-owners of Egypt. Being free in America is not that simple. No matter how vociferous and boastful they become in their insinuations that they are free, in actuality they must admit they are not free. Remember the making of a slave required the help of the entire system and that system will never submit to completely freeing its dead prey (the negro), because even in the despicable state that African Americans are presently in, they are still seen as a threat.

There had to be an infrastructure clandestinely designed to maintain Black subordination whereby the leaders could forever rely upon it to uphold the injustices of bigotry and racism. Simultaneously, the hypocrites pacified the masses of African people with false promises. The entire infrastructure is race-oriented and is not about to be dismantled. The religious system, the educational system, the economic system, the political system and the social system are all active parts of a racist system of government. How many times have you heard a minister say "God has no color" or "It doesn't matter what color God is"? In actuality, the Bible scholars, the picture selectors, the image makers, the movie producers and religious scriptwriters have perpetuated the deception of a white Jesus for hundreds of years. They are fully aware that Jesus and the ancient Hebrews were not white. But the white establishment had no intention of letting African Americans know the truth, and presently have no intention of dismantling the system. At this stage of the game, eradicating the injustices perpetrated against African Americans will not occur by switching from the European Jesus image to a Black one. There has been too much damage done. We would have to put the Black image on every wall for the next four hundred years to undo the damage.

Black America is 400 years behind — certainly not by choice but by purposeful intention — to keep us, the former standard bearers of God, from ever regaining our rightful places as leaders in this world. Perhaps you consider yourself free, but that means free within the framework of the existing system, not free from it.

At this stage in history it should be clear what the story is, especially after watching so many of those you thought to be great leaders, fall by the wayside. The Black leader, in his attempt to be impartial, has become ineffective, for no genuine African American leader can serve the interest of the system and the interest of the African American community at the same time. It is an illusion to think they can serve the system and belong to us. For this reason there is no genuine leadership in the African American struggle today. In reflection you must reluctantly admit that those leaders who have moved up in the governmental or social hierarchy have a tendency to be automatically distrusted, for no man can serve two masters. To be an American is not the prophetic destiny of the African American. Prophetically, the Euro-gentile world is our rod of correction in the Plan of Redemption of God Almighty. How long before you realize that you cannot remain a negro and be free in God? At the culmination of the true struggle for freedom you will not be a negro. We may further discuss what you will be, but the fact that you won't be negroes is not debatable.

> "The negro in western civilization, because of his environments that force upon him an inferiority complex, is the most stubborn individual to discipline within the race. He has but little, if any, respect for internal racial authority. He

cannot be depended upon to carry out an order given by a superior of his own race. If the superior attempts, in his presence, to enforce the order he is undermined and accused of `putting on airs.' If the order is entrusted to a lieutenant he in turn changes the order to suit himself and endeavors to constitute himself the superior individual. In my experience, as head of the largest serious negro organization in the world, I have found that to every hundred orders given to be executed for the absolute good of the organization and the race, not two per cent of them have been carried out in their entirety. This lack of obedience to orders and discipline checkmates the real worthwhile progress of the race. This accounts for the negro's lack of racial nationalistic ideal. The only cure for him is his removal to an atmosphere entirely his own, where he would be forced under rigid civil and other discipline to respect himself and his own racial authority."[5]

The Honorable Marcus M. Garvey

"The people that walked in darkness have seen a great light; they that dwell in the land of the shadow of death, upon them hath the light shined."

"And in that day the deaf shall hear the words of the book, and the eyes of the blind shall see out of obscurity, and out of darkness."

Isaiah 9:2; 29:18

For those who understand these words and who desire to be free, you have been given enough material here to make a clear assessment of the problem. There has to be a repossessing of our African soul. Just as the slave had to be taught how to be a slave, so must the Sons and Daughters of God be taught how to be free in God. It is not sufficient to pray for forgiveness for a specific sin. There now has to be a whole new way of life. All of the old negro mentality has to die, for there won't be any new wine put into the old bottles. We must now look into the mirror at the pale, bleaching cream countenance and jeri curl, and hate what we see, for it is a reminder of our negro past. We must renew our countenance, and retrieve our thick hair and restore our African beauty. These will be the first blows delivered in the "War in Heaven."

The Love Teachings of Jesus

The resurgence of Black America spells the revival of the light (intelligence) of God, the essential element and prerequisite for the redemption of the world. To prevent this revival, the teachings of Jesus Christ and the prophets have been purposely misinterpreted and distorted and are used daily to perpetuate ignorance among African Americans and the Black world in general. Black churches, as they now exist, are nothing but mechanisms of pacification, designed to divert our attention from the everyday problems of the world. We are taught to consider a heavenly life after death as the essence of our beliefs, and not a heavenly life here on earth. The slave-and-missionary-church structure, theology and related programs were created to "hedge up with thorns" the way back to God, not to ensure our safe arrival. The reasoning behind this clandestine and covert scheme of present-day world religions and spiritual movements is to make sure that the God-appointed Saviors of the world remain covered in darkness, in order to assure the continuing rule of the ungodly.

Jesus emerged on the world stage at a time when speaking in parables was necessary because his ministry was revolutionary. Jesus was careful not to overtly offend the rulers of the land. His intention was to reach his people (the Black Israelites), who were the principal cause for his advent. He spoke spiritually (in parables) to his people in the presence of the Roman and Edomite spies who sought to hear provocations that would prompt charges of rebellion. However, Jesus' message was far beyond his enemies' comprehension. He sought to establish a cohesiveness within the oppressed nation of Israel because their strength and unity had been fragmented by the Roman and Edomite oppressors. Jesus understood the inner forces which separate an oppressed people and cause them to betray one another while serving the interest of the oppressors.

In his teachings to the Black Israelites, he informed them that they were the light (intelligence) of the world (St. Matthew 5:14), indicating that if the world is in darkness, there is no intelligence or light. Jesus further stated in St. Matthew 5:13, that "ye are the salt of the earth; but if the salt have lost his savour, wherewith shall it be salted? It is thenceforth good for nothing, but to be cast out, and to be trodden under foot of men."

Jesus was a revolutionary leader, and like any tactician he certainly had a plan. Many of his teachings were tactical instructions, not emotional commandments. He analyzed the cruel Roman and Edomite enemies; he knew the tactics of the oppressors. Without this knowledge, he could not have formulated a workable plan. His foremost objective was certainly to end the Roman occupation and to bring freedom to the Black Israelites. Yet, Jesus' number one concern was that they unite and love one another. Is this not a prerequisite for the success of any liberation struggle? Let us analyze the strategy and the truth of the love ethic of Jesus:

> *"But I say unto you, That whosoever is angry with his brother without a cause shall be in danger of the judgement; and whosoever shall say to his brother, Raca, shall be in danger of the council: but whosoever shall say, Thou fool, shall be in danger of hell fire.*
>
> *Therefore if thou bring thy gift to the altar, and there rememberest that thy brother hath ought against thee;*
>
> *Leave there thy gift before the altar, and go thy way; first be reconciled to thy brother, and then come and offer thy gift.*
>
> *Ye have heard that it hath been said, Thou shalt love thy neighbor, and hate thine enemy;*
>
> *But I say unto you, Love your enemies, bless them that curse you, do good to them that hate you, and pray for them who despitefully use you, and persecute you."*

> ### *St. Matthew 5:22-24; 43-44*

First, Jesus analyzed the moral responsibilities which the Black Israelites had for one another. Upon seeing the strife and dissension, he admonished them to get their own house in order, to develop a true concern for the well being of one another and to hold no grudges or animosity in one's heart toward one's brother. Does this seem highly unusual? Well it should not, because if there was a plan of redemption for African Americans, and a redeemer was walking through the ghettoes, would he not be appalled at the Black-on-Black crime? Would he not begin his ministry by objurgating the brothers and the community? Would he not admonish you to cast aside all differences, solve all grievances, forgive all offenses and "love ye one another"? How do you feel he would address the murdering, raping, stealing, drug addiction, alcoholism and prostitution in the community?

Jesus was very forceful with his words: "Either get the family and community problems solved, or don't bring your problems or yourself to the Temple." Jesus told the Israelites that if they brought that ignorance to the Temple they would be in danger of "hellfire." Hellfire was the terminology used at that time to express how the disobedient were to be handled. In other words, either get it together or be dealt with. All revolutions have to have a clear-cut policy of how those found to be stirring up dissension are to be chastised. Whatever the terminology used today, the message would still be the same — "where there is unity and genuine concern for one another there is strength."

Jesus could, under no circumstances, have meant "Love your enemies" as handed down in the perverted Christian theology of Europe. This precept was, first and foremost, intended to inspire the Israelites to overcome all obstacles and not leave a stone unturned in their pursuit of love and unity among themselves. He certainly did not mean this as the authorization to form a coalition with their enemies, the Romans. Slave-oriented Christianity has fed you the emotional portions of Jesus' doctrine only, with the intent of making you docile in your acceptance of slavery. No sound mind would reason that Jesus was adjuring the Israelites to trust in Rome. If we accept the emotional tenets of the doctrines of Christianity then we should ask ourselves the following questions. Should we invite the enemy to our strategy sessions? Should we inform him of our plans? Should we ask his approval of what we have decided to do against him? Did African Americans refuse to fight in Vietnam because they loved their enemies? Did Black regiments give Jesus' teachings an emotional translation in the First and Second World Wars or in the Korean War?

Let us be realistic; you have fought and killed America's enemies in four major wars. No teaching or doctrine has prevented you from achieving excellence on the battlefield for America; but in the struggle for your freedom, the love teachings of Jesus become strictly emotional and passionate. That is beyond a contradiction, it is hypocritical! Jesus' message, "compel you to walk one mile, go with him two," or "turn the other cheek," was not meant to render you helpless before your enemies, make you totally submissive or have you show obeisance before God's adversaries.

The problems at that particular time in history are very similar to the problems of Black Israelites in America today. When Jesus began his ministry, there existed all kinds of groups, all translating the Holy writings in order to justify whatever it was they wanted to do. There were moderates, liberals, extremists and religious zealots, all vying for control of the masses. There was chaos and confusion; the people were weary from false hope and false teachings.

When authority over a people is exercised by groups and organizations instead of by a central command, there is a tendency to follow programs which do not aid the overall liberation struggle, thus the loyalty of the people is limited to that particular group. This kind of authority weakens and fragments, causing animosity, fear and outright hostility to override the order of the day. If the church had a central-command governing body, it would be an immediate, powerful redemptive force among Blacks in America. Instead, there is ideological confusion; each church goes its own way, attempting to avoid the responsibilities of government. The powerlessness of churches today stem from Blacks' inability to change. They continue making the same mistakes. It is like the blind leading the blind. The majority of our contemporary leaders have been and are ministers. Ironically, while these ministers "teach the Bible," "preach the Bible," and supposedly "herald the Good News," they are as a rule, accepted by the "powers that be" because they uphold worldly doctrine. That is quite a contrast from the Men of God of old who heralded God's word. These men were examples of "those afflicted" for teaching God's truth. Certainly, the preachers of today cannot be classified as "those afflicted" for teaching God's truth.

There has to be a doctrinal revolution as we keep foremost in our mind that when a people truly seek to be free, and struggle in God's name, God is bound by His nature to help them succeed. God will never leave a people to be oppressed by His adversary if the people desire to be free to serve Him. The key to succeed in a movement under God is then to decide: free to do what; for whom? Except that you desire to be free to worship God, then there is no benefit to His freeing you, but if you sincerely desire to serve God, then His whole planetary system will respond and aid you in that struggle. The devil cannot keep any man a slave that desires to worship God.

Jesus saw the problems stemming from the day-to-day competition between organizations for membership. This competition brought with it the pitfall of having to renounce other groups or organizations. There were even those who spoke only to their fellow members. They were actually hostile to other segments of the community. This led to internal strife, confrontation, and self-abuse. This competition prevented the rise of an authority to challenge the oppressive Romans.

*"For if ye love them which love you, what reward
have ye? Do not even the publicans the same?*

*And if ye salute your brethren only, what do ye more
than others? Do not even the publicans do?*

*Be ye therefore perfect, even as your Father which is
in heaven is perfect."*

St. Matthew 5:46-48

The old tactic of the enemy of God, "divide and conquer," works every time. The oppressor always encourages the establishment of many diversified organizations. Then, the same enemy keeps dissension in the midst of the people as the organizations continuously strive to protect their personal flocks by any means necessary. We now find an immediate contrast to this confusion in the example of the Catholic Church, a powerful social, political and economic force in America and Europe. The Vatican of Rome exercises authority over Catholic churches all over the world. All priests come under the leadership of the Pope of Rome. There is no such structure in the Black Church. As a matter of fact, most Blacks tend to fear power being allotted to one person. If you mentioned the need to formulate a governing body for African American churches, you would be scorned unmercifully for daring to suggest that power of such magnitude should be in the hands of Blacks. All of the churches with group-oriented mentalities are far from God's word today. The enemy always escapes while we keep a wary eye upon our brethren who may be trying to take our members. Doesn't it make sense that if African American churches were under a central command there could be no member-snatching because there would be but one membership?

The Bible, starting from the accounts of Moses and continuing to the testimonies of Jesus of Nazareth, is a prototype of a struggle for liberation. Jesus was confronted by the everyday problems of life, while yet applying the skill and understanding of God in the freedom struggle of a people. He began to go back to clarify the teachings and meanings of the law and prophecies which had long been lost. Today the basic life-guiding and life-giving principles of the law and the prophecies have been lost, and in their place have come more than 2,000 different religious denominations, all vying for control of the multitudes. Jesus knew that those deeply involved in unrighteousness would raise great opposition, and not understand, because "these things would be hid from the wise and the prudent and revealed unto babes." Jesus began many explanations with the words "you've heard that it has been said...," or in other words: "you have been taught that..." He used this as his lead-in to explain that the interpretations of the teachings of the prophets were purposefully distorted by the so-called wise and prudent in order to mislead the people. In one instance, Jesus said, "you've heard that it has been said love thy neighbor and hate thine enemies." Those that were perpetrating this distortion were the ones that wanted to stir up rebellion and a physical confrontation with the Roman occupiers. Yet, nowhere in the books of the law is such a commandment written. Furthermore, to even deduce that interpretation from any other commandment would be virtually impossible.

If it sounds somewhat strange that the adverse groups were preaching doctrine strictly from their own personal textbooks, it really should not, because the same textbooks exist today in slave-oriented Christianity. The European missionaries have been preaching and teaching that our black pigmentation was a result of "Ham being cursed by his father, Noah, and turning Black." The European missionaries have taught this diabolical lie with such demonic energy and consistency that, no doubt, they have forgotten that there is nothing even similar to that recorded in the Bible. For centuries this lie has been taught by the European missionaries for their own racist motives, while in truth, every curse spoken of in the Bible dealing with the pigmentation of the skin has stated that the *cursed* ones were turned *white*. In fact, it was Miriam, Naaman, Gehazi, Uzziah and the hand of Moses that were all *cursed and turned white*. Therefore, it is obvious that *they were originally Black*. Love your black pigmentation for nowhere in the Bible has a man ever been cursed to turn Black.

Jesus went on to clarify the teachings of the law. He said, "But I say unto you, love your enemies, bless them that curse you; do good to them that hate you, and pray for them which despitefully use you, and persecute you." Now let us review the source from which both sides claim to have found support:

> *"Thou shalt not curse the deaf, nor put a stumbling block before the blind, but shalt fear thy God; I am the Lord.*
>
> *Ye shall do no unrighteousness in judgement; thou shalt not respect the person of the poor, nor honour the person of the mighty; but in righteousness shalt thou judge thy neighbour.*

Thou shalt not go up and down as a talebearer among thy people; neither shalt thou stand against the blood of thy neighbor: I am the Lord.

Thou shalt not hate thy brother in thine heart: thou shalt in any wise rebuke thy neighbor, and not suffer sin upon him.

Thou shalt not avenge, nor bear any grudge against children of thy people, but thou shalt love thy neighbor as thyself: I am the Lord."

Leviticus 19:14-18

"And if a stranger sojourn with thee in your land, ye shall not vex him.

But the stranger that dwelleth with you shall be unto you as one born among you, and thou shalt love him as thyself; for ye were strangers in the land of Egypt: I am the Lord your God."

Leviticus 19:33,34

The message is clearly, for all practical applications, the same as we find in the love teachings of Jesus. The substance of the message is: put no stumbling block before the blind; there is no respect of person or position in righteous judgment; do not lie on your brother; do not allow the shedding of your brother's blood in quarrels; do not hate your brother; rebuke him if he is wrong. Do not be vengeful against your brother; hold no grudges. Love thy neighbor and the stranger as thyself. These were your guidelines for dealing with the "God Family" and their problems, utilizing the guiding principles of Brotherhood and Oneness. There were those who were making mistakes on the path to the Father, who were experiencing problems of growth or who simply lacked understanding. They are of the "God Family."

When you were a child or young adult in the household with your brothers and sisters, sometimes there was resentment or dissension which occasionally led to a physical confrontation. If you got the upper hand, you would ready your fist to deliver crushing blows, but understandably you could not. Each time you brought the fist down, you would break the force of the blow, for in your heart you knew your brother or sister was not an enemy. Then, "Mother" or "Father" would come, sit you down and "preach the gospel." This was certainly a serious matter, but it was in the family. So, your parents admonished you to get it together, not hold grudges, nor seek revenge at a later date. You would say, "I hate him; I'll kill her; I'll hurt him," or "we can't live together," but even with the outpouring of all your harsh words and feelings, there was an inherent feeling which limited the injuries which you could cause your brother or sister to sustain. There was always someone in the family who had some bad habits that needed correction; still "Mother" and "Father" knew, even as Jesus of Nazareth, that except the angry feelings were immediately extinguished, they would soon become an all-consuming, unquenchable fire.

Then there is the external enemy, the adversary of God, the one that opposes all that is good or right. He is not of the "God Family," neither does he have any desire to be. He is dedicated to the destruction of God's family and creation. He is the standard of evil. The world has been deceived into carrying out his diabolical plan of destruction under the guise of scientific development and technological advancement. For him the love teachings of Jesus have a different meaning, a meaning that is not exactly the same as that of the enemy we have identified in the "God Family." To understand this, we must go deeper than the superficial emotions that are evoked in the use of the term "Love." When you were a child and inquired as to what love was, the answer usually given was "it's an emotion," "a feeling," or "it's just something inside everyone that can't be explained in words." How could it be that something upon which so much rests and depends, cannot be explained or given a lucid meaning?

In the Biblical, prophetic and Godly message, love is doing things, doing the right things to and for one another. It will never be any more or any less. Now that the great love definition mystery has been cleared up, we can proceed to break the remaining barriers erected by the enemies of God. Love is an expression used very loosely to mean different things at different times to different people. When you say that you love ice cream, it has absolutely nothing to do with passions or emotions. When you say to your mother "I love you, Mother," you don't mean the same thing as when you say to your wife "I love you, my dear wife." Nor are you alluding to the same thing when you say to your daughter, "I love you, my dearest daughter."

You have used the same word four times, but each time meaning four different things. You have never taken the time to explain these meanings, except briefly to your wife, but you assume that everyone must know that you did not mean the same thing. You kiss your mother on the cheek as your expression of "Love of Mother." You kiss your wife on her lips, passionately, as an expression of "Love of Wife." You place a little kiss on the forehead of your daughter, as an expression of "Love of Daughter." When a friend that is close to the family states "it does not seem as if you love your mother," he is certainly not implying that you should take your mother to bed as proof of your love. However, there is something unsaid between the two of you which allows you both to understand what is meant, even without a detailed explanation.

Was not the same thing expected by Jesus of his followers when he taught the Israelites to "love your enemies?" "Love your enemies" could not mean the same as it does within the context of the "God Family." It did not mean to strike up an affectionate relationship with your enemies. Jesus never expected you to come forth with such an absurd interpretation of his teachings. Had the brother felt that his friend meant that he should express passion in love of his mother, he still, by his nature, could not have performed such an ungodly act. A similar example can be found within yourself. Even after centuries of continuous indoctrination, you still don't love the devil like you love God. Neither do you love your enemies or God's enemies like you love the "God Family." That alone, should make you know that Jesus did not mean "love your enemies" in any emotional way. Jesus' admonishment was strictly tactical and revolutionary. Lest in the end, you would be as a dog that returns to his own vomit. That is, initially you were a serious revolutionary, sworn to rid yourself of your enemies by any means necessary. However, at the climax of your struggle you have returned to the tyrannical master to beg for the crumbs that fall from his table. It is evident that Jesus did not mean that we should love our enemies in an emotional way. His words were just tactical, strategic and revolutionary. Moreover, he simply meant that we should love an enemy with an enemy's love.

If you were the owner of a horse, how would you express your love for your horse? Would the horse be allowed to eat with the family? Would you give him the choice things of your table, or would he be given what would be termed as "garbage?" Would he stay in your house, defecate and urinate on your living room floor? Is this how you would express the "love of horse?" When you hear the expression "love your horse," the term love may be alright, as long as you never forget he is a horse in all of your dealings. If, by nature, you know not to bring your horse into the house as a member of the family, why can't you understand that Jesus expected you to understand, by that same nature, what was meant by the term "love your enemies?" If by chance, God forbid, that you heard a cry and dashed from your house to find your horse attacking a child of the family, by nature you would do all in your power to save your child,... even if it meant killing the horse.

Whenever you are doing what is right, it is an expression of love, or the love of God. Whenever you are doing what is wrong, it is an expression of hate, or the hate of God. People have become so adept at hiding behind the term "love" while carrying out the deeds of hate, until now they can no longer differentiate between true love and hate. We can no longer allow the cunning adversary to deceive us with his clever selection of words. We must, in God's name, characterize all things according to the Divine definition of "God's Family."

If a man can come home, open a package of cigarettes that has written on the carton "sure death; positive cancer" and politely offer the pack to his wife, saying "Have one honey," he is void of understanding. It does not matter what the terminology is, he *hates* his wife. Can't you picture her sitting there, puffing away, as he states: "I sure love you!" Little does he know that giving her that cigarette is an expression of hate of his wife and hate of God. It is the same with the wife who pulls out a glass and the bottle of gin, guaranteed to consume his liver and drive him to his grave, and then says "This is for you, my beloved." These two individuals are deadly enemies, who are locked in a death struggle. While continuously saying they love one another, they spend the entire day killing each other or committing suicide.

It is no small wonder then that children as they grow older do not know how to love their parents or even relate to them. After years of watching their parents kill each other under the false assumption of loving one another, by doing things like drinking liquor and smoking cigarettes, children succumb to the confusion and the hate game of the enemy of God. We, as a people, no longer need that kind of "love." It is an evil, cold, devilish love. We must return to the "Love of God" — doing only what is good and right to and for one another. If, when studying the gospels, one does not use the Old Testament as a reference, or if you depend entirely upon the literal, written word, you will not be able to form a correct interpretation of the love teachings of Jesus. Therefore, I have put you in a position where you will be able to test the validity of your past understanding, by bringing to bear a multiplicity of factors, many of which you may not previously have been aware.

What is written can only be applied constructively when you are uninhibited by a religious compulsion to assume that every word was meant to be taken literally.

> *"And there went great multitudes with him: and he turned, and said unto them,*

If any man come to me, and hate not his father, and mother, and wife, and children, and brethren, and sisters, yea, and his own life also, he cannot be my disciple."

St. Luke 14:25,26

Again, if we interpret literally the "Love thy enemies" to mean something emotional and affectionate, we would, after reading this verse, use that same measuring rod to say that Jesus taught us "hate thy family." The words are explicitly clear, when taken literally. There *is* a hate that is required to be a follower of Jesus. Yet it would become an unquenchable fire, certainly an unimaginable impediment, if you tried to "love your enemies" and "hate your family or friends." The spiritual, revolutionary interpretation of this scripture is that we must not get so bogged down in so-called "love" for family or friends that we forget our Father's work. Likewise, we cannot get so bogged down in hating our enemies that we, again, forget our Lord's work. These explanations of truth about certain elements of Jesus' teachings are not an attempt to weaken the message; where I have had to challenge traditional beliefs, it has not been with any hostile intent. On the contrary, they are to fortify your faith and to give you strength through a better understanding of his revolutionary message.

Slave-oriented Christianity, as handed down from Europe, has purposely distorted the character and teachings of the carpenter from Nazareth. Jesus' strength was founded upon his perfect faith in the law and prophecies, a deep concentration of will and purpose, and astuteness in planning and Divine insight. When clearly understood, these attributes will only more vividly allow us to see what God saw in this African Messiah. Jesus could be tender and compassionate, but he was not the soft, "peaches-and-cream" Messiah depicted in European literature and teachings. He had a capacity for action which matched the greatness of his vision. His non-flinching, authoritative message had a profound effect, favorable or unfavorable, on those who came in contact with him.

"And the Jews' passover was at hand, and Jesus went up to Jerusalem,

And found in the temple those that sold oxen and sheep and doves, and the changers of money sitting:

And when he had made a scourge of small cords, he drove them all out of the temple, and the sheep, and

*the oxen; and poured out the changers' money, and
overthrew the tables;*

*And said unto them that sold doves, Take these things
hence; make not my Father's house an house of
merchandise."*

St. John 2:13-16

Very few of you know this Jesus, the physically powerful, fearless,
dedicated servant of God, who made a whip and drove the merchants from
the Temple! Can you picture Jesus fighting in the Temple? How would you
classify what was taking place: Jesus, whip in hand, overturning tables
laden with money and physically throwing the moneychangers from the
Temple? What would be Jesus' reaction today if he paid a visit to all of the
churches established in his name? Do you feel that Jesus would say "you've
made my Father's house a valuable business" as he uncovered the bank
accounts of the moneychangers? Would today's preachers and ministers
be greeted with an embrace or with the whip?

The imperative here, for your understanding, is that Biblical men of
God are quite a contrast from the muddled images pushed by slave-oriented Christianity. From Moses to Jesus, the Bible holds no record nor does
it bear any testimony of docile, soft, cowardly Men of God. Understanding
the true character of the Men of God helps us to understand Jesus' interpretation of "hate thy family." His message was simply that we must be
totally dedicated, or we must step aside. We must demonstrate non-com-
promising dedication to God's work of redemption. Whatever it is that you
have to suffer on this path is the burden you must carry as you continue the
journey. Jesus selected the more forceful term "hate" as he considered the
commitment required to succeed in the redemptive struggle.

We are instructed in Saint Luke 14:25, 26 that "...thou shalt love the
Lord with all thy heart, soul and might." This is the greatest of all the
commandments of God Almighty. This love supersedes the love of man for
his wife, father, mother and children. This same love is the armor required
to be a soldier in God's army. Anything less is unacceptable by God. One
must forego all other business for God's business. The love of God is the
ultimate expression of love; there is none higher. Therefore, when Jesus
said you must "hate" your family for him, he only meant that the struggle
was a struggle for all of the people, not just an isolated family. Jesus' struggle
was for a New World Order in which all men would enjoy peace, justice,
truth and mercy. He did not mean that one has to discontinue loving their

families. To do so is unnatural and, generally speaking, unlikely. Jesus was a powerful revolutionary with an understanding of the caliber and fortitude of the soldiers needed to fight the awesome Roman, Edomite, and Israelite adversaries. He certainly did not want someone in his ranks who would be offended because they had to temporarily, and often times permanently, renounce their families. Therefore, by saying "you must hate your family for my sake" (or for the sake of the cause and he *was* the cause), Jesus wisely rid himself of weak, fair- weather soldiers. He sought the real revolutionaries.

Remember, if the doctrine or ideology of the enemy is embraced by a member of the fleshly family or people, inevitably, that particular member is dangerous. If the oppressor of the people controls the thinking of a member of the family, the oppressor need not worry about what he will do. This family member's every action will be to please the oppressor. Again, Jesus admonished the young man to hate his family, because if the family did not side with him then they would struggle against him. What could be the feelings for an African American family today that yet believed in the Euro-gentile world? If the angels of God approached such a family, how would the angels react to such a gross inclination? Jesus made it clear what to do. Simply shake the dust from your shoes and depart, and leave such a family's fate to the angel of destruction.

Another illustration of "hate" is that which God has for Esau. In Malachi 1:2-3, God made it perfectly clear: He loves righteousness and hates evil. There is one way — one path that is the right way, the right path. Contrary to that is wrong. There are no alternatives. It is written that "broad is the way that leads to destruction and narrow is the path that leads to life and few are those that will find it."

Therefore, the great ingathering of God Almighty won't bring, in most cases, every member of a family. Again, it is written that one from a city and two from a family will be saved. Thus, when the Messiah comes and commands you to forsake family, friends, job and riches for His sake, don't be offended. It is prophetic and inevitable that, if necessary, you must "hate" your family for the sake of the cause, because freedom and salvation *are* the cause. This is the blueprint for revolution.

Righteous Cycles, Seasons and Set Times

For every pain, sickness or disease, or for that matter, any problem, there is a cause. Violating the cycles of God brings on these troubles. The present plight of Black America indicates how out of cycle African Americans are. The sad state of Black people's affairs was brought about by their violation of God's laws and cycles. Black people were initially chosen by God to guide the world out of its state of ignorance, but instead they chose to join the world of iniquity. Because of their provocation of God, Black people are not only abhorred by all nations, but are foolishly out of step with the rhythms and patterns established by God for perfection in each of their lives.

> *"My people hath been lost sheep: their shepherds have caused them to go astray: they have turned them away on the mountains: they have gone from mountain to hill, they have forgotten their resting place.*
>
> *All that found them have devoured them: and their adversaries said, We offend not, because they have sinned against the Lord, the habitation of justice, even the Lord, the hope of their fathers."*
>
> ***Jeremiah 50:6,7***

Everything created in the righteous order of God Almighty is recycled into the earth. Violation of that order leads to disorder and death. The body, for instance, upon death, disintegrates or is cycled back into the earth. The perfect gauge to measure the righteousness of man's creations is simply the earth's acceptance or rejection of that organism. Evil creations — poisonous gases, synthetic materials, radioactive particles, plastic etc. — are not readily recycled.

The natural body, created by God, is so intricately constructed, yet so righteously ordered by God, that the use of any unnatural products becomes detrimental to life and health. The Children of Israel (Black America) were instructed to wear only garments of natural materials such as cotton, silk and wool, and that these materials were not to be mixed with nylon, dacron, banlon, polyester, etc. To wear natural products is to be obedient to

God's laws and orders, which in turn, enhance the health and longevity of the body.

Man was created in the image of God. In other words, man is a god. All of the celestial and terrestrial bodies were created to be subject to man. Therefore, man's deviation from the right path — his obstruction and deformation of God's righteous cycles, have thrown the entire universe into chaos. The present world state (wars, erratic weather, polluted air, water and food, etc.) is a result of man's violation of God's righteous cycles and seasons. A fruit, grown out of season or taken from a tree before it has ripened, has not completed its cycles and has not conformed to its specific season for growth.

In the same manner, God has established specific cycles and laws for man to live by. A complete cycle of pregnancy is nine months; an early or late delivery spells complications. Abortion violates the order or cycles of pregnancy. Inevitably the body will experience repercussions in the form of severe physical and mental problems. The transplantation of organs is unnatural, and breaches the natural cycles of the body. Similarly, men were not to have sexual relations with men, nor women with women. This is a gross breach of God's natural order. Furthermore, dogs, cats, birds and fish were naturally equipped by God to thrive outdoors, not indoors. Animals locked in the house and in zoos can be equated to man being imprisoned in the worst kind of dungeon or maximum security prison.

To reach perfection, everything must complete its circuit or cycle. Otherwise, it is deemed imperfect, abnormal, premature, queer, etc. Thus, you must pray and struggle to regain entry to the everlasting cycles of God, and moreover, to become a Saint in God's Holy and everlasting Kingdom for the Kingdom of God *has* come.

The Kingdom of God is no Biblical myth created in the minds of "religious fanatics." The tenets of the Kingdom of God operate upon the principles of Love, Truth, Justice, Mercy, Equity and Peace — *in practice.* The Kingdom of God has been established by practical men who possess the wisdom of Divine law (the instruction of God), the knowledge of prophecy (the Plan of God), and the understanding of faith (the power of God). In the Millennial Age, participation in the Kingdom of God is the *natural birthright* of everyone, but the forces of evil in today's world continue to hold so many in the bondage of ignorance — leading them to death. You now hold in your hand a principal weapon of the planetary corrective force: **NEW AGE TRUTH** — the right knowledge of reality; a light on the pathway back to everlasting life! Only after a cleansing — after the removal of the waste (corruption) within your world (body) — will you be ready to ingest that which will give you life. Not until the removal of unrighteousness can a place be prepared and room be made for righteousness. Furthermore, the righteous cycles of life can never be returned to the "body" of the world until men return themselves to these natural cycles.

Today in the Millennial Age, the choice between evolution and extinction, between life and death, is set before each man. Thus, it must become clear that to say someone has to teach you a proper and righteous diet and digestive cycle, is not merely in reference to your *personal* health and well-being, *but that of the entire planet.* The commitment to change is the only guarantee of admission to everlasting life.

A call to return to righteous cycles may seem to some like a call to "revolution," but we are talking here about the higher business of the intervention of God into the affairs of men. *Evolution will take place* — with or without your cooperation or participation!

The Divine government of righteousness in the New Age has been prophesied and has come as surely as the sunrise follows the coming of dawn. Yet, surely today's world is filled with waste and corruption. Misguided world leadership and ignorant philosophers have fed the wrong diet (teachings) to the "systems" of the universe, bringing about a world afflicted! That diet, which has so sickened and corrupted the body of the world, has been grown in the soil of the satanic principles of force, greed, selfishness, ambition, and hate.

Just as the earth refuses to cycle out synthetics created by mankind, which, thereby, cause harmful pollution, likewise has mankind's synthetic (imperfect) systems of governing led to his self-engineered annihilation. It is an accepted fact that none of the existing social systems work. The Euro-gentiles would most certainly like to find a way out of the quagmire which has trapped their societies, but without having to acknowledge God. If they could accomplish that, they would have no need for God's Plan of Salvation. The very Plan of Salvation came into being because of the Creator's Divine foreknowledge that man would lead himself into a predicament from which he could not extract himself.

Man, today, is rushing at breakneck speed along a collision course with extinction. Only an immediate return to the righteous cycles of God can save him from himself. Everything suffers under wicked rulers — man, vegetation and beast. Everyday we witness more and more species of natural vegetation and animals added to the list of those facing extinction. The terrible irony is that the greatest culprit and agent of their death is man — either through his ignorant misuse of the environment, or his arrogant pursuit of "sport" and "trophies." Certainly the "death" of nature means the death of man! Man — lost in the wickedness of unrighteous cycles — has become suicidal.

Man treks through the frozen wasteland of the polar regions wielding bats to club seals to death for recreation and money. He has killed almost all of the elephants of the world just for their ivory tusks. The rhinoceros is under threat for his horn. The Japanese slaughter thousands of dolphins because the dolphins eat their fish. Even the great blue whale — the largest creature on this planet — is almost finished because of man's oil spills and air pollution. Death is everywhere. No one escapes!

> *"And except the Lord has shortened those days, no flesh should be saved; but for the elect's sake, whom he hath chosen, he hath shortened the days."*
>
> ### St. Mark 13:20

There are those who in their own simple way see this approaching apocalypse and demonstrate their fear of God by seeking His help, His truth, and His salvation. Others are searching diligently for ways and means of escaping this holocaust outside of the realm of God's plan, but they shall not succeed, because God is on their trail, and there shall be no hiding place.

The world of man is constipated from the continuous consumption of poisoned doctrines, poisoned philosophies, and poisoned ideologies. Consequently, the consumption of these poisons has broken down the organisms to the point that they cannot properly function. As a result, the world is suffering from the terminal disease of wickedness. This is why these words of **NEW AGE TRUTH** which you are reading now are not merely words, but are the *first steps in the world-healing process!* As you digest and assimilate this information, you become eligible to join the **EVOLUTIONARY CORRECTIVE FORCE**: those whose spirits (minds and hearts) have been formed by and given the protection of the Divine principles of Love, Truth, Justice, Mercy, Equity and Peace. The **CORRECTIVE FORCE**, having cleansed the internal environment (mind), and restored balance to the internal ecology (body), can then pass on the salvation of self-healing to others and finally to the whole world through enlightened world leadership and the promotion of intelligent philosophies. Thus, the earth will be restored to the natural state of Divine health and well-being God has intended. If you take heed, you will see in your lifetime that the righteous cycles of life will overcome the unrighteous cycles of death forever, because the acceptance of Truth is likened unto the consumption of wholesome mental food which causes your mind to develop on one accord with the mind and purpose of the Creator. The Divine government of tomorrow will be based upon consumption today of the Divine diet — naturally and spiritually.

The Kingdom of God has come to restore the dominion of the people of God over God's creation, and to return man to the proper cycles of life. By doing so, man will receive manifold blessings that shall open his eyes to the everlasting truth: that *God's way is best.* This is the time when the wisdom of God will judge the wisdom of the world; when the knowledge of God will judge the knowledge of the world; and the understanding of God will judge the understanding of the world.

God has pre-established righteous cycles which control the elements — fire, air, water and earth. These cycles also control the seasons of the cycle of birth and growth, joy and happiness, the renewing of the spirit, and spiritual elevation. An in-depth study of the cycles of life will render a deeper knowledge and understanding of the basic principles of life and the Creator; and how to use them to keep the world in a spirit of Holiness. This spirit produces more Holy thoughts which form the ideas that produce actions which are never contrary to the will and intention of the Creator. These actions cannot be misinterpreted in any way to influence man to think wrong or do wrong against himself, his fellow man or God.

The evil one was very clever to lock us into his cycles of death wherein we grope as a "blind man at noonday." However, throughout the Holy Scriptures there is an allusion to a great dividing, which will also be a great deliverance. We must take note that at every great deliverance there was a *separation* instead of an *integration*. As a matter of fact, the Hebrew Nation began with the setting apart of Abraham from the society and people which he knew. The Holy Bible also teaches us that we must "separate the clean from the unclean, and the Holy from the profane." Therefore, if deliverance begins with separation, we must differentiate *our* objectives from the objectives of the Euro-gentile world. We must first separate our morals, principles, values and perceptions; then, we must conclude the cycle by separating ourselves.

"And after these things I saw another angel come
down from heaven, having great power, and the

earth was made bright with his glory.

And he cried mightily with a strong voice, saying, Babylon the great is fallen, is fallen, and is become the habitation of demons, and the hold of every foul spirit, and a cage of every unclean and hateful bird.

For all nations have drunk of the wine of the wrath of her fornication, and the kings of the earth have committed fornication with her, and the merchants of the earth have grown rich through the abundance of her delicacies.

And I heard another voice from heaven, saying, Come out of her, my people, that ye be not partakers of her sins, and that ye receive not of her plagues;

For her sins have reached unto heaven, and God hath remembered her iniquities."

Revelation 18:1-5

Whatever happened to sound judgment and rational thinking? You must, Black America, start over as a child; you must learn all things anew. You must be re-educated and re-taught the ways of God. The scriptures state: "The love of this world is the hate of God," and your ways are not God's ways. Your values and morals are of the world; you measure and determine your wealth according to the way of the world; your dress is according to the way of the world; you eat and drink according to the way of the world. Therefore, if God hates this world, He hates your morals, values, wealth, dress, food and drink. This is certainly the reasoning behind the requirement — "You must be born again."

After man returns unto the Divine and Holy cycles of life, he will immediately be transformed (born again) in his manner of thinking and doing. God's righteous cycles are designed to change man's sense of values, giving him a new spirit and feeling of oneness (a feeling of being a part of something and someone). As man moves into his step-by-step, day-by-day cycle for growth, he will see life as a part of him, having definite meaning and purpose. Yet he will seek it being simple and not complicated. He will quickly learn the values of love and understanding by living them daily in oneness with others. He will see that the beauty of the brotherhood is better than living in competition and hostility.

The Sons of God, after their fall from the cycles of light to the cycles of darkness, began to do the works of darkness. They did not keep the law of life nor pursue it for correction and edification. Notwithstanding, they suffered tremendously for walking contrarily and stubbornly away from the Almighty God. The Sons of God are now governed by cycles of error in which there is continuous pain, suffering and death, because they are governed by men in whose hands are powers of evil and deceit, and who do not love the Creator. These evil doers have convinced men that it is possible to do all manner of evil things and still live. They cause men to continuously fill their bodies with food saturated with adverse spirits, thereby causing much suffering. Satan has darkened their minds to truth while promoting his evil ways.

Thus, the Children of Israel (African Americans) followed the ways of perverseness and corruption. They forgot the law of purity and Holiness in God. They considered not that these sicknesses and afflictions were of the power of darkness that sorely pressed upon them and of the spirit of error which governed them. Their understanding of God has been confused. The Sons and Daughters of God violated the universal law, therefore they were sorely oppressed by God in the house of their enemy so that they would swiftly seek Him with prayer and repentance for their salvation. No government, party or system can bring salvation unto the Children of God. Certainly, they should realize this. Their salvation is only of God. There is nothing or no one who can exist in a state of adversity to the Living God...not even satan. They have locked themselves in a prison with ungodly people, and only this truth can set them free.

You, Children of Israel (African Americans), are locked today in a mental and spiritual prison. Your prison is Proctor and Gamble, General Motors, I.B.M., Ford, positions and titles. These things have bound you; they have taken control of your time, and there is no freedom without the control of time. People that are truly free in God become creative only when they control their own time. They know and understand their own spirits and cycles. They also understand the cycles of the major elements of their natural and human environment. By making the necessary calculations, they control their time and fix set periods and seasons. Only when we return to this kind of self-destiny will we be able to feed and nourish our Black souls. As we come alive again as a people, we shall have time eternal, because we shall control time.

Free, creative people remember where and from whom they came as individuals and as a nation. They remember that they had vision. They remember the experiences, both pleasant and unpleasant, that helped them to discern who their friends are *and* who their enemies are. Free people love their nation and are not afraid to acknowledge that they are a part of it. In order to achieve this kind of freedom, you must be cycled back unto God, wherein you will receive the strength to cast off the mentality of a prisoner. Without the faith in God, your first thought at the moment of trouble will be about preserving your individual job or position, not understanding that the taskmaster will cause instability in many places and families, attempting to cause a deep fear...of being **FREE**.

If you were free in God, you would not destroy your natural environment, nor your God-given outdoor friends. You would not be party to a system in which every minute of every day, acres of rain forest fall because of man. It is believed that rain forests, which have not changed for millions of years, may disappear before the end of this century. In our race to automate, we have created machinery that can clear tons of trees and animals in only a few hours. Astronauts orbiting the earth have provided evidence that concludes that at the rate we are destroying our forests, all that will remain in *fifteen* years will be a few island-like forests in a sea of barren land.

If these statistics do not stir up a sincere feeling of concern for your life and environment, then nothing will. Can't you see that mankind has proven his inability to rule over God's creation?

These trees are the victims of devil worship, which engulfs the planet and imprisons all men and nature in the cycles of death and destruction. Nothing and no one has escaped. The earth certainly does mourn.

> *"How long shall the land mourn, and the herbs of*
> *every field wither, for the wickedness of those who*
> *dwell in it? The beasts are consumed, and the birds,*
> *because they said, he shall not see our last end."*
>
> ### Jeremiah 12:4

Now ask yourself, what do they do with all of those trees? A considerable amount of them are pulp trees, used to manufacture paper for affluent societies. We cannot consider it progress or affluency when three friends who work together approach a newsstand, each purchasing a daily newspaper which they each spend 30 minutes reading; and, after which they either lay it on the desk or throw it into the trash. That newspaper spends the other 23 hours and 30 minutes of the day in vain, completely useless.

A recent survey in a New York office that employed 250 workers, noted that 190 employees purchased the daily newspaper. These workers each devoted less than 15 minutes reading constructive news items. (A large percentage purchased newspapers just for the sake of perpetuating the white collar image, and didn't read them at all!) Here are some comparative statistics:

Overall Average

	MEN		**WOMEN**
12 min.	Sports	10 min.	Checking sales (food and clothing)
5 min.	Celebrity columns	5 min.	Celebrity columns
1.5 min.	Horoscopes	2 min.	Horoscopes
3 min.	Car advertisements, parts, etc.	1 min.	turning pages
1 min.	turning pages	8 min.	Sports pages
7.5 min.	the rest of news items	4 min.	the rest of news items

African American Men

17 min.	Sports pages
5 min.	Celebrity columns
2 min.	Horoscopes
1 min.	turning pages
5 min.	on all other items

African American Women

It was stated that Black women read so little from the news contents that it was amazing that they bought a newspaper at all. They read horoscopes, celebrity columns and humor pages...totaling an average of 13 minutes!

The other twenty-three and one-half hours of the day, the newspaper was in the trash cycle. During the day, when these same employees were questioned about the contents of the newspaper, five percent could only give a three minute oratory on national issues; another five percent could only give a one-and-a-half minute oratory on international items. The other ninety percent could only quote the score of their favorite sports event.

African American concern for African news was very depressing. On days where there were major items of importance on Africa, one percent read them. Another two percent saw them, and a shocking ninety-seven percent did not even know that these articles were in the newspaper!

The survey continued with the request that ten percent, or 19 employees not buy a newspaper and instead read their friend's or fellow employee's. The first day was relatively smooth. By the third day there was subtle refusal ("You're tearing up my paper" etc., and "I don't know where it is" or "I haven't read it yet"). By the fifth day the purchasers felt they were being exploited by those that were not purchasing. By the seventh day, there was outright selfishness and hostility to the non-purchasers. The result was an office meeting in which they were told, "You have money like everyone else; if you want to read the newspaper, then you should purchase one for yourself!"

The conclusion of this study was thus: all of the items read in the newspaper could have been encompassed in four pages instead of the 42 that were printed. The amount of constructive reading required only 15 minutes. The needs of that office could have been met with six newspapers instead of the 190, and a righteous mentality.

The prophecies testify — everything suffers under wicked rulers. There has to be a people raised up free in God. Only then will relief come to God's afflicted people and planet. In these days of complex ideologies, confusing religious and political philosophies, and strange human behavior, it is evident that the objective has certainly been to destroy the way that leads unto God. Indeed, every way not totally destroyed is hedged with thorns.

What happened? How did we get so far from God and His cycles of life? The answer is simple: it is through education that people and societies are transformed. You have been educated away from God. It is time for the people to take a serious look at the educational and religious teachings being given to them. Righteousness is the true key to man's success. Therefore, education in Holiness is the answer to the death and destructive course the world has set itself on today. The education of this world prepares you for this world. It teaches you how to perpetuate the systems of the world, and has prepared the people to accept unrighteous standards in their day-to-day living. Education has always set the pattern for living because it sets the pattern for thinking. Therefore, education can be good or bad, righteous or wicked, a builder or destroyer. Worldly education has made you ignorant and disrespectful of nature and the ordinances of God. You, with your diplomas, degrees and numerous other certificates are like those who have eyes but see not the creation of God.

You have been given ears that hear not the Word or Plan of God. Evidence is widespread, because the educated, who have the eyes and ears of the world, operate the schools, sit in the high seats of government, officiate the religions and fashion the social, economic and moral structures of the people. The world is corrupt and everyone pretends not to know why. The answer is simple: satan has educated the world to fulfill and answer the academic needs of evil.

> *"Go and proclaim these words toward the north, and say, Return, thou backsliding Israel, saith the Lord, and I will not cause mine anger to fall upon you; for I am merciful, saith the Lord, and I will not keep anger forever.*
>
> *Only acknowledge thine iniquity, that thou hast transgressed against the Lord, thy God, and hast scattered thy ways to the strangers under every green tree, and ye have not obeyed my voice, saith the Lord.*
>
> *Turn, O backsliding children, saith the Lord; for I am married unto you; and I will take you one of a city, and two of a family, and I will bring you to Zion;*
>
> *And I will give you shepherds [educators] according to mine heart, who shall feed you with knowledge and understanding."*
>
> **Jeremiah 3:12-15**

I want you to stop and think for a moment. Very few of you have ever reflected on why you believe what you do and why you follow the customs that you do. You were born into a world filled with traditions. You have accepted them without seriously questioning their origins.

> *"And God called the light Day, and the darkness he called Night. And the evening and the morning were the first day."*
>
> **Genesis 1:5**

God began the new day at sunset, but the pagan custom of the Euro-gentiles begins the day in the middle of the night, as measured by a mechanical device.

The devil has deceived the whole world. God began the week at the setting of the sun on the seventh day (Saturday), (Exodus 20:8,11). The pagan Euro-gentiles begin the week a half a day later at Sunday midnight.

God began the months with the new moon, but the devil has induced the world to use his calendar dates instead of the celestial body. God began the year in the spring when nature is bringing forth new life everywhere, during the month of Aviv, (the first month of the Hebrew calendar year and which itself means spring)...(see Exodus 13:4 and Leviticus 23:5). But the world now follows the ancient Roman custom, where the new year begins in the middle of dead winter, with the month of January, named after the Roman deity Janus.

God gave us a true rest day, the seventh day (Saturday), designed to keep us continually in the knowledge and true worship of the one God. It was also set aside as a memorial to God's creation. However, the Europeans have pushed upon a deluded world the observance of a day on which the pagans worshipped the sun. The first day of the pagan week, called Sunday, is the day on which the pagans worshipped the all-conquering sun. It is not the Lord's day, and has absolutely nothing to do with the resurrection of Jesus, to which its existence is attributed. Sunday was designated as the first day of the week according to pagan tradition because of the adversary's refusal to accept the way of life set forth by God Almighty. The day used today as the Sabbath was originally called Sun Day of Worship. But to deceive the whole world, they made it one word — Sunday, and said it was the day of the Lord. But we can plainly see when we simply separate and give it original form, that Sun-Day is still the day of the pagan sun worship. No people have changed their god or manner of worship except the Children of Israel, the Sons of God.

Never in the history of the world have the Euro-gentiles accepted the prophetic God of the universe, the God of Israel, as their Saviour. They have always found some way to negate His existence or lessen His importance. This is all a part of the Great Religious Conspiracy against the Sons of God, the lost sheep of the House of Israel, Black America. The world very tacitly uses the name Jesus while continuing to use all of its ancient customs which were and still are an abomination before God.

Greek mythology and ancient Rome's pagan holidays have been balled-and-chained upon a heedless, deceived world. New Year, Easter and Christmas — every one a pagan holiday, every one used to stimulate the sale of merchandise in the commercial markets — have absolutely nothing to do with the worship of God!

> *"Then the Pharisees and scribes asked him, Why walk not thy disciples according to the tradition of the elders, but eat bread with unwashed hands?*
>
> *He answered and said unto them, Well hath Isaiah prophesied of you hypocrites, as it is written, This people honoreth me with their lips, but their heart is far from me.*
>
> *However, in vain do they worship me teaching for doctrines the commandments of men.*
>
> *For laying aside the commandment of God, ye hold the tradition of men, as the washing of pots and cups; and many other such things ye do.*
>
> *And he said unto them, Full well ye reject the commandment of God, that ye may keep your own tradition."*
>
> ### St. Mark 7:5-9

Did God err when He established His cycles, set times and seasons? He certainly did not, for God's plan is a way of life. His laws or instructions are a way of life wherein if a man will keep and do them he will live because life is a whole series of righteous actions and thoughts. It is the opposite of devil worship. Let us now consider the cycle of the seasons of celebrating and feasting (holidays).

Have you ever thought to question the origin of the pagan holiday "Christmas" and its historical perspective? First of all, the exact date of Jesus' birth is entirely unknown as all authorities acknowledge, although most agree it was most likely in early fall. Nevertheless, if God had wished us to observe this season and celebrate Jesus of Nazareth's birthday, He would not have so completely hidden the exact date. Jesus was not born on the 25th of December, neither did the Apostles or early followers celebrate his birthday. Neither was it instituted by Bible authority. The celebration of Christmas came to the world from the Roman Catholic Church, and has no other authority. It was instituted in the 4th century A.D., the offshoot of an old Roman pagan festival which was in existence long before the birth of Jesus!

*"Thus saith the Lord, Learn not the way of the
nations, and be not dismayed at the signs of heaven;
for the nations are dismayed at them.*

*For the customs of the peoples are vain; for one
cutteth a tree out of the forest, the work of the hands
of the workman, with the axe.*

*They deck it with silver and with gold; they fasten it
with nails and with hammers, that it move not.*

*They are upright like the palm tree, but speak not;
they must needs be borne, because they cannot go.*

*Be not afraid of them; for they cannot do evil,
neither also is it in them to do good."*

Jeremiah 10:2-5

The prophet Jeremiah has certainly left no stone unturned in his description of this ancient pagan holiday. We can certainly discern that this is
the custom of what is today called "Christmas."

In the fourth century, A.D., Constantine, emperor of Rome, made Christianity the religion of Rome. The pagans that followed brought all of their
idolatrous customs with them; they only changed the names. For example,
the 25th of December was already celebrated as the birthday of the sun
god. When the Romans became Christians, they simply changed it to the
birthday of the Son of God by making the "U" an "O." I ask you, can a
leopard change his spots? Then, in a similar manner, no matter how long
you call a cat a dog, he's still a cat. You may now try to reason, "Even
though Christmas was a pagan custom honoring the false sun god, we now
do not observe it to honor a false god. We observe it in honor of Christ."
For those that reason on that wise, the prophet states:

*"Take heed to thyself that thou be not snared by
following them, after they are destroyed from before
thee, and that thou inquire not after their gods,
saying, How did these nations serve their gods?
Even so will I do likewise.*

*Thou shalt not do so unto the Lord thy God; for
every abomination to the Lord, which he hateth, have
they done unto their gods. For even their sons and
their daughters they have burned in the fire to their
gods."*

Deuteronomy 12:30,31

Some of you will be shocked at this truth; some will be offended. However, I must show you your transgressions, how you are bound in sin, so that you may weigh, evaluate and make the necessary changes for your return unto God in word and in deed. Before men can settle any spiritual controversies with God, men must first come to the realization of what causes problems. Then we must come into an understanding of what solves problems: knowledge of Truth and Justice, knowledge of what is right and what is wrong. There is no way that African Americans, the most religiously sincere people in the world, could remain under the sentence of bondage if what we were doing was right! Our problems stem from our controversy with God, and in our search we found *religion and not righteousness.* We were taught to *say* God, but not to worship God; we honor God with our lips, but our hearts are far from Him, for our ways are the ways of adversity.

You work all year and buy your children toys and gifts. Then you lie by telling them that a fat, rosy-cheeked European came riding through the sky on a sleigh of reindeer, landing on your roof to then come sliding down your chimney with a big bag of toys; and if that is not enough, he then goes back up the chimney and away he goes! All year long you are offended if your child tells a lie, then at Christmas time, you, yourselves, tell the Santa Claus or "Jolly-Old-St. Nick" lie (Old St. Nick or Nicholas was a Roman Catholic Bishop of the fifth century). It is no wonder that when they learn the truth, they also tend to see God as a myth. You have substituted the Truth of God for a lie, and you love it!

> *"And this is the condemnation, that light is come into the world, and men loved darkness rather than light because their deeds are evil.*
>
> *For everyone that doeth evil hateth the light, neither cometh to the light, lest his deeds should be reproved.*
>
> *But he that doeth truth cometh to the light, that his deeds may be made manifest, that they are wrought in God."*
>
> ### St. John 3:19-21

> *"But when they in their trouble did turn unto the Lord God of Israel, and sought him, he was found by them.*
>
> *And in those times there was no peace to him that went out nor to him that came in, but great vexations*

were upon all the inhabitants of the countries.

*And nation was destroyed by nation, and city by city;
for God did vex them with all adversity.*

*Be ye strong, therefore, and let not your hands be
weak; for your work shall be rewarded."*

II Chronicles 15:4-7

Your work shall certainly be rewarded! Let us assemble our families
and loved ones; let us pray prayers of repentance. Let us enter into a
covenant that we shall no longer follow strange customs and worship strange
gods. The God of the universe established set times and seasons which
were to keep man in harmony with Him and His Creation. The Holy Days
or Feast Days given to the Children of Israel in the Law were in fact God's
festive days and not theirs. These festive days were spiritually given to all
men as a sign of sanctification of God's Holy name. Jesus acknowledged
and kept God's Holy Days and none else. As a matter of fact, they are the
only festive days that both the prophets and Jesus give credence to in the
Holy Scriptures. One of the High Holy Days will be used as a sign of
acknowledgment of God's Kingdom and rulership during the Millennium.
The Feast of Tabernacles (Feast of Ingathering) is to be celebrated by all
nations or they shall taste the immediate wrath of God.

*"And it shall come to pass that everyone that is left
of all the nations which came against Jerusalem shall
even go up from year to year to worship the King,
the Lord of Hosts, and to keep the feast of tabernacles.*

*And it shall be that whoever will not come up of all
the families of the earth unto Jerusalem to worship
the King, the Lord of Hosts, even upon them shall be
no rain.*

*And if the family of Egypt go not up, and come not,
that have no rain, there shall be the plague, with
which the Lord will smite the nations that come not
up to keep the feast of tabernacles.*

*This shall be the punishment of Egypt, and the
punishment of all nations, that come not up to keep
the feast of tabernacles."*

Zechariah 14:16-19

These days have not and cannot be abolished. Most people accepting the modified version of slave-oriented Christianity have reasoned that all the annual Sabbaths and feast days have been abolished. Yet history shows that as Christianity held fast to its ancient roots and origins, all African (particularly Northeastern African) scholars observed and taught the observance of the annual Holy Days given by God. It was not until after the Middle Ages that new ordinances originating in Rome began to come forth. The African scholar disappeared, and a new European scholar arose that gave no respect to the truth, nor did this scholar desire to worship according to ancient African Hebrew customs. As we consider the reasons for the establishment of a chosen people, we should not imagine any motive for their existence beyond the reason given by God. They were a special people because they were given a way of life that generally differed from that of their neighbors. However, their law and way of life was not for them alone, for the essence of their being chosen was that they might be a light (sign of God's intelligence) unto all the nations.

Why then, has satan worked so hard to separate the purpose of ancient Israel from the minds of the people? Was it not to pave the way for the institution of new laws, customs, traditions, feast days and Sabbaths in his honor, and not God's? Who gave him the right? For the earth and the fullness thereof belongs to God. Therefore only He or His representatives can take away or institute, all according to the Will and Plan of God. The ancient ceremonial regulations were only temporary additions to the law, awaiting the necessary growth of the people in their comprehension of the substance of God's law (instructions). When we read of the instructions for washing the clothes and the body, followed by the offering of a burnt offering or sacrifice, the message is simply that cleanliness is Godliness; and, fire or heat was always used to drive away or destroy disease or bacteria (as illustrated by the fact that the body, when attacked by a virus, creates heat — fever — to fight to destroy its presence). Testimony to this phenomenon is the fact that even the Word of God is referred to as a fire, the purpose of which is certainly to destroy all evil presence.

In the days of our fathers, fire (sacrifice or offering) was symbolically used at the discovery of any plague or disease. It was also used for healing or purification. Would it not be the same if at the onset of a problem, disease or defilement that the Word of God was offered up to make war against evil? After the victory, certainly we should hear "Hallelujah, Hallelujah" as the word (fire) offering before our return to our normal functions among the people of God.

Do not use the ancient sacrifices as your excuse for rejecting God's law, because they were added only as similitudes and substitutes until such time that God's people would grow in their comprehension of the true sacrificial requirement: to be a totally perfect moral character, and to give of one's self unto God.

The body, properly cared for, is the most perfect healing mechanism ever created. With proper care, within the cycles and seasons of God, it will dispose of all of its waste, both solids and liquids. The body has a defense system which will mobilize itself instantly, and secrete antibodies which will attack and destroy any virus as well as repair all injured tissues or organs. It was originally created to function and last forever. What people are walking around with today is a very poor similitude of the original physical form because the body has not had the loving care which it required. Instead, it has been beaten and attacked with the ferociousness of an insane enemy, whose purpose was to destroy totally this great creation of God. Although the body has not yet been totally destroyed, the adversary has however, beaten it into submission, simultaneously destroying its resistance to disease; whereby it no longer functions within the life cycle of God, but in the death cycle of its adversary.

If it could be totaled, the moans and groans which have been heard and the pain which has been felt by the human body during the last two hundred years of rule of the modern Euro-American, would greatly surpass all the moans, groans and pain of the preceding five-thousand, eight hundred years combined. There has never been a time in history as it is now when it could be generally stated that *everyone* is sick, suffering or dismembered (35 million operations are performed yearly in America alone). Before the coming of the Euro-gentile dominion, man, beast and the creation had never suffered so much and so regularly: the axe is taken to the trees, the gun to the birds, and the scalpel to man. A century ago Victor Hugo wrote:

> "War will be dead, the scaffold will be dead, hatred will be dead, frontiers will be dead, royalty will be dead, dogmas will be dead, man will begin to live. But here we are, and war is not dead, the scaffold is not dead, dogmas are not dead, and man does not know how to live. His mind, trained in science, is applying his education to the perfection of weapons of death. Because man's capacity for destruction has become almost unlimited, the need to rekindle his awareness of a higher purpose in the human destiny is all the greater."

Only Truth, Justice, Mercy, Love of God and Righteousness will bring about the necessary change in the societies of today, not technological advancement and scientific research. In these, the days of the Kingdom of God, all the above attributes will become the law of the land; from them the plant of Peace will begin to grow and flourish.

> *"Until the Spirit be poured upon us from on high,*
> *and the wilderness be a fruitful field, and the fruitful*
> *field be counted as a forest.*
>
> *Then justice shall dwell in the wilderness, and*
> *righteousness remain in the fruitful field.*
>
> *And the work of righteousness shall be peace; and*
> *the effect of righteousness, quietness and assurance*
> *forever.*
>
> *And my people shall dwell in a peaceable habitation,*
> *and in sure dwellings, and in quiet resting places."*
>
> ### *Isaiah 32:15-18*

There is no technology available to prevent the killing, maiming, robbing, dope peddling and exploitation of one another. Scientists will not find a cure for broken hearts, heart ailments and heart attacks. Neither will they be able to cure cancer or find a "safe" pill for birth control. Consider the mindlessness of men and the darkness of governments that employ thousands and spend hundreds of millions trying to find a safe, healthy way to alter or prevent God's will from being fulfilled. Trying to circumvent God is a plan destined to failure. I state clearly, emphatically, and authoritatively, there is no injection discovered or yet to be discovered which will allow mankind to continue smoking, polluting and consuming poisons while not being afflicted with cancer. There is no safety in wickedness.

Sadly, this pattern of ignoring the cycles of God while having the illusion of "progress" has repeated itself, even on a worldwide scale. One of the greatest protections of African and other "Third World" people from today's rampant diseases has been the Africans' natural rest pattern: to bed early, to rise early and relaxation after meals. In most African countries there is a two-to-three-hour midday break (lunch), but the more industrialized and European-oriented a country becomes, the more the natural, traditional protections disappear. Ultimately, if a traditional African has not made it to the "big city" and learned English, then he has not learned to say "cancer." Thank God! Yet, so-called Third World or "underdeveloped" countries are continually being seduced to embrace the "progress" of the

West. Shamed into rejecting the natural as primitive, backward or lazy, they allow themselves to become "developed" away from the righteous cycles of life — and to "progress" toward the unrighteous cycles of death.

Meanwhile, the offending society attempts to bury or conceal its guilt. Let us consider how the cigarette manufacturers attempt to conceal their criminal offense by offering you its great all around "life insurance policy." "Complete coverage" they call it. You are so beguiled and blinded by these "benefits" that you cannot see the true criminal or his victims.

The multi-national R.J. Reynolds cigarette manufacturers (whose assets were the objective of a $25 billion corporate take-over recently) also provide life insurance policies. To be sure, the company also contributes large sums to cancer research — as if they did not know that cigarettes are inextricably linked to cancer and are destroying your health (life)! Reynolds and other cigarette manufacturers brazenly write this on their (your) package, gambling that in spite of the warnings, their policies, contributions and seductions (advertisements) will keep you blinded to the fact that they are criminals — and you are their victims. So, they go on providing compensation for what they are causing — certain you are going to need it — powerlessly caught up as you are in the unrighteous cycles of death. Thus satan, with his last gasp of breath, is attempting to gain more time, whereby he can totally destroy God's earth and people. In satan's attempt to prevent the rebellion of the people, he gives the impression that he is concerned about their health and well-being. Through the invention of great, wicked machines which satan's workers connect to their patients' brains, kidneys, hearts and livers, and through satan's wonder drugs, the people have been seduced into not considering that satan's way of life-death is responsible for their horrible, sickly predicament.

The world, deceived by modern Christian teachings (which have their origins in Europe), believes that God's laws (instructions) have been abolished. I grant you that the law will never be as it was in the days of Moses, but the spirit of the instructions of God is eternal. There was much more than the sacrifices contained in the laws (instructions) of God. There were laws of principles, laws for building strong character and morals, instructions for cleanliness and hygiene, together with instructions for maintaining good health.

The one person that should certainly take heed when good health is mentioned is the woman, because within the human family, no vessel has undergone so much abuse as that of the woman's body. It is a wonder that she has any body left at all, after the chemical aerosol sprays and deodorants used externally, and the cancerous tampons and douche concentrations used internally. She has had her tubes tied, her ovaries removed, foams sprayed internally, pills swallowed, hysterectomies, mastectomies, caesarians, and abortions.

She has waged war against God and lost. All of the abominations mentioned could have been prevented simply by believing and following God's instructions; but instead she rebelled against Adam and followed the law (instructions) of the devil and made herself an enemy of God. It is no wonder then that today *all* women are suffering from what is called "female sickness." Disease exists in the female sex organ at a ratio unparalleled in history. Venereal disease has become so widespread and pandemic, until certain viruses are now being passed on to the young daughters, who have become victims of their mothers' disobedience unto God; subsequently, those in their early and pre-teens are now experiencing "female troubles." Some of these viruses are virtually incurable, and when detected, the women are advised to discontinue childbearing.

One disease, affecting both men and women in epidemic proportions, is AIDS (Acquired Immune Deficiency Syndrome). AIDS is a disease which suppresses the body's natural resistance to the host of potentially harmful viruses and germs which invade the body daily, leaving the victim susceptible to any number of ailments, the least of which become life-threatening. Affecting many millions of people, AIDS is one hundred percent fatal...with no cure in sight!

AIDS first received recognition in the early 1980's as a disease striking white homosexuals in the United States. Widespread fallacies rooted in racial bigotry surfaced in the immediate hysteria following its appearance, which linked the virus to Africa and Africans (via the central African Green Monkey and Haitian refugees), theories which were later proven false. AIDS is now known to be a heterosexually-transmitted disease which strikes disproportionately among the African/African American population, primarily women and their offspring.

The face of AIDS has grown darker, younger and increasingly more feminine. The dreadful malady has dealt Africa a severe blow, where it has decimated the ranks of the urban, educated, professional elite — cutting deeply into many a country's leadership pool with the effects of a protracted war. Consequently, AIDS is thought by many to be a product of Euro-gentile biological warfare research, employed against the African world. This is indeed a distinct probability when we recall the use of small-pox-laced blankets in the United States' war against the American Indians or the carnage wrought by the use of the cancer-causing defoliant, "Agent Orange," in Viet Nam.

Yet, the fact remains that AIDS (and other venereal diseases) are the end result of the carefree lifestyles, promiscuous attitudes and permissive environment promoted during the "sexual revolution" of the 1960's and '70's. Sexually liberated, we are now "free" to contract any number of evil afflictions. The subsequent rise in female troubles, gonorrhea, syphilis, herpes, chlamydia and AIDS has made the sexual revolution a modern-day "Trojan Horse."

How can we see diseases of this sort and not consider them a plague upon the people? In former times something so widespread would have immediately caused people to begin repentance and seek God for an understanding of what they had done wrong. Today, there is no true fear of God, because God is only seen in the abstract and not the absolute. Religion has left you void and in darkness concerning God, Truth and Worship. Everything suffers: your mind, spirit and physical body.

> *"Notwithstanding, I have a few things against you,*
> *because thou allowest that woman, Jezebel, who*
> *calleth herself a prophetess, to teach and to seduce*
> *my servants to commit fornication, and to eat things*
> *sacrificed unto idols.*
>
> *And I gave her space to repent of her fornication,*
> *and she repented not.*
>
> *Behold, I will cast her into a bed, and them that*
> *commit adultery with her into great tribulation,*
> *except they repent of their deeds.*
>
> *And I will kill her children with death; and all the*
> *churches (people) shall know that I am he who*
> *searcheth the mind and hearts; and I will give unto*
> *every one of you according to your works."*
>
> ***Revelation 2:20-23***

To what should we attribute the many complex genital diseases that plague man today? People do not just "happen" to get sick; there is a cause for every effect. There has to be a comprehensible reason, whether accepted or not as to why there is so much sickness, disease and suffering in the world today. The problem is that satan is always very careful to steer your thoughts away from any feeling of true guilt. You never once consider that possibly you are breaking or violating the laws of God. If you did, you would naturally think of the Ten Commandments, or the Spiritual Law. You have completely forgotten that there are physical laws also that regulate physical health and well-being. If these laws are broken, it is considered a transgression of the law and a penalty is exacted, usually sickness or physical suffering of some kind.

How does man seek a cure for a plague like AIDS without seeking to understand whether he is violating the Everlasting Law of Life? It is doubtful whether many know that there are laws that govern the genitals and sexual activity. The cause of sickness, even AIDS, is the transgression of the cycles and physical laws that God has set in motion to govern our human bodies. These laws are just as real as the law of gravity, and the penalties for violating them are just as sure.

Many of the aforementioned ailments are a result of improper sex habits, i.e., sexual relationships out of cycle with God's set times and seasons. During the initial seven-day cycle of menstruation, the vagina, cervix and womb are vulnerable and covered with blood spots. (A woman's menstruation cycle lasts for seven days starting from the time her blood issue begins. It does not end with the ceasing of her flow, because some women only flow three or four days. Her body is in menstruation for seven days). When the blood spots are mixed with secretions and man's sperm, they form a deadly acid called "pad" which coats the vagina, cervix and womb thus weakening the tissues. We find a verification of this danger in God's instructions of quarantine. According to the law, if during sexual intercourse, the woman began her issue of blood, and this blood touched the man's genitals, he was quarantined for seven days. This period of time was to allow for close observation by the physicians and priests for the development of any symptoms of venereal disease. It was considered to be a danger of such magnitude that even the thought in a man's mind to approach a woman in her issue for sexual intercourse was considered evil. Moreover, if a man and woman purposely had intercourse during her menstruation, they were both expelled from the Israelite Nation, and no longer considered Holy unto God.

Why was so much emphasis placed upon forbidding the mixing of blood, sperm and secretions even five thousand years ago? God's way of life is like a shield against evil: without it you are vulnerable to any and everything. In today's world of promiscuity — "everything goes." * This mentality is exacting a high price on us in terms of deformed bodies and minds. God's instructions would have prevented the plagues that are upon us today. How does it make you feel to know that your body is rotting with disease that could have been prevented with a little chastity and Holiness? Men and women are spreading more disease today through sex than at any time in history. Even the great God-given pleasure of sexual intercourse has been made a curse. As you lay there in bed now, you are not so anxious because the two of you stare suspiciously at each other wondering...does she/he have "it" or not? I have no comfort to offer you, only pity. According to statistics, most likely he/she *does* have "it."

Thus, copulation during the seven-day cycle of menstruation prepares the way for the onset of venereal disease and/or cancer of the cervix and uterus. Few women, and hardly any men are aware of God's instructions for the prevention of venereal disease:

> *"And if any man's seed of copulation go out from*
> *him, then he shall wash all his flesh in water, and be*
> *unclean until the even.*

> *And every garment, and every skin, whereon is the*
> *seed of copulation, shall be washed with water, and*
> *be unclean until the even.*

> *The woman also with whom man shall lie with seed of*
> *copulation, they shall both bathe themselves in water,*
> *and be unclean until the even.*

> *And if a woman have an issue, and her issue in her*
> *flesh be blood, she shall be put apart seven days;*
> *and whosoever toucheth her shall be unclean until*
> *the even.*

> *And everything that she lieth upon in her separation*
> *shall be unclean; everything also that she sitteth*
> *upon shall be unclean.*

> *And if any man lie with her at all, and her impurity*
> *be upon him, he shall be unclean seven days; and all*
> *the bed whereon he lieth shall be unclean.*

"Modern western society still preserves some old myths about menstruation, all of which can be ignored. It is perfectly safe for the menstruating woman to bathe, shower, swim, wash her hair and have intercourse, and take part in any other activity she wishes."[6]

Thus shall ye separate the children of Israel from their uncleanness, that they die not in their uncleanness, when they defile my tabernacle that is among them.

This is the law of him who hath an issue, and of him whose seed goeth from him, and is defiled therewith;

And of her who is sick of her impurity, and of him who hath an issue, of the man, and of the woman, and of him that lieth with her that is unclean."

Leviticus 15:16-20; 24; 31-33

"Also thou shalt not approach unto a woman to uncover her nakedness, as long as she is put apart for her uncleanness.

And if a man shall lie with a woman having her sickness, and shall uncover her nakedness, he hath discovered her fountain, and she hath uncovered the fountain of her blood; and both of them shall be cut off from among their people."

Leviticus 18:19; 20:18

What is the substance of the instructions to wash and be unclean until evening after copulating? Is this just a ritual or does it have some significance to good health and strength? The words "unclean" or "defiled" was the terminology used when something was not fit for use in its proper cycle of Holiness. ("Holiness" means something sanctified or set aside for a specific use in righteousness. It cannot be used at just any time to do anything). The term "holiness" was commonly used to denote something which required regulating or setting aside for a season or period of time. Also, in order that measuring times would not be complicated, God simply said one would be unclean (not ready for use) until evening. (Evening in the proper cycle of God, begins with the setting of the sun).

The significance of these instructions was to make man and woman aware of the need to wait a period of time between copulations. It was established primarily to prevent men from copulating with other women and women from copulating with other men on the same day (as in prostitution), an indulgence which is a prime source of venereal disease.

The sperm of man and the vaginal secretion of woman requires time to dissipate after sexual intercourse; therefore, one is instructed to wash with water and wait a period of time before copulating again. The dissipation requires a number of hours. To eject another sperm in the woman's vagina before the last sperm has dissipated would be like mixing dangerous acids, thereby causing a volatile reaction. A continuation of this process will certainly lead to venereal disease and cancer of the cervix and/or penis. In medical studies it has been substantiated that uncircumcised men have a higher incidence of infection or cancer of the penis, while their wives or mates have a higher incidence of cancer of the cervix. This is attributed to poor hygiene — a conclusion which is partially true, but it is not the whole truth. The whole truth, as I have previously stated requires the acknowledgment of the triumph of God over man's attempt to avoid keeping God's laws and instructions of hygiene. The world today is in its sorrowful state because it has been made God's adversary.

The actual cause of cancer of the penis and cervix is smegma, (a thick secretion of both man and woman which accumulates under the foreskin of the penis or around the clitoris) a result of poor hygiene, the man not being circumcised or from sexual promiscuity. The body fluids required to help in the dissipation of this smegma cannot reach those areas. Consequently, the old sperm or vaginal secretions accumulate and remain. As daily sexual intercourse continues, the old sperm or vaginal secretions which do not dissolve, are mixed with the new. During copulation, heat is produced, causing a chemical reaction and the release of an acid-like virus into the woman's vagina and onto the man's penis. It is from this agent that the cancerous sores begin, resulting in venereal disease, weakening of tissues, and in some cases, cancer of the penis and/or cervix. Furthermore, cancer of the penis and cervix have a higher incidence in hot climates because of the increased heat produced during sexual intercourse and the longer time required for the cooling of the body.

Nighttime has been associated with the sexual act from the beginning of time. Nighttime is also the time of the lesser light, the moon. Why is there a prevalent feeling that "nighttime is the right time to be with the one you love"? This feeling also coincides with the Biblical instructions "wait until evening." A good reason for waiting is that the vagina will be lubricated and the testicles will most likely be refilled with fertile sperm. This is tied directly to the cycle of the moonrise. Now we can see the wisdom in the instructions of the Omnipotent God, unto whom all praise is due forever. According to His instructions, washing after copulation and abstention from sexual intercourse until evening allows for the dissipation of old sperm, the refilling of the testicles, and the lubrication of the vagina, which protects both your health and life.

It has always been insinuated that the celestial bodies were a source of strength and agility. However, the understanding about the movement of these bodies within the universe has had a tendency to take on mythical overtones which, in the end, left us in possession of something we could not quite explain. Therefore, we called it a myth. People must understand again that God has kept the mysteries to Himself, but the how, when and where of the things which we must do are made clear unto us. One source of strength and agility is the moon, because it is the moon which causes the formation of fertile sperm and the refilling of the testicles. The rising of the moon stimulates the action by which the testicles are refilled, and the vagina lubricated, therefore ready for use. The amount of sperm has a tendency to increase with the growth of the moon, reaching its zenith on a full moon. This is why a full moon usually stimulates romance, not just because of its utter beauty, but mainly because of the pressure within the testicles and the lubrication inside the vagina on a full moon. As the moon subsides, the standard amount of sperm is still produced but the increasing quantitative process begins again only with the new moon.

Man's health, life and well-being are tied directly to the celestial bodies. Exposure to moonlight and sunlight are essential. No man, woman or child can stay imprisoned in their home sitting before the television set and expect to be healthy. Not only does television destroy your mental well-being, but your physical well-being also.

Everything used in Holiness is used properly within the cycles of life. When the organs are used properly, they function without end, for Godliness eternalizes. One of the false impressions the world has given to men is that the more times he copulates in one day, the stronger he is, when in truth, the opposite is true. Multiple copulating between moonrises is a vanity, because as copulations increase, the sperm weakens drastically. Venereal diseases and other ailments can in most cases, be traced back to improper sex, or to not understanding God's instructions for the prevention of such ailments. I should also make note here that the firmness of the erection of a man's penis depends upon the amount of sperm in his testicles, and not his age. As a rule, man's penis deflates after sexual intercourse. This occurs because he has ejected his sperm. His movements or amount of activity mean absolutely nothing in terms of the firmness of an erection. (Mental state can also affect his firmness). If a man maneuvers upon a woman and does not ejaculate, he can re-erect his penis a number of times, for the high quantity of sperm is still present. After it is ejected, the penis naturally softens. The only thing which has changed is the amount of sperm in his testicles. Elderly men, or all men for that matter, who are having problems erecting their penis, should seek ways of building their sperm content and not get caught feeling sorry for themselves because of age. Under normal circumstances as long as the moon rises, testicles should refill, causing the penis to become erect. In many instances, a shortage of sperm can be attributed to a blockage of the replenishing passage to the testicles, caused by waste or cholesterol build-up from improper eating habits, or a blockage of the mind, clogged by fear, worry, anxiety and the wickedness of the world.

In today's world of sickness, disease and death, lies have caused both men and women to continue to mutilate, abuse and misuse their bodies. Therefore, we find that the primary cause of man's multiple ailments is man himself. He no longer follows nor cherishes the way of life and God; instead he cherishes the way of death and satan. If a man and woman would maintain a positive relationship with God through cleanliness of mind (proper spiritual relationship), cleanliness of body (proper hygiene and eating habits), and rest, they could fruitfully copulate all of their days, even forever. Today man leans to operations and antibiotics to correct his physical ailments, consequently complicating the matter and aggravating the problem because he has been deceived. Man in this world, under the rule of satan and under the influence of error, seeks no solutions which require an acknowledgment of and allegiance to God, the Creator of the Heavens and Earth. If God's laws (instructions) have been abolished then you had better inform your body, for it has not been taught to accept anything other than God's proper treatment and care.

How long must the Sons and Daughters of God suffer the pains of ungodliness in the decadent world of satan, the arch adversary of God? You are being destroyed for lack of knowledge of God! You have rejected God's instructions for that which does not and shall not profit.

Another prime, although somewhat comical, example of the unrighteous cycles of death and the gross foolishness of man is what he has done to the poor chicken. You see, it is natural for a hen to lay one egg per day during daylight hours. Then mankind discovered that if you kept the hens thinking that it was still daylight, they would lay another egg at night. So men snap on large lights at sunset and the poor chickens keep on laying — becoming the victims of deception and wicked invention.

However, Divine Justice takes over, for the eggs produced by this process are not fertile, because they were not brought forth with regard to the natural cycles of the Living God. Yet, because of the increased production, there is increased consumption of these eggs. Nutritional "experts" recommend that you increase your consumption of eggs in order to satisfy your need for protein. As the years pass, increased egg consumption leads to high cholesterol levels, causing heart attacks and death due to the clogging of the arteries and veins feeding your vital organs. In addition, the excessive protein intake becomes carcinogenic to the body.

Thus, with natural cycles being just, the chicken which man abused came back and abused him. He forced the chicken to operate under strenuous and unnatural conditions. The insomniac chicken, in turn caused man to live and work under strenuous and unnatural conditions. Justice is always the Divine balancer of any wicked deed of man. It never sleeps. Man was healthier when the natural (righteous) cycles were followed, because his egg consumption was lower. The end result, therefore, is that man is once again the victim and the inventor is the criminal. But the **TRUTH** shall bring him before the throne of the Living God for Divine judgement.

The wicked inventor uses the same tactic on man that he uses on the poor chicken. He installs the same big lights in your home and places of work in order to keep you hatching away during your normal hours of rest. Therefore, at sunset you click on your lights and continue your pace, never acknowledging the natural change in cycle which was to bring about a decrease in activity, thus preparing you for your needed rest. You forget that it is night time with your bright lights. You reject the call to slow down and to enjoy the night. You become a victim of deception and the end result is nervous tension, poor digestion, sickness, pain and death. You were not taught that the activities of tomorrow depend upon the strength restored to your organs while you rest at night. How well you function, how much you enjoy your surroundings and your fellow man — all depend on how well you rest at night.

The electric lights keep you unbalanced, and soon, like the poor chicken, you will be producing, but will not be fertile. Justice prevails, for the body you would not allow to rest soon will not allow you to rest. The body which you would not allow to follow the cycles of God will soon — through sickness and malfunction — not allow you to follow the cycles of man. That body which you took out of the cycles of God (life) shall soon take you out of the cycles of man (death). Thinking you had become wise, you became a fool, because you made your own body your enemy. In the same manner in which you have polluted your own water, your own air...in the same manner in which you have poisoned the food you eat, you have set out to alter or destroy everything that God has given you — yea, even your own life!

The cycles of God are a way of life. In the beginning, the Creator set forth the "Way of Life" for man. Man was to live and function within the cycles of life. Then, deceived by satan, man began to feel that he had his "own mind," not understanding that man was created in the image of God and given the "God Mind." Now, man finds himself trapped in the pit which he has dug; he has to now seek to understand God's Divine cycles, seasons and set times and be obedient unto them. This will bring about the purifying of his body and mind, allowing God to return to his temple.

Truth at all levels had been cut off, changed or destroyed by corrupt-thinking men and nations who have abused it for selfish purposes. The Plan of God through the Kingdom of God, is to return man to Truth and Truth to man; whereby Truth will bring man to his Creator, in Peace, Love, Harmony and Divine oneness. The Kingdom of God is dedicated to the restoration of man to God Almighty and His Divine plan of life. Through teaching and living the Divine laws, statutes and commandments, every man may know how to live in harmony with his part of the plan, keeping him in place with the eternal plan of the Creator as it has been charted by Divine prophecy.

It should be clear unto all men, that satan, the arch enemy of God, in his moment of power and dominion could not provide Peace, Happiness, Truth, Mercy and Love. Therefore, satan deceived men so that they could not see his failure. He projected himself as a god, but he could not rule as the True God had ruled over His creation. Under the rule of err and satan, men cherish death instead of hating it. Satan has even convinced men that in their graves they would be in their finest hour, journeying on to Heaven. The Sons of God were taught to accept wars, unhappiness, lies, injustice, inequity and hate — the fruits of satan's dominion over God's creation — as normal.

No force functions as it did under the Divine authority of God. Everything now enhances death. The polluted minds of evil, controlled by satan, do not even allow the land, air and water to perform their life-giving tasks for man. Nothing and nobody works right for wrong. There is no Heavenly existence under evil rulers. Moreover, satan has made the Heavenly bodies not to appear unto man as they did in the beginning — in perfect cycle as a source of power, energy and rejuvenation from God Almighty. Satan has caused them to appear as planets that could contain a higher way of life than that on earth, with people thereon. He caused man to seem small and inferior in comparison to these beings; thus, making the heart of man seek after that which does not exist, rather than to seek after the ways of the

Living God, and meditate upon the secret truths of His law. God requires all men to keep His laws and to live within the cycles of life, because they are a sign of loyalty and obedience unto Him.

The righteous cycles of God were formed in the beginning and given to man through inspiration, dreams, and visions, as the guidelines for the way of life designed by the Creator to promote a happy and peaceful existence, free from sickness and death, the consequence of gross errors, ignorance, wrongful teachings and the inability to know and understand truth. Those who seek God will hear the truth and grow to live it and use it as a daily companion, guide and judge. God's plan is to help those who have become blinded by ignorance and false teachings to see how Truth creates Peace, Justice and Love, and destroys the thoughts that create wars, injustice and hate. The world, in its reevaluation, must look at itself as illiterate and incompetent in its knowledge, wisdom and understanding of the laws, principles and cycles that govern life.

Let us investigate the law or cycle of the season of childbirth, as well as prenatal and postnatal care. In the book of Judges, we find the instructions for a woman of God during her conception:

> *"And there was a certain man of Zorah, of the family of the Danites, whose name was Manoah; and his wife was barren and bore not.*
>
> *And the angel of the Lord appeared unto the woman; and said unto her, Behold, now, thou art barren, and bearest not; but thou shalt conceive, and bear a son.*
>
> *Now therefore beware, I pray thee, and drink not wine nor strong drink; and eat not any unclean thing."*

> ### *Judges 13:2-4*

Manoah's wife had to first understand that she was to bring forth a special child, with a special mission for God. This mission is the same for all of God's Sons and Daughters. "Ye are the light of men; ye are the salt of the earth." So the angel instructed Manoah's wife, who was symbolic of the women of God's kingdom. "Beware," he said, "of what you eat, drink and think during conception, because your child is a special child unto God." As the vessels delivering God's goods — His children, His creations — women must be especially conscious of their thoughts, (they must be pure and divine, not wicked and unholy); of their words, (for though they be invisible to the eye, the spoken word carries the force of a raging storm);

and what they consume, (the food we eat determines how alert, cunning, and intelligent we are or how slow, inept and ignorant we are).

I reflect upon my childhood spent in the southern United States. I would hear my grandmother say to the young daughters in conception: "Be careful what you say child, because you will mark that baby." Or if a dog or cat suddenly appeared, disturbing the young mother-to-be, grandmother would state, "Honey, don't you get mad (at the cat, dog, etc.) because you'll make that baby come out looking like that." Did she mean that the baby would look like the cat or dog? Even grandma didn't really know totally what she meant. She always seemed to have a reservoir of understanding and wisdom for which she could not assign an origin beyond "my mother taught me," but she knew and believed those things to be true. In her own simple way she knew that the mind of the mother would become an integral part of the mind of that child. One of the least understood factors governing prenatal embryo development is the profound effect that the mind of the mother-to-be has upon the embryo's development. A large part of the mental and social ailments of children have been caused by the state of mind of the mother during conception. As grandma would have simply said, "you have marked that baby."

Few women in conception, because of the chaotic, wicked world in which we live, have the feeling of contentment and real peace of mind upon which a spiritually healthy child is predicated. Women in conception must be taught again to control their thoughts during the initial, critical nine months of the baby's life because they are responsible for building the mind of the child to come — building the mind of a Dr. Martin Luther King Jr. or Nelson Mandela rather than a tyrant like Ferdinand Marcos or Jean Claude "Baby Doc" Duvalier.

In the days of the Kingdom of God, we understand and respect grandma's wisdom. From the day of confirmed pregnancy, the priest pays regular visits to the mother to read the Word of God unto the mother and her unborn child. He teaches the unborn child the principles of life and makes known what will be expected of him after birth. As the priest reads to the unborn child, the readings also soothe and develop thoughts of Holiness in the mind of the mother.

The effects of these initial teachings will be seen in this decade as children are again taught innocence and given a childhood. People who reject the law (instructions) of God can never achieve the promise of life and health for themselves nor their children. They have deceived themselves into believing that the more materialism they make available, the happier a child will be. We fully reject this untruth, because in these days of overflowing materialism, the state of the children has never been worse. There are childhood killings, suicides, drug addiction, mental retardation, anxiety, alcoholism, depression, disrespect of elders and gang warfare among the world's children. Things have never been worse for children. The parents and the children are constantly visiting their physicians, psychologists and psychiatrists seeking cures for their mental illnesses and fears, but only a return to God by African people and by all men will bring peace of mind and oneness with God.

When we see the children born today to those mothers who smoked, drank alcohol, ate rotten food and thought only about money and materialism, we can easily understand what has happened to them. They were destroyed from the womb. The degenerate minds they possess are the degenerate minds of their mothers. They have no childhood. They know no innocence. They are sipping beer at five, drinking alcohol at nine, taking dope by twelve, and hustling to fulfill their materialistic lusts by thirteen.

They have been programmed into unrighteous cycles of death and illness even from the day of their birth. The manufacturers of unrighteousness in the spirit of err and deception — operating by the satanic principles of force, greed, selfishness, ambition and hate — plan and prepare these children for an early adulthood and a premature death! They begin by preparing the wrong diet for the newborn child, making you believe that "Carnation" or "Pet" milk is as good as mother's milk. Aside from *naturally* being for calves instead of for human babies, these and all other packaged, processed "baby foods" contain chemical preservatives (embalmers) and addictive refined sugar. Your early childhood addiction to sweets and "junk food" starts in the cradle. Then you are treated as if your late teens and early twenties are the "prime of your life." You can expect to notice the signs of the regressive process in your late twenties — "middle age spread," decaying teeth, thinning hair, etc. — which are actually due to your earlier terrible diet of sugars, chemicals, junk, etc. You are told you are "over the hill" at 40. With your sexual agility and vigor decreasing, you begin to deactivate yourself. Once you are inactive, you are in preparation for the final phase — you are ready to be "put out to pasture." If you live to age 65, you "retire" to wait for your pension and your funeral.

The "experts" and their statistics have always told you how long you are supposed to live. You hear continuously their projected life expectancy rates: the life span of African American males is 60 years; African American females, 65 years; white males, 70 years; white females, 72 years.*

Little did you consider that you were simply being led where your leaders desired you to go. Then, when you do see these things happening, you have heard them so much that you accept them as "natural" occurrences. From the Carnation milk of your cradle to the carnation flower of your grave, you have been psychologically groomed — and physically doomed — to fulfill the unrighteous cycles and seasons of death, and you accept this as "normal."

Always remember that every mental condition, sickness and death is *caused*; it is not just something which happens. If you accept these things as normal, you will not attempt to alter or eradicate them, thereby giving them a permanent habitation among the Sons of the Kingdom, in opposition to the prophetic Word and Plan of God. I admonish you to consider grandma's words, because they were final remnants of the wisdom from the elders of Israel. Now, if to disobey those instructions has brought a curse, will not obedience bring forth a blessing?

Let us make our young daughters wise in God in order that they may live in God's Kingdom, because misguided world leadership and ignorant philosophers abuse and insult life and the whole of God's creation through unbalanced, unrighteous cycles of death. Continuing on in our investigation, we find the postnatal instructions for a Holy people.

> *"And the Lord spoke unto Moses, saying, Speak unto the children of Israel, saying,*
>
> *If a woman have conceived seed, and born a male child, then she shall be unclean seven days; according to the days of the separation for her infirmity shall she be unclean.*
>
> *And in the eighth day the flesh of his foreskin shall be circumcised.*
>
> *And she shall then continue in the blood of her purifying three and thirty days; she shall touch no hallowed thing, nor come into the sanctuary, until the days of her purifying be fulfilled.*

---

*Life expectancies in African and other "Third World" countries are appallingly low. In the poorest of "sub-Saharan" African nations, African males will rarely survive into their forties!

But if she bear a female child, then she shall be unclean two weeks, as in her separation; and she shall continue in the blood of her purifying three score and six days."

Leviticus 12:1-5

If a woman would receive the proper care after childbirth and allow the total healing process to be performed by the body itself, she would be greatly rewarded by God. First of all, there would be no menopause, no need for caesarians; bladder and kidney problems, resulting from rough sexual activity during her days of separation, would be unknown; lower abdominal pain and excessive gas would disappear; and she would be able to bear children as long as man could give them. Let us briefly consider this last statement.

Have you ever given thought to the fact that a woman's conception cycle usually ends with menopause, which commences between the early to mid-forty years, while a man can impregnate, in most cases, all of his days? When we agree that the sole purpose of man's seed is for procreation, and not for the physical pleasure, (although the physical pleasure is an added blessing of the Eternal, blessed be He), then either the man would have to cease to copulate or be continuously given younger women that he might fulfill his days of copulation. Neither of these were practiced, because there was no need. In the early years of the creation, the woman could conceive as long as the man could impregnate, year after year without end. There was no menopause. Noah was five hundred years of age when Shem was born, and all of his years were nine hundred and fifty. Many of our fathers were over one hundred years of age when their first child was born. They then proceeded to bring forth sons and daughters all of their hundreds of years.

Many attempt to discredit the Holy writings of the Old Testament, which point out that men lived like trees. They attempt to dispute the life span of man in the early stages of his fall from grace. The scriptures describe the length of the lives of men like Adam (930 years), Seth (912 years), Enosh (905 years), and Methuselah (969 years). These were years no different than the years you know to be. For then, as now, the sun and moon, the day from sunset to sunset were used to determine the seasons: "And God said, let there be light in the firmament of the Heavens to divide the day from the night, and let them be for signs and for seasons and for days and years..." The men of that day were still close to the righteous cycles of life. But even in that day Noah was warned when he was 500 years old that unrighteous cycles would begin to shorten man's life. Genesis 6:3 — "And the Lord said (to Noah), My Spirit (righteousness) shall not always dwell with man for that he also is flesh: Yet his days shall be an hundred and twenty years." Here we are today, convinced by so-called "medical professionals" that we should be happy to reach "three score and ten" (70 years)!

But in a world built upon deception, the Truth is disguised as the patient and the lie appears as the physician. They have made good health and long life sound strange and be rejected, while sickness and death seem natural.

We find the Biblical account of men producing children in the very early years after the flood, and continuing to reproduce for four and five hundred years thereafter.

> *"These are the generations of Shem: Shem was an hundred years old, and begat Arphaxad two years after the flood:*
>
> *And Shem lived after he begat Arphaxad five hundred years, and begat sons and daughters.*
>
> *And Arphaxad lived five and thirty years, and begat Salah:*
>
> *And Arphaxad lived after he begat Salah four hundred and three years, and begat sons and daughters.*
>
> *And Salah lived thirty years, and begat Eber: and Salah lived after he begat Eber four hundred and three years, and begat sons and daughters.*
>
> *And Eber lived four and thirty years, and begat Peleg:*
>
> *And Eber lived after he begat Peleg four hundred and thirty years, and begat sons and daughters."*
>
> ### Genesis 11:10-17

Do you think that these men were continuously seeking out younger wives? Certainly not! The women they married initially could bare children all of their days. Their bodies were strong and still close to the cycles of God. Those days are not gone forever; those days are sure to return as women turn back to the laws (instructions) of God and halt their war against Him. After childbirth, there can be no sexual intercourse during her days of separation (40 days for a boy child and 80 days for a girl), nor can there be any strenuous activity. A man's sperm in the womb of a woman during a woman's days of separation is as dangerous as a toxic chemical spray. I must add that this great damage to the body did not occur in a day, but is the result of long seasons of abuse and misuse. Hence, neither will the healing process come in a day, for you must be cycled back onto the path which leads to these innumerable blessings.

Moreover, the Word of God came unto Ezekiel saying, "Son of man, eat that thou findest; eat this roll (book) and go speak unto the House of Israel (people of God). So I opened my mouth (mind) and He caused me to eat that roll (message) and He said unto me `Son of man, cause thy belly to eat (mind to absorb) and fill thy bowels with this roll (message) that I give thee.' Then did I eat it; and it was in my mouth (while reading) as honey for sweetness."

As you read this message, it will be as sweetness, but it may be like a bitter herb to you when it gets into your stomach. When it is time to digest it, then the real work begins. You'll know the cleansing process has begun when your stomach begins to cramp a little. Sometimes it will cause you some pain; but you know that bitter herbs are your most potent cleansers, for they rid you of all the waste. You must endure the little cleansing discomfort. After you are thoroughly cleansed, you'll feel like a new person and will realize that the waste was really your problem and will be glad when you flush it away.

The process of elimination has already begun in God's Kingdom, the alternative to this wicked world of sin. The God of our Fathers, Abraham, Isaac and Jacob, is a Great Redeemer and He's also known as a "jealous God." He is a God that likes to prove Himself (though not out of necessity). Even now He is waiting to prove that He can heal all sickness, open every womb, create eternal joy, and cause men to live forever. Let us now go as clay unto the Great Potter to be fashioned according to His will, that all the world may know that our God... "He is God and there is no other."

Heaven and Hell
(The Truth and The Myth)

When God created His Sons, He created them in His image, in the image of His Holy Spirit and with the attributes thereof, enabling them to understand and fulfill His Divine will and glorify Him. They had no knowledge of good and evil; no care and worry. Their crops failed not, and their harvests were full. Their children were born in Holiness; their seed failed not. There were no barren daughters. Pain and affliction they knew not. Righteousness was no endeavor, and truth needed no searching out or investigation. Their minds were heaven; their surroundings were paradise. The Sons of God were not victimized by the lust of the flesh, but rather were willing subjects of the will of the Most High God. Everything in their lives was reasoned and purposed with the will and glorification of the Most High God in mind before it was enacted or transpired.

The Daughters of God, the epitome of grace and Godliness, were the essence of beauty in the hearts and minds of the Sons of God, and were often looked upon as the flowers of the Kingdom. There was an inner beauty, which shone forth from their souls. The Sons and Daughters were riding upon the winds as gods and goddesses. They made thought into substance, created realms, worlds and people, and in Righteousness they brought forth life. Their domain was without end, for the earth and the fullness therein was theirs. The desire of the Most High was that His Sons forever remain on the mountaintop or in the high, elevated place wherein they would not be subjected to the will of satan or come under his power and dominion.

This high, elevated place is the "God Mind" of the Sons of God; it is Heaven. It is the dwelling place of the Most High God, His Throne of Glory.

God gave His Sons the dominion over all living things. All the fowl of Heaven made their nests in peace; the beasts of the field brought forth their young and all the nations under their shadow did dwell. In the world of the Sons of God (African Hebrews, who later became known as African Americans), love did abound; unhappiness and sorrow had no habitation. Yet, my God , my God, how did a people who sat so high come down so low? How could those with a world like this, turn aside from the path of God, to become subjects in the world of His adversary?

> *"Hear O heavens, and give ear, O earth: for the Lord hath spoken. I have nourished and brought up children, and they have rebelled against me.*
>
> *The ox knoweth his owner, and the ass his master's crib: but Israel doth not know, my people doth not consider.*
>
> *A sinful nation, a people laden with iniquity, a seed of evildoers, children that are corrupters: they have forsaken the Lord, they have provoked the Holy One of Israel unto anger, they are gone away backward.*
>
> *Why should ye be stricken anymore? Ye will revolt more and more; the whole head is sick, and the whole heart faint.*
>
> *From the sole of the foot even unto the head there is no soundness in it, but wounds, and bruises and putrefying sores. They have not been closed, neither bound up, neither mollified with ointment."*

Isaiah 1:2-6

What seemed to be impossible did happen; the fall came. The Sons of God moved backward: a complete 180 degrees just as the prophet stated. In place of the "God Mind" there came a mind so wicked that it could be compared with a cancerous, running sore. Instead of Heaven, there was hell and in place of the surroundings that were paradise, there came the flaming fire of the ghetto. The beautiful flower had withered; the strength of the Sons had dried up, and all that passed by mocked and jeered; "Ye are the salt of the earth; but if the salt have lost his savour, wherewith shall it be salted? It is thenceforth good for nothing but to be cast out, and to be trodden under foot of men." Thereby, the Sons of God fell away from their heavenly Father into the hands of lust, deception and iniquity. They lost sight of "inner beauty," the beauty of the soul. The power of the spiritual sense and vision was taken away. They could only see with the carnal eye of the flesh. They were now like their new master, satan, the great deceiver. Satan could see the handwriting on the wall, but being void of the wisdom of God, satan could not understand the message.

He therefore sought out one of the Hebrew Sons of God that was still in possession of the "God Mind" to help him. Before the great fall and the calamities which followed, all of the Sons of God could read the handwriting on the wall. The Sons could see unto the heavens, for they were free to roam the high places of God. The Sons were not bound by the Spirit of Err. Their spiritual eye was open; they could see all things. After the fall of the Sons, their dominion was taken away, and in place of the collective "God Mind," there were left as a sign, only a few of those who could still manifest the former natural attributes of the Holy people.

There was always an ensign or reminder of the former greatness. There were enough signs to remind us that God had not forgotten us, although we had forgotten Him. The seers, the prophets, the judges and the great lawgivers were all a continuous reminder of former glory. Isaiah, the prophet, wrote: "I and the children whom thou hast given me are for signs and wonders in Israel from the Lord of hosts." (Isaiah 8:18)

They reminded us through word and deed that we are now governed by those very forces which we once controlled. There was a time when no negative force could harm us, for we were the former of all things. But now in our low, hellish existence, the waters will drown us, the strong winds will destroy us, the earth will not yield her increase, the sun will scorch us, the animals will attack us, and the fowl of Heaven do fear us so they sing no pleasant tune unto us.

Your power and dominion have faded away and are all but forgotten. The memories of the power of your forefathers have purposely been destroyed and the former deeds of the prophets of God are called miracles, in order that the Sons will never know of the power bequeathed unto them. The power of the Sons of God is purposely mythicized to place it beyond reach. You can no longer recall that Noah brought the rain; that Moses commanded the dark to remain over Egypt, ordered the hail to fall, summoned the locusts and sent them away.

Before the invasion of the minds of Godly men by satan, these were common exploits by the Sons of God. You never consider that Moses stopped the flow of the Red Sea and divided the waters from the waters; then Joshua, his commander and successor performed the same feat at the River Jordan. The great fish could not consume Jonah. The ravens fed Elijah, who also held back the rain for three years; then, at his command, it came. Samson manifested the strength of a god; Solomon the wisdom of the Lord. Jesus walked on the water as on dry land, and stilled the tempest. When the prophet and Son of God, Jesus, controlled the wind (tempest) upon the raging sea, what was he controlling? He was controlling an inner element of his composition: wind, spirit, his very soul. He was, in essence, the wind! It was no great task for him; indeed it was a small one, for he said, "These things and many more shall ye do if ye believe on me." He was the Word spoken into the wind. He was the Spirit of God.

But the fallen Sons of God said he was a blasphemer and insane. Why? It was because they looked upon him with the natural eye. There satan hid, deceiving their minds, blinding them to the Will of God. They could only see a man, for the Spirit of Err possessed them. Jesus said, "They know not what they do." He knew that they were not their own, as also he knew that the will that they wrought was not the will of their own.

Space will not allow the detailing of the many exploits of the Sons of God in their heavenly state. The point that must be made here is that these were not always isolated occurrences, nor miracles; these were the ordinary powers of the Sons of God. They became rare manifestations only because the people turned away from God, His authority and power. Now the Sons are trapped, helpless in hell, buried among the dead. They are weak before their enemies because they do not know the source of their strength, much less how to manifest it. The devil has invaded the high place, disguised himself as an angel of light and installed the Spirit of Err as the ruler. This Spirit knows no limitations or bounds in its quest to bind and destroy the Angels, Saints and Elect of the Kingdom of the Most High God. We must, therefore, become as serious in our efforts to merit God's salvation, as the Euro-gentiles have been in their efforts to merit God's destruction.

Man has become unbalanced in his acceptance of such common statements as "No one is perfect," or "Everyone has some good in them." What is meant by these statements? To say that "everyone has some good in them" is to imply subtly that we accept the evil in them also; that "no one is perfect" is to insist upon the acceptance of imperfection. The prevailing thought in the world today is that no one can do what is right! Have you once considered why these thoughts prevail? It is simply that in the world of satan, no one is allowed to feel that he can meet the high standards of God. This mentality is the opposite of the Truth in God. Let us draw from an example of a victim who has lung cancer caused by cigarette smoking. How did he arrive at such a horrendous end? First of all, he had to work to earn money to purchase his cigarettes because they are not given away. Secondly, he had to walk or drive to a location which sells the little packs. Thirdly, he had to open his pack, remove the object, place it in his mouth, take out his little fire stick and light his cigarette. He then puffed, inhaled and exhaled smoke. He had to go through this process not just one day, one month or even one year; he performed this ritual with intense regularity for long periods of time. Moreover, and most ironic, is the fact that the conclusion of this process was known by the victim at the onset.

What does this individual merit from God for his supreme effort to destroy his temple? How easy it would have been to just not smoke and thereby be healthy! In truth, the victim has earned the right to his lung cancer after such a tremendous effort. Can you comprehend how complicated it is to be evil? It is the doing of evil that requires the great effort; to do right is simple and natural.

Let us also consider what happens to those who are weak in God when they attempt to stop smoking. First, we observe that this inorganic, non-talking, non-breathing, non-walking roll of tobacco has complete control over the smoker's weak mind. Therefore, the business world, including the tobacco industry, manufacture chewing gums, pills and sprays to assist him as he vainly attempts to stop smoking. He is afraid to be around the frightening little cigarette; he suffers on into the night as the soul-less, little monster drains all of his energy until finally, weak and beaten, he succumbs to his little tobacco ruler. Our analogy confirms that the weak are prey to all things and to everyone.

The adversary of God has succeeded in convincing the world that righteousness is full of unwarranted hardships. The mindless generation is as determined to serve satan as they are to disobey God. The mindless are the prey; they suffer continuously. Satan has deceived the "inner man" within the Saints of the Most High God, causing them to even overrule the spirit within them which was subject unto the Will of God.

The Holy Spirit, which is the Most High, will not dwell peacefully in an unclean house. The house is the soul. When the mind is dedicated to the Spirit of Err or evil, the Holy Spirit then leaves that body because it will not remain in the habitation of evil. If the brain is unclean and cluttered from the educational and intellectual doctrines of the world and its institutions (which is, consequently, the dogma of the devil), then the Holy Spirit, which controls all spiritual matter, will find no resting place in that body or mind. In order for mind and body to be occupied by the Holy Spirit you would first have to undergo a cleansing process. God said, you cannot put new wine in old bottles, neither can you put a new patch on old clothes. Satan and all of his dogmatic doctrines have to be cast from the minds of the Sons of God. The everlasting light of God and His Truth must be put there instead, which will expose all of the dark doctrines of the devil. Consequently, we have come to know there is a war that has to be fought in the high, elevated place — the "God Mind," or heaven.

There is no higher dwelling place than the minds of the Sons of God. This is where satan strives and struggles with the Sons of God, and even with the Almighty Himself, in order that he may eventually sit upon the throne of God Almighty and inherit His Kingdom. Satan also had inner vision of great proportions, and was able to understand prophecy; but satan was err disguised as truth, ignorance disguised as wisdom, and regression disguised as progress. His success depended upon the existence of no comparisons or alternatives. Therefore, even greater than the physical bondage of the Sons of God, is the mental bondage.

Before satan can capture a soul, he must first conquer the mind and then the body. Thus, he deceived the people of God and caused them to commit iniquity within their temples, "the dwelling place of the Holy Spirit" whose throne is the high, elevated place of the mind. Just as the earth is God's footstool, the Heavens are His throne, i.e. God walks upon the earth and thinks above the earth. Heaven, little children, is not the place beyond the clouds as taught by slave-oriented Christianity. Heaven is, was and always will be, in the minds of the Sons of God. There never has been nor will there ever be for God's creation, another Heaven. The Heaven beyond the clouds where you go after death, replete with pearly gates and everlasting life, originated in Roman doctrine and Greek mythology. These false concepts of Heaven, sadly enough, are deeply rooted in the minds of the Holy people.

The old dragon, called Lucifer, made you ignorant of God. Lucifer taught that you would die and go to Heaven, although in all your scriptural reading, death has never been connected with ascension. In death you *always* descend. You don't go up; you go down. No one dies and goes to Heaven; you die and go to hell, and if you are not resurrected, that is where you remain! Everything in God's plan is about life. Jesus said, "God is the God of the living, and not the dead." To what God are you referring when you state that all of the dead people go to Him? Furthermore, who is it that has bequeathed all of the graveyards unto the Almighty? Is it so hard to discern that this concept of dying and going to Heaven is an unholy lie?

When Israel was cast away from God, it was because they had become engulfed in iniquity. Their sins had become so great that a total moral rebirth was required. Only then would their iniquity be purged. Being cast away was their death in God. Their reconciliation would be a rising from the graves that lay among the wicked nations that worship not the Living God. Upon their return to God, they would accept a high and Holy way of life; it will be a life pertaining to Heaven — a heavenly life. When Jesus of Nazareth said, "You must be born again," he meant Nicodemus had to die in the world, that he might live in God. Nicodemus had to actually die, (reject the old teachings or mentality), in order that he might, afterward, receive the Spirit of God. How does one be born again, except that he die? Rest assured that Nicodemus was not one whose flesh had returned to the dust of the earth.

I must, in God's name, lay bare your minds, expose your thoughts and show forth their origins in order that you may understand. Those separated from the Truth of God are either knowingly or unknowingly linked to the mind of satan. Those who worship the devil are spiritually dead in God. The influence of devil worship is everywhere. Satan has so blinded the minds of the Sons of God that now the message of God and the messengers of God appear strange and foolish in this spiritually darkened world. Jesus spoke and said "The prince of this world (the devil) cometh and I have nothing with him." Again, he said "He was in the world and the world knew him not." How could one be in the world and the world not know him? Surely, Jesus would have to have been physically different or have borne a great spiritual unlikeness to the other inhabitants of the world in order to rate such description. He spoke further, saying: "I came unto my own, but they rejected me." Who were his own and why did they reject him? The Sons of God had fallen unto such a low state until they did not even recognize one of their own nor did they understand Jesus' simple testimony.

Thus, in you are the words of Isaiah the prophet fulfilled. You have eyes, but they are carnal so you see not the vision or the Plan of God. You have ears, but you hear not the doctrine of salvation. The Sons of God now are like our forefathers in the days of the advent of Jesus. They have fallen to a very low state. They then, as now, were looking for a great physical deliverer to come riding in to crush the Romans. They did not understand that the problem was spiritual. The first war to be fought is a mental war, a war in the High, Holy Heaven of their minds. Know ye not that there has to be thought before substance? Right minds will bring about right conclusions. Your wrong, devil-oriented thought patterns have kept you a prisoner to your adversary. You are trying to use the adversary's mind against himself. The adversary has not equipped you to defeat him; neither has he given you the sense needed to outsmart him.

When Jesus came, the Word of God had been abused, misused and Hellenized (made Greek in character) to such an extent that even basic truth was seen and taken out of context. I recall that Jesus said, "Ye worship ye know not what. We know what we worship; for salvation is of (with) the Jews (Israelites)." There is so much in those words that must be understood. What Jesus was actually saying is that salvation is to be found within the framework of the teachings and instructions given to the Children of Israel. Jesus believed and taught that and only that. He gave credence only to those teachings. From the beginning he stated, "I have not come to destroy the law and prophecies but to fulfill." When he saw the many factions and doctrines, he was amazed that something so simple could be made so complicated. Thus he stated, "You don't know what you're worshipping." The same thing exists at this time among the Holy people of God who are trapped in the dispensation of the captivity in North America (Babylon). The resurrected Sons of God, the African Hebrew Israelites, have come to the world, but the world does not recognize them, for they come not with the accepted plan of salvation and freedom. Moreover, they were not friends with the prince of this world (satan).

The foremost problem in the time of Jesus was not the physical presence of the Romans, as now the foremost problem is not the physical presence of the Europeans. The apex of the problem is the spiritual presence of satan, who possesses the minds of the Holy people. It sounded strange when Jesus continued to attack, first of all, the people's understanding of God's doctrine. The first fight was with their captive, demon-possessed minds. These minds had to be taught to "seek ye first the Kingdom (God Mind) and its righteousness, and then all other things shall be added unto you."

Before we can envision any spiritual matters there has to be a vision which brings into focus truth, justice, mercy, peace, love, compassion and a kingdom wherein there is wisdom and understanding of all matters. Total love, submission and obedience to the Will of God Almighty ties a knot and seals the bond that interlocks and interweaves spirit to spirit, and God Almighty to His Sons.

A comprehensive study of anything cannot be done without discipline of the mind. Discipline of the mind cannot be attained without inner vision. The coming of the Kingdom of God manifests the tools which allow you to take apart and investigate every faculty of your mind. This investigation could not be made with a carnal mind possessed by satan — a mind investigating itself with itself. This investigation could only be carried out upon the return of the "God Mind." Only the living know the dead; only the destroyer knows the destruction. Initially, the Sons of God neither recognized nor understood the doctrine taught by Jesus of Nazareth, because the faculties of God were inactive in their minds. God commanded them to follow Him by faith, give Him a chance, and the understanding would come. God would resurrect the "God Mind," causing a new birth and a new way of life. Their resurrection would be their coming out of the world. The world would not recognize the resurrected Saints of God, because they would no longer be serving the interests of the world, automatically making the Saints outcasts, as are all seekers of another place, in this case seekers of another world whose builder and maker is God.

As the Sons of God were sent to gather His sheep and to make war with the dragon, they were admonished to keep the vision of the Kingdom of God before them, and keep their inner spiritual senses attuned to God; for if it were possible, the devil would deceive even the very elect. The Plan of Redemption calls for a redefining of all things instituted during the captivity, with the understanding that these things were given to perpetuate our captivity. We must reject, intellectually, all authority that is hostile to God's Kingdom. Armed with the "God Mind," and with our very survival at stake, we must bring all things to be judged, evaluated, maintained or discarded. Where people have been living a lie, it is understandable that only the Truth shall set them free. The minds of the Holy People must be washed, rinsed and disinfected of the impurities of sin and thousands of years of adverse thoughts and actions imposed upon them by satan, the arch enemy of God, in order for them to ascend from the hellish world of their adversary and re-enter the High, Holy and lofty mountain of the Most High God.

You must come down from the mythical Heaven in order that you may ascend again to the Heaven of Truth. The Old Deceiver has ploughed up the way that leadeth back unto our God, but has left broad the way that leadeth unto destruction. He has deceived the whole world.

The world today is perishing in its sins, because God is bringing every work into judgement. Why has it been so important to change the Truth of God? Why turn your minds away from your surroundings? Your mind has been made your enemy, because it no longer discerns Truth. You are under the total influence of the Spirit of Err; your ears are dull; your heart is as a stone with no feeling or desire to search out the Word of God and follow His messengers. You are swift to understand evil, but slow to comprehend what is right. These are the reasons why this "war in heaven" has to be fought.

It seems rather ironic that a supposedly religious people could believe so many things that simply have no Biblical or prophetic origin. Yet, they simultaneously reject as being false, the true written word of the Law and the prophecies of God which were worshipped by their Savior. There is no Biblical basis for the belief of the "die-and-go-to-Heaven" lie. As a matter of fact, if we were to accept literally the Biblical records concerning the ascension, we would find that all of those who were taken were alive, not dead. Elijah ascended by a whirlwind as he journeyed with Elisha; Enoch was taken as he walked with God; and Jesus as he administered the blessings upon the Disciples. If we were to accept these as literal occurrences, the truth would still be the opposite of the baseless teachings of slave-oriented Christianity. All of the above-mentioned men were alive and active when they were taken, not dead and in their graves.

> *"And it came to pass, as they still went on, and*
> *talked, that, behold, there appeared a chariot of fire,*
> *and horse of fire, and parted them both asunder;*
> *and Elijah went up by a whirlwind into heaven."*
>
> **II Kings 2:11**

> *"And Enoch walked with God: and he was not; for*
> *God took him."*
>
> **Genesis 5:24**

> *"And it came to pass, while he (Jesus) blessed them*
> *(the Disciples), he was parted from them, and carried*
> *up into heaven."*
>
> **St. Luke 24:51**

We must know the origin and author of these doctrines of lies: he who has established himself as the definer of the Word of God, who dresses himself in the sheep's clothing of religion, saying daily "God, God, God," but whose every work is continuously evil. We were to know satan by his works: "by their fruits we shall know them." If two men were standing before a bush, and the one plucked a flower and said to his friend: "This orange is for you," would not the friend say unto him: "This, my brother, is a flower, not an orange. Furthermore, this bush is one that *by nature* produces flowers, for behold the many flowers thereupon?"

What should we call the tree which produced an economic system which keeps agricultural produce at a stable, yet exorbitant price by destroying tons of excess food while people starve? What should we call the tree which has produced the atomic bomb, the hydrogen bomb, the nitrogen bomb, the neutron bomb, and has accumulated enough weapons to destroy the entire planet many times over yet still manufactures more? What shall we call the tree which has produced the diaphragm, the tying of fallopian tubes, the removal of ovaries, vasectomies, "the pill," unisex clothing, tampons, and the laws allowing homosexuals, lesbians, transvestites and others to wantonly exist?

Someone continues to bring forth evil fruit, saying that it is alright when it is all wrong; saying it is edible when it is poisonous; saying that it is God when it is the devil. How do we know? By his fruits you shall know him! The Sons of God have been deceived, yet they continue to cling unto those things that are wicked and not of the Spirit of the Most High God. As it is written, "The shepherds who feed my flock, outside they appear as harmless as lambs, but inside they are as ravenous wolves, ready to devour my sheep." Furthermore, all that say "Lord, Lord" will not enter the gates of the Kingdom, nor those professing to believe but who in truth are hypocrites.

The Sons of God were not deceived by surface beauty before their fall. They loved that beauty which cometh from within and shineth out: the inner beauty of the soul which is subject to the Will of, and in complete submission to the Spirit of, the Most High God. The Sons of God did not judge carnally according to the sight of their eyes; using Divine logic and reasoning, they judged according to the spiritual attributes of God. We recall that in the beginning, satan was a coward, afraid to stand before the "God Mind" of Adam. Satan preferred to do battle with Eve, fearing the impregnable spirit of Adam. Satan has never forgotten his weakness and even now is attempting to exterminate Adam because he greatly fears his presence. The Black man in America, even in his lowly state, is despised and feared by the entire European family of nations. Satan has always used indirect ways and means in his quest to accomplish the genocide of the Black male. We can see evidence of this, because in every statistic in America, the Black female is preferred over the Black male, a preference that goes all the way back to the creation when satan had decided to challenge God.

We find another instance of satan's crafty use of the woman as he manifests his plan of attack against God and the Black male. After the fall, the Sons of God became attracted to the daughters of men. Could it be that the daughters of men were more spiritually appealing than the Daughters of God? Of course not! It was because the eyes of the Sons of God had been opened to physical lust and the daughters of men were promiscuous, vain, haughty, and rebellious, full of the spirit of harlotry and beguilement. They beguiled the Sons of God, took their souls captive and caused them to lust after them and to become lost. We find God reprimanding Adam thusly: "And unto Adam he said, because thou has hearkened unto the voice (instructions, ways) of the woman and hast eaten of the tree of which I commanded you, saying, Thou shalt not eat of it; Cursed is the ground for thy sake, in sorrow thou shalt eat of it all the days of thy life." (Genesis 3:17) Satan made the daughters of men to outwardly appear very beautiful and enticing in the eyes of the Sons of God, (which were opened to the knowl-edge of evil after their disobedience unto their Heavenly Father, the Almighty God). Yet as satan worketh iniquity, evil and death, so doeth the Most High God worketh justice, goodness and giveth life; for as satan openeth the eyes unto evil, so does the Most High openeth the eyes unto good. The evidence is clear. The Sons of God were no longer using the righteousness of God or their relationship with God as the measuring rod for selecting a bride or helpmate, because the Sons of God, beguiled by satan's plan, were unable to look into the souls of the daughters of men and determine that their hearts were not right with God. Thus, the Sons of God became deceived and their souls were made to cling unto those things which were not of the Spirit of the Most High God.

There was once a very strict, unwritten law, that all women had to be brought before the Father (parents) for approval. The decision was moreso the parents' than the child's, as long as the children remained under the wings of their father (which in most instances they did) until marriage. If a father disapproved of a marriage, it was absolutely forbidden. This approval process was symbolic of bringing the bride-elect to the Throne of God before the Holy union could take place, in order that God (the Father) could search the heart of the prospective helpmate.

Before the fall into oblivion, the Righteousness of God was the measuring rod for all things and people. The prevailing thought was always: "Abba, (Hebrew for father), what do you want me to do? Thou art the potter, and I am the clay. Fashion me in a manner that is pleasing unto you." The "God Mind" has been replaced by the "satan mind," but the resurrected Sons are now engaged in the "War of Restoration." This is the war of wars. The Sons of God have come to cast satan, the devil, down from his throne in the minds of men. It is now as it was during the time of Daniel, the prophet and beloved Son of God, that "the handwriting is on the wall," stating **"MENE, MENE, TEKEL, UBENAI AL,"** which is interpreted thusly: **MENE** — God has numbered thy kingdom, oh satan, and finished it; **TEKEL** — Thou art weighed in the balance and found wanting; **UBENAI AL** — Thy kingdom is divided and given to the Sons of God. At the time of the interpretation, Belshazzar, grandson of Nebuchadnezzar (ruler of ancient Babylon), appeared to be unconquerable. Even as it is now, the host of the gentile armies appear undefeatable to all of those who can focus only on the flesh, and to those who have no spiritual sense to understand or interpret the things which they see occurring all around them.

The natural eye, without spiritual sense, is very deceptive! If you allow yourselves to become subject to the natural eye, given unto the desires of it, or further be absorbed by the sights which you see, then, verily ye shall be destroyed, for the inner mind is for salvation. Insight means to look further than that which is observed and understood by the carnal mind under the influence of Err. In God's Plan of Redemption, vision is a prerequisite; for the Most High, working by signs and standards, shall bring into fullness the salvation of His chosen people (Black people in America).

When ye shall see the budding of the trees, know ye that summer is nigh. One must be cautious not to wait to see this "budding" (the wrath of God and impending destruction of the Euro-gentile world) with the natural eye. In order to be saved from this fate, one must hear the plane engines roaring and see the bombs falling *before* the actual event takes place. To wait to receive a visual confirmation of such an event with the natural eye would be tantamount to suicide! There are always two immutable things: a thought or vision (the spiritual) which is soon followed by the *substance* of that thought or vision (the physical). The first destruction of America is the spiritual destruction which is seen with the spiritual senses of the "God Mind." This destruction must be seen in a spiritual vision in order that men might be saved by coming out of that world. It has to be preached and acted upon just as if the event was actually taking place. You recall that Noah moved by faith to build the ark many years prior to the sighting of the first rain. Yet, his spiritual vision (coupled with his faith and works), enabled him to escape the coming destruction.

The angel of God comes heralding, with a loud voice (a voice of authority), "Babylon the Great (America) has fallen, has fallen" — that is to say, has been destroyed. (Revelation 18:1-2) The angel then describes the land after the nuclear holocaust as being a place of only evil — "the habitation of devils and foul spirits and all unclean (contaminated) things" — meaning clearly and emphatically that after the physical destruction, there will be nothing or no one to save. Those seeking salvation will be saved during the first destruction — the spiritual destruction. How could you possibly think, that as the planes are roaring overhead and nuclear weapons are raining down, that a plan of salvation could be activated? What could be said or done at that time? You must believe by faith; you must see things even before they appear.

God makes known His plans to His servants, who then warn the people of the apparent danger and give instructions as to what they must do to escape the wrath of God Almighty.

What is it that has signaled the imminent destruction of America? The revelator states quite clearly, "Her sins have reached unto Heaven" — a continuous, multiplicity of sins against God, His creation and His people. At the time when the angel is preaching that America has been destroyed, the people are still there. Therefore he states, "Come out of her my people, that ye be not partakers of her sins, and that ye receive not of her plagues (or physical destruction)." Every great destruction is preceded by the warnings of the prophets or angels (messengers) of God. As it is written, the choice of life and death has been put before the people in order that they may decide. If the wrong choice is made, consequently, that price has to be paid. He that has ears to hear, let him hear.

The source of the great damage which has been done to the people of God is in the mind. It is here that all things begin or end. It is here that men die and it is here that the resurrection must take place. It is in and for the mind of God's people, that the Sons of God must fight the prophetic, God-initiated "War in Heaven." (see Revelation 12:7)

Let us now journey back to the days of the prophets to receive and understand the scriptural references to Heaven. In Heaven, you would expect to find the people in possession of the mind of God. You will know that they possess the mind of God by the fruits of their thoughts continuously showing forth the attributes of God as they love and live in harmony with His Creation.

> "And the Lord said unto Moses, go unto the people, and sanctify them today and tomorrow, and let them wash their clothes,
>
> And be ready on the third day: for the third day the Lord will come down in the sight of all the people upon Mount Sinai."
>
> "And it came to pass on the third day in the morning, that there were thunders and lightnings, and a thick

cloud upon the mount, and the voice of the trumpet exceedingly loud; so that all the people that were in the camp trembled.

And Moses brought forth the people out of the camp to meet with God; and they stood at the nether part of the mount.

And Mount Sinai was altogether on a smoke, because the Lord descended upon it in fire; and the smoke thereof ascended as the smoke of a furnace, and the whole mount quaked greatly.

And when the voice of the trumpet sounded long, and waxed louder and louder, Moses spake, and God answered him by a voice.

And the Lord came down upon Mount Sinai, on top of the mount: and the Lord called Moses up to the top of the mount; and Moses went up."

Exodus 19:10,11,16-20

"And the people stood afar off, and Moses drew near unto the thick darkness where God was.

And the Lord said unto Moses, Thus thou shalt say unto the children of Israel, Ye have seen that I have talked with you from heaven."

Exodus 20:21,22

"Righteousness exalteth a nation: but sin is a reproach to any people."

Proverbs 14:34

"For though we walk in the flesh, we do not war after the flesh:

(For the weapons of our warfare are not carnal, but mighty through God to the pulling down of strongholds;)

Casting down imaginations, and every high thing that exalteth itself against the knowledge of God, and bringing into captivity every thought to the obedience of Christ;

*And having in a readiness to revenge all disobedi-
ence, when your obedience is fulfilled."*

II Corinthians 10:3-6

Let us now meticulously follow the footsteps of the prophets as the light of the Holy oracles guides us up the path to God's eternal Heaven and dwelling place. First, we find Moses bringing the people to the nether region of the mount to receive instructions about how they should sanctify themselves for the third day, when God's presence would be felt and heard upon Mount Sinai. From these verses we may also discern an all-important lesson in sanctification (to be Holy; to separate; set apart), for God requires such from all of those to whom He will reveal Himself. There are always special preparations of Holiness preceding the feeling or hearing of God's presence. Without these preparations we are warned that death is imminent. Even today, every mind not prepared and sanctified unto God at the appointed time will be destroyed.

In the subsequent verses we find the fulfillment of God's promise, because the presence of God comes down upon Mount Sinai. God's presence is likened to a great furnace; His words are as fire. God called unto Moses, and Moses answered Him by voice. God then instructs Moses to inform the Children of Israel that He has talked with them from Heaven. Here we find our first comprehensive guidelines in determining the prophetic location of Heaven, from a most authoritative source — God's own words and voice. What was Mount Sinai? What is the connection between this mountain and Heaven? Simply thus: Mount Sinai is a great mountain, a very high mountain and Heaven is merely a high, elevated place. Mount Sinai was called Heaven because it was a high, elevated place. Heaven is always high, upward or an elevated state in contrast to hell being low, downward or a depressed state. These scriptural writings were given for the edification of the Saints of God in this day, that the people may find their way back unto God. He is not a mysterious God, because He already stated that the mysterious things He keeps unto Himself. He is a God that can be found.

The Holy oracles were not written to deceive men, but to be a light on the path as the Sons of God seek to come out of their deep coma of ignorance of God, their Father. The Sons of God have been without the *true* God and the teaching priests for seasons without end (II Chronicles 15:3). However, only if you are sincerely seeking, shall ye find Him. Ask, and it shall be given; knock, and the door shall be opened. If you are truly crying out unto God, you will understand these things which are written, and know of a surety that they are true.

Our next reference is found in Proverbs: "Righteousness exalts a nation, but sin is a reproach (shame, disgrace) for any people." Here it is explicitly clear that to do what is right will move you upward; it will elevate you or take you to the *true* Heaven, the thought pattern of the "God Mind." The elders would always say that if you do right, you go to Heaven. They knew this, but could not explain the true prophetic meaning. They were very near to the truth in their spoken words, but their minds were far, far away. If to do what is right will exalt or elevate, then common sense should reveal that the reason you have not lifted yourselves from the pits of damnation and degradation is because you are not going about it the *right* way. You are using your institutionalized thought patterns or "devil dogma," and it has not worked because it is not right. The Proverbs further state that your reproach (shame, disgrace) is your continuous sin against God. The devil has deceived the people of God by using the Power to Define. He has caused you to look upon your curse as a blessing, your ignorance as intelligence, and your death as life. Never forget that he is the father of a lie; he has been lying since the beginning and will be lying until his end.

Look around you at what is defined as progress. You never stopped to seriously consider: "progressing" to where? You have made the destiny of your enemy your destiny also. Look at how your families have progressed — away from one another. Your children have progressed into early adulthood. Your wife has progressed to the point that she does not need you. Your people have progressed to such dubious achievements as punk-funk kings, murder kings, rape kings, homosexuals, bisexuals, transvestites, and all of the things we never knew as Africans. These are our new "achievements" as we continue to progress in the modern world. The Sons of God have become a mindless generation. They have no knowledge of their past, no control over their present and no desire to plan for a future.

Let us consider what is called progress in the institutionalized thought patterns of the medical profession. You read daily of the well-equipped medical schools and their capabilities to turn out more and more doctors, nurses and surgeons. The progressive reports usually note the opening of a new school or the expansion of existing facilities. For example: "This year there will be ten thousand new interns, surpassing last year's total of eight thousand." This news is met with joy; everyone praises the medical establishment. Yet, should we consider the announcement of an additional hospital wing with one thousand more beds or the news that this year they are adding 20 new, well-equipped hospitals as "progress"? You have been taught to accept this progress with a sigh of "things are sure getting better." But think: are they really getting better? Have you considered that there must be patients for the two thousand more doctors as well as occupants for the additional thousands of beds? Should that news be met with joy or sadness? Praise or scorn?

Let us imagine the headlines in a *truly* progressive society. They would read: "The Local Hospital is being demolished for lack of patients. It will be replaced by a four square mile park and playground for children;" or "Harvard Medical School is closing down its surgeons' training facilities for lack of demand for surgery;" or "Fifty percent of all doctors are out of work; high unemployment among dental surgeons." Sounds strange doesn't it? Certainly, because in your dead, lowly state, you cannot imagine something like that. If you could, you, with your institutionalized thought patterns, would certainly seek to define it as being wrong. Nevertheless, the former headlines are sure signs of regression, while the latter would be progress. So be it. But the question remains — progressing to meet what destiny? Will the forces of satan be pleased when everyone has a hospital bed and requires his own personal nurse and doctor? In truth, both movements can be defined as progress: one in evil and one in God. You make the choice: the high of Heaven or the low of hell.

> *"For my people are foolish, they have not known me;*
> *they are sottish children, and they have no under-*
> *standing: they are wise to do evil, but to do good*
> *they have no knowledge."*
>
> ***Jeremiah 4:22***

If you turn back to God and do what is good and right, you will be lifted up from the pits of the captivity, and given a new abode in Heaven with God. The Holy writings further confirm that, "the way of life is above to the wise" (Proverbs 15:24), meaning that a wise way of life is found in Heaven. It will lift you from the society of the dead. The way of life of the wise, the righteous, the Sons of God, is the *true* "high." It is far from and above ignorance; it is where you eat like you have some sense, dress Holy and raise children in innocence. You will walk with your head in the clouds, amazed at the good things of God. The right way of life is truly Heavenly.

When we read the latter part of Proverbs 15:24 we find a very sharp contrast: "...that he depart from hell beneath." Hell is always low. The elders once pictured it as being a place beneath the ground. Again, they knew, but without the instructions of God, they could not define "hell" accurately. They knew subconsciously that hell was the same place that the dead reside; they knew it was a low place inhabited by the dead. They expressed it as best they could without the clear prophetic understanding of God's word. Their analysis was somewhat correct, however hell is not beneath the earth, literally. It is below Heaven, and is a place where the people have the minds of the devil and are dead in God. To escape from hell, you must be resurrected: given a new, living mind, and taught again how to live in God and with God. You must begin with a new, wise and right way of life. As you continue progressing in God you go higher and higher. At last, when your heart is pure, ye shall see God.

Your inner mind will cause you to say: "It's time for us to raise up and get out of the pits of America." However, except that you are aware that "raising up" and doing right are synonymous, and that by your pronouncement you mean a return to right and to God, then your revelation is a vanity and your efforts will be ineffective. Only the "God Mind" can deliver Black people from the abyss of hell. Everything else is destined to fail. This is according to the irrevocable word of God Almighty.

The Children of Israel (African Americans) are trapped in the pits of hell, where they stumble as a blind man at noonday. Your thought patterns are continuously evil all the day long. Only God's right way of life will deliver you.

To build a New World, we must build a new thought pattern. The world of tomorrow will not resemble the world of today. Your present thought patterns were created in the Euro-gentile educational institutions to perpetuate the system for which you work. For instance, when you hear the phrase "rich nation," you rattle off with the lightning speed of a computer, the names of America, Britain, France, Japan and Germany, because this is the institutionalized thought pattern of the world today. In the same manner, when asked to name some poor nations and any African country is mentioned, you pass the test. Who established the value system whereby we measure rich and poor nations? What are the criteria used? We question the logic of calling big, filthy, dope-infested, crime-laden, poverty-filled America a symbol of wealth, while small, clean, friendly, drug-free, almost crimeless Liberia is called a poor nation.

We also question the value system used to determine industrialized standards wherein we immediately equate "high standards" with large factories assembling and manufacturing everything imaginable under the sun, of which, at least fifty percent have no definite requirement in the life of man. In the process, they plunder and consume the earth's resources at an alarming rate. On the other hand, a small, productive unindustrialized (by world standards) community like the West Bank of Israel produces items to meet most of its essential needs without large, destructive factories. These institutionalized thought patterns give the impression that creativity began with Europe; prior to that there were only savages doing savage things; that there existed a clothes-less, food-less, production-less world. Further investigation leads us to the conclusion that anything that operated sensibly was considered backward; anything based upon God's cycles was out of tune; anything that was right was labeled wrong.

Let me remind you there were great, strong building structures (e.g. the Pyramids, the Temple of the Queen Sheba at Axum, Ethiopia and the temple-pyramids of the Mayan Indians) before the coming of the polluting, health-destroying steel mills. There were textbooks being manufactured long before the arrival of forest-destroying paper mills. There was spun gold, silk, cotton and fine wool clothing manufactured long before the coming of the ecologically-unsafe synthetic clothing produced of today. However, these works were virtually unknown because they were not destroying enough of God's creation to gain credibility. The sense of balance, the sense of reason, the spirit of the "God Mind" present in the building of our ancient civilization were lost by the Sons of God during the great fall and the seasons of the great dispersion.

Spiritual sense bears no relation to worldly intellect! Wisdom, knowledge and understanding of "all things" come directly from the storehouses of the impregnable spirit of the all-seeing, all-knowing, all-wise Lord of Hosts. God spoke against worldly intellect when He said, "I shall make their wise men as fools." This amounts to a condemnation of what the world terms "higher education." It is an evil intellect which makes you rationalize and deem reasonable the cancerous death blow of cigarette smoking. You are ready and qualified to tear apart anyone who even alludes to the closing down of the factories which manufacture this curse. You, being void of the Spirit of God and possessed with the Spirit of Err, make all sound judgement appear wrong, backward or uncivilized.

> *"With my soul have I desired thee in the night; yea,*
> *with my spirit within me will I seek thee early: for*
> *when thy judgements are in the earth, the inhabitants*
> *of the world will learn righteousness."*
>
> **Isaiah 26:9**

How much intellect is needed to understand why one should not smoke? The world has literally made you too smart — to live. You are too smart to stop smoking because you are free to do as you please. The devil has given you the Spirit of Err and taught you to intellectually explain and defend your unrighteous life-style. You are the intellects that have explained away breast-feeding of the human offspring as unfashionable, time-consuming, backward and not fit for the modern world. You know every key word or key phrase to use as you apply your "higher education" to tear apart righteous living. No intellect needed? How much intellect is needed to understand and explain why a mother should feed her child the milk which accumulates in her breast instead of that which accumulates in the udder of a cow? What has to be added to the statement: "Human milk is better for the child and breast feeding is naturally right"? How many classes are required to prove that to give cow's milk to humans is wrong? Why is it that so much proof has to be given to disprove these senseless, wicked acts? Simply because you are a worldly intellectual. You are too intelligent to accept at face value the fact that human milk is better for humans than cow's milk.

The Spirit of the Most High is not of the world. Neither can it be reckoned by your brain alone, because your brain is flesh and has no control over itself, and can be activated by the Spirit of Err. The devil was in need of a tangible soul, but this he could not create. To gain a tangible soul to show forth his intellect and to challenge God, he had to tamper with the creations of the people of the eternal, Almighty, Living God. Once the devil invaded God's heavenly domain, he had to destroy all "common sense," (often called "mother wit"). The Sons of God were actually too wise, even with only remnants of the "God Mind," to accept their captors as being superior. In the initial years of slavery, it was common to hear the oppressors say the slaves had too much "God-given sense." Senses are tools which God gave us to govern our minds and bodies. They enable us to see, hear, taste, smell, touch (or to feel). The elders called our exceptional ability to know or sense the unknown or unseen, "common sense," — the uninstitutionalized ability to perform tasks correctly. This kept alive the words: "He sure is blessed by God." This unseen God or Instructor was beyond the comprehension of the slavemaster, therefore he knew these remnants of "common sense" had to be destroyed. "Common sense" is defined in the Webster's New World Dictionary as "good sense or practical judgement;" the word "common" means "belonging to or shared by all."

Where did the slave get "good sense" prior to Western education? It now sounds very strange to know that we were collectively very intelligent in the initial years of slavery. Consequently, the slavemasters killed those wise, intelligent fathers and mothers and institutionalized the minds of the children so that now the once commonly-known, correct knowledge has all been destroyed. With the thought patterns of this system as they are, our common sense has been destroyed. Once you knew how to survive on nothing. Now, if the supermarket closed for a week, you would perish. It was once "common sense" to give a child his mother's milk. Now, you really do not know what is best.

Therefore, things that were once very simple to understand have now become complicated. Without "mother wit" you really cannot understand why Blacks are not free, why we must control our own land and why we must have self-determination. You are now a worldly intellectual, qualified to tear to shreds all sound judgement. You can reason away why we are continuously catching hell. You can show all of the "good things" we have in New York, Los Angeles, Detroit and Newark. You might possibly explain away the incredibly high rates of incarceration for African American males. I must humbly confess that I am not one of those worthy to sit beside such intellects, because my answers are too simple. In my confession, I must say it does not make sense to me that all of the "brothers" are in prison. It does not make sense to me why our people are still in New York, Los Angeles, Detroit, and Newark. It does not make sense to me why our people stay there catching hell in Hell. I am just one of those who still relies on "common sense."

When you turned away from God, you fell. Where did you fall? Consider that you have journeyed from Paradise to the poverty and degradation that is characteristic of the ghetto. As one falls from Heaven, his next abode is automatically hell beneath. The great earth-shaking fall was your fall away from God. When you possessed the "God Mind," your thoughts were continuously to do good to and for one another. You were a caretaker of God's creation. Your creativity was Holy; your inventions were Godly. Your meat was the fruit of the trees. You loved the herbs of the field. You lived with and loved your brother; you knew the value of life and the pleasure of people. Outside of the worship of God, the greatest joy is joy found among a people who love one another. The Sons of God did fall. They turned from God and from one another. As a result, they are trapped in hell in a very low state of existence, surrounded and besieged by the adversaries of God.

There is no need now for further ignorance, because the Kingdom of God has come to make the way straight. It is the beacon that shines from the mountain top to give light unto all of those lost in the world of obscurity and adversity.

"The heathen are sunk down in the pit that they made: in the net which they hid is their own foot taken.

The Lord is known by the judgement which he executeth: the wicked is snared in the work of his own hands.

The wicked shall be turned into hell, and all nations that forget God."

Psalms 9:15-17

"Therefore my people are gone into captivity, because they have no knowledge: and their honorable men are famished, and their multitude dried up with thirst.

Therefore hell hath enlarged herself, and opened her mouth without measure; and their glory, and their multitude, and their pomp, and he that rejoiceth, shall descend into it."

Isaiah 5:13,14

Here, we find David further clarifying what the elders were trying to imply by saying that hell was beneath the ground. It is the heathen nations that dwell in this low point, in pits below the ground. They dug these pits to avoid living under the rule and authority of God. Mankind, thinking that they could chart their own course, decided to compete against God. "Therefore, they say unto God, depart from us; for we desire not the knowledge of thy ways. What is God Almighty, that we should serve him? What more can we profit by praying to him?" (Job 21:14, 15) Again, mankind lost as he found himself snared in his own evil. You, being very naive and lacking an understanding, have looked in amazement, wondering what would be the next dose of evil. Had you forgotten that hell and hellfire are the elements of the abode of the devil? The fire does not disturb satan, but those victims trapped in Hades suffer continuously. He, the devil, has taken evil in stride, for evil is his habitation; but to the Sons of God, it is torment without end. Now, however, satan's foot is snared, because the Sons of God have escaped and he realizes that he must burn alone in hell. The devil lost his favorite pastime. The season of torment of the godly seed has ended.

In the beginning, there was no hell, but the wicked escaped not the wrath of God. God turned them and their habitation into hell. Hell is where laws are passed to protect gays and homosexuals, and where bakeries specialize in making genital-shaped products from dough! Hell is where they cut out men's hearts, kill children, dance the "butt," and where your child comes home and declares that she's the "freak of the week"! Are all of these things, and many more, the result of one demented individual? Certainly not! This is the devil's evil system. American democracy claims to be "of the people, for the people and by the people." Who is Uncle Sam? Uncle Sam is spiritually every man, woman and child in America. Uncle Sam is the government that represents the people. It is a totally hellish, evil system used to deceive the entire world. There are no prophetic good people in the evil system. Good people have to come out of her to be saved. There can be no good people in hell. Hell is made up, totally, of evil people. If someone was good, he would not remain in hell. All those of God must sanctify themselves in Spirit and Truth and come up out of hell, or accept the consequences. Hell is just the opposite of God's Kingdom.

The Kingdom of God is a righteous structure. If a wicked person appeared and could not find fuel for his wicked fire, he would have to seek another place. He has absolutely nothing to do with the purpose and plan of the righteous structure of God's Kingdom. People trying to do what is wrong in God's Kingdom would appear insolent, and the structures within the Kingdom would cast them out, spiritually and physically. It is the same in hell. All people saying and desiring to do right things are ostracized and made to appear crazy. One gets nowhere in his attempt to change the system, because the system itself has to be destroyed. Therefore, when the Children of Israel turned away from God, they became subjugated by their adversary.

God's punishment for His people was to cast them down into the pits of the base, heathen nations — the prophetic hell — the low place governed by people that are governed by the devil. God's people now dwell among the nations that have forgotten God. The people of God are destroyed because they have no knowledge of God's way of life. They have forgotten that working harmoniously with the creations of God means open communication with the Creator, thus insuring automatic protection against every type of evil invasion or attack. However, a broken line of contact with God leaves one naked and vulnerable to attack by every vile and wicked force in the universe.

God's people have fallen from Heaven. They have come down so low that they no longer recognize their Heavenly Father. Open thine eyes that thou mayest see, thy heart that thou mayest feel; open thy mind that thou mayest understand, and take heed to these words, that thou mayest pray, for God has not cast thee off forever.

Isaiah, the prophet, lamented at seeing the condition of his people as they fell further and further from God. Isaiah reasoned: My people, with all of their pomp and glory, descended into hell, causing hell to enlarge herself and increase her influence, (Isaiah 5:13-14) i.e., the adversary used the Children of Israel to further his evil cause. He used their minds and skills to further his evil ambition. Black America, the people that were walking in darkness, became a tool in the hands of all evil people, cunningly put on the front line of satan's war against God. The Sons of God bend their tongues like a bow for lies, they are not valiant for the Truth, instead proceeding from evil to evil, and they know not their Heavenly Father.

The Sons of God, with their glory, multitudes, pomp, and rejoicing, have descended into the pits of New York, Chicago, Baltimore, Detroit, Los Angeles, Philadelphia, Atlanta, Jackson and Buffalo. Oh, that my head were waters and my eyes a fountain of tears that I might weep day and night for the slain of the daughter of my people! How have a people that were once so high, come down so low?

The Sons of God are now a prey unto all the beasts of the field. The adversary has invaded the High, Holy and Sacred place and made the Sons of God ignorant of God, haters and despisers of what is right in God. He transformed your soul to comply with his evil specifications; he taught you to think and act against yourself; he made you to do all the things which God did hate. Once the mind was taken into captivity, the body could offer no resistance. For it is the spirit that quickens (gives life); the flesh profits nothing. You are whomever's spirit you possess. Therefore, if there exists in your mind a heavenly state, it is because the Spirit of God reigns. In other words, the mind is the place where the great battle is fought. The mind is the High place of man. The mind creates Heaven or hell. Whenever God is no longer acknowledged in the minds of men, nor His instructions followed in their works, the people lose all moral responsibility to themselves, their neighbors, and to the Almighty. Consequently, they become corrupt. This was the crux of the spiritual breakdown among our fathers *and*, the prelude to the Great Fall. Now, we have come to the end of that age. The Sons of God are engaged in the Holy War of Redemption, the war for the salvation of every bird, bee, elephant, pulp tree, the air, the water, and the souls of all men. We have come to bring into judgement every evil work and invention. The War in Heaven has to be fought.

The Deliverer is not equipped with carnal weapons of war, but with the weapons of God's Truth, to dissect, reject and bring an end to all ungodly influence. All things must be brought before the resurrected Sons of God for redefining, for this authority is theirs alone. Naturally, one would not expect the solicitor of customers to confess that his product is not the best. So it is likewise with satan. The master deceiver is not the one to inform his patrons that his place is hell. He too, will no doubt claim, that *his* domain is heaven; that America is the best place to be. To differentiate is the job of Truth. What will be the test? The devil is deceiving constituents. Someone is telling the "Big Lie." Jesus said that satan was the father of a lie, but what has he been lying about? Since he is the arch enemy of God, we can presume that first and foremost he has been lying about God, His plan and way of life in righteousness. We do not have to enumerate to know that he lies about all things that pertain to Godliness.

We now come to the book of Revelation, and examine what could be the most important verses relative to God's Plan of Redemption: Revelation 12:7-12. These verses relate to the entire arena of Heaven, hell and the mental captivity of the Elect of God. They must be understood. We find John the Revelator viewing the struggle at the end of days, at the end of the Euro-gentile dominion. He saw Michael and his angels fighting against the dragon and his angels. The prophetic War in Heaven is not a military struggle; it is spiritual warfare in the minds of the Sons of God.

> *"And there was war in heaven: Michael and his angels fought against the dragon; and the dragon fought and his angels, And prevailed not; neither was their place found any more in heaven.*
>
> *And the great dragon was cast out, that old serpent, called the Devil, and Satan, which deceiveth the whole world: he was cast out into the earth, and his angels were cast out with him.*
>
> *And I heard a loud voice saying in heaven, Now is come salvation, and strength, and the kingdom of our God, and the power of his Christ; for the accuser of our brethren is cast down, which accused them before our God day and night.*
>
> *And they overcame him by the blood of the lamb, and by the word of their testimony; and they loved not their lives unto the death.*

Therefore rejoice, ye heavens, and ye that dwell in them. Woe to the inhabiters of the earth and of the sea! For the devil is come down unto you, having great wrath, because he knoweth that he hath but a short time."

Revelation 12:7-12

Who are the devil's angels? They are many and varied. To begin, there is the African American middle-class, who, when opportunity has presented itself, has exploited the Black masses as ruthlessly as have whites. They have no interest in the liberation of their fellow Black brothers.

Then, there are the majority of the religious leaders, theologians and sociologists who do not desire to discover the truth concerning the Redemption Plan of God Almighty for Black people in America. There are the groups and organizations which have allowed themselves purposely to be deceived and blinded to the simple Truth of God, because they cannot change their old doctrines and traditions, their charters and church constitutions for the real truth, because the truth means change. Meanwhile, the masses of the poor continue to suffer from generation to generation, worshipping lies and erroneous teachings just to satisfy the ego of those who sit over them, many of whom just do not want to be disturbed from their station of complacency. They desire to keep their positions in the church, community, or organization. Therefore the masses are taught lies instead of the truth of the Most High God. These teachers and perpetrators of falsehood are known prophetically as "The Angels of the Dragon," and are lined up squarely behind the devil.

We find Michael and his angels, (the resurrected Sons of God), fighting against the devil in the High place, the prophetic Heaven, in the minds of the fallen Sons of God. Make no mistake about it, this is no war somewhere beyond the clouds. No one is in space battling with laser blasters, light sabers, space shuttles or atomic weapons like in the movie "Star Wars." Bows, arrows, spears and tanks are the weapons of cowboys and World War II movies. The war I am referring to is very near, even in your very souls; it is a war in and for your mind. In your vision of salvation, what did you see taking place? When God comes to save, does it not mean there will be war against those who are destroying? What is salvation other than to be saved from the devil and his evil way of life? That being the case then, is God coming to save some physical bodies and take them somewhere to build another world such as this? Certainly not!

Let us now see a vision of two wise generals in battle for the possession of a kingdom and all of its wealth. The ruler of the kingdom approaches
the one general with an offer of his own car. The wise general refuses,
knowing that to agree to this offer would leave him in possession of only a
car. The ruler then approaches the second general with a proposal to give
him a house. He, too, refuses for the same reason as the first general. It is
evident that both of these generals realize that there is a much more important ultimate objective and to capture it, *all* of the ruler's possessions must
fall into the hands of the victor. The prize possession, which is inclusive of
all other things, is the ruler's mind. Whomever wins the ruler's mind will
then automatically possess the ruler's house, car and all the other wealth of
the ruler's kingdom, including his soul. Therefore, what is the one thing
worth fighting for? The mind. There is nothing else of greater value. There
is war in heaven. God has come to save the minds of the Sons of God; the
physical body will, then, willingly follow.

Let us not mythicize this war, because it will have all of the characteristics of the physical war: there will be pain, suffering and death. The pain
will be in having to cast off your lifelong beliefs and values. It will be a
painful experience to confess that you have been wrong and have been
deceived. There will be suffering from the wounds you will receive in the
houses of your friends and family as they witness the change that will take
you out of their world. There will be death, the killing off of your old per-
sonage, because the old you is your enemy. He has to die.

We see John the Revelator alluding to this in his writing: "The Dragon
and his angels were cast out of heaven for they prevailed not against the
Sons of God." Again, we find the devil being cast down into a low place. In
all of your teachings, it is doubtful that you have ever known that the devil
was up in Heaven, stirring up trouble in the High place where all of the
great things of God came into existence. Once satan invaded the High
place, he proceeded to use the minds of the Elect of God to bring forth
works of deception. Thus, he deceived the whole world.

The deceived Sons of God who now call themselves by the stigmatized
name "negro," did not realize that "negro" did not denote a nationality, but
the personality and character of satan. The "negro" is a product created by
the devil. The devil knows his product like he knows himself, because the
negro is in the image of the devil. Satan knows the negro's every desire and
ambition, because satan created him. Satan foresaw how to establish the
negro's neighborhoods, what foods to put in the negro's stores, how many
liquor stores to put per block, how many rib joints and exactly how the

negro would spend his money and where. Satan can give a yearly projection of the number of rapes, murders, shootouts and cut-ups in the negro community. He knows that negroes will never turn against him, for to do so would be to turn against themselves. How could one so accurately determine the marriages, divorces, birth and death rates except that he knows well his product? Satan has built the proper world for his product, because he knows their deeply-ingrained, evil thought patterns.

The devil could not build a world for the Sons of God. Their minds belong to God and only He knows their hearts. God foretold that He would prepare a place for His Sons so they could be received unto Him. The Sons of God have now re-entered the Heavenly High places and are at war with the negro personality and character. However, Pharaoh refuses to let our people go. Therefore, we must fight to save our people, using the skill and understanding of the "God Mind." The negro personality and character has to be destroyed, because it is the problem of our people. It is of hell, and has to be removed with the thrust of the Word of God. After the old mentality is cast down, we will hear the loud, rejoicing sound of happiness and greatness saying "We're saved; we've been saved!" Then strength will be returned unto the Sons of God. What had been cast down that caused so much joy?

If we were saved after casting down the negro mind, then it was the negro mind that had been destroying us as a people. If we became strong after we repossessed our minds, then our weakness was our old negro thought patterns. The great burden has been the enemy's presence in us. We could not see our way because he possessed our eyes. We could not feel one other because he possessed our hearts. We would not help one another because he possessed our hands. We were a completely "possessed" people, having been earlier dispossessed by God for our disobedience to Him. This is why there was a great rejoicing in Heaven. We rejoiced at the seeing, feeling, and helping of one another. It was like unto the long-awaited homecoming, the great camp meeting. *This* is the manifestation of the Kingdom of God!

The struggle for total freedom encompasses seven principal considerations:

    1.   The byword will be "beautiful" once the struggle is over, but for now the struggle seems repulsive.

    2.   Joy and laughter will overwhelm us when the

struggle is won, but when it is begun, there will be weeping and moaning.

3.   There will be harmony and unity at the conclusion, but in the beginning discord and division.

4.   With the victory there will be wealth and abundance for everyone, but until the victory is achieved, there will be shortages and poverty.

5.   We will have health and life at the consummation of the struggle, but in the beginning there will be suffering and death.

6.   We will have a land, a language and a culture in the end, but in the beginning we will just have a plan.

7.   At the culmination it will seem as if it were not hard after all, but now it appears like an impossible dream!

Thus shall the prophets words be fulfilled: "Humility before Honor."

Endnotes

[1] Ostling, Richard. "New Grounding for the Bible?" *TIME.* September 21, 1981. Vol. 118, No. 12. New York: Time Inc.

[2] Johnston, Sir Harry H. THE NEGRO IN THE NEW WORLD. New York and London: Johnson Reprint Corp.,1969.

[3] *TIME.* "Cooks Tour: French Kitchen Diplomacy." February 20, 1978. Vol. 115, No. 8. New York: Time Inc.

[4] Woodson, Carter Goodwin. THE MIS-EDUCATION OFTHE NEGRO. Washington, D.C.: The Associated Publishers, Inc., 1933, 1977.

[5] Garvey, A. Jacques. GARVEY AND GARVEYISM. Kingston, Jamaica: United Printers Ltd., 1963.

[6] The Diagram Group. WOMAN'S BODY, AN OWNERS MANUAL. Paddington Press Ltd., 1977. New York.

Special Prayers and Lamentations from Jerusalem

For People of African Descent

"And he spoke a parable unto them to this end, that men ought always to pray, and not to faint."

St. Luke 18:1

One of the oddities of the times when Jesus of Nazareth was preaching at Jerusalem, was that the people had forgotten how to pray. One of the peculiarities of these times is that African Americans have forgotten how to pray.

> *"And it came to pass that, as he was praying in a certain place, when he ceased, one of his disciples said unto him, Lord, teach us to pray, as John also taught his disciples."*
>
> **St. Luke 11:1**

"If they sin against thee (for there is no man who sinneth not), and thou be angry with them, and deliver them to the enemy, so that they carry them away captives unto the land of the enemy, far or near;

Yet if they shall take it to their hearts in the land where they were carried captives, and repent, and make supplication unto thee in the land of them who carried them captives, saying, We have sinned and have done perversely, we have committed wickedness;

And so return unto thee with all their hearts and with all their soul, in the land of their enemies, who led them away captive, and pray unto thee toward their land, which thou gavest unto their fathers, the city which thou hast chosen, and the house which I have built for thy name.

Then hear thou their prayer and their supplication in heaven, thy dwelling place, and maintain their cause."

I Kings 8:46-49

"And the Lord said unto him, I have heard thy prayer and thy supplication, that thou hast made before me; I have hallowed this house, which thou hast built, to put my name there forever; and mine eyes and mine heart shall be there perpetually."

I Kings 9:3

"Prayer for My People"

Father, Thou - even Thou - art God. Thou -even Thou -art God alone. Thou has made Heaven the "Heaven" of heavens with all their hosts; the earth and all things that are therein; the seas and all that is in them, and Thou preservest them all, and the host of Heaven worship Thee. Thou art the Lord, the God that did choose Abram and brought him forth out of Ur of the Chaldeans, and gave him the name of Abraham and found his heart faithful before Thee and made a covenant with him to give him the land of the Canaanites. To give it, I say, to his seed; and Father, Most Holy One, thou has performed Thy word, for Thou art righteous. But they, our fathers, dealt proudly and hardened their necks and hearkened not to Thy commandments, and refused to obey Thy instructions, and neither were mindful of Thy wonders that Thou did among them and in their rebellion, they chose to follow the strangers that were around them, of which Thou had said, Thou shall not be like unto them.

But Thou art a God ready to pardon, gracious and merciful, slow to anger, and in Thy great kindness Thou did not forsake them. Nevertheless, they were disobedient and rebelled against Thee and cast Thy law behind their backs and slew Thy prophets which testified against them to turn them unto Thee. And they wrought great provocations. Therefore Thou delivered them into the hands of their enemies who vexed them, but in the time of their trouble when they cried unto Thee, Thou heard them from Heaven, and according to Thy manifold mercy Thou gave them saviours to save them out of the hands of their enemies. But after they had rest, they did evil again before Thee. Therefore Thou left them in the hands of their enemies so that they had the dominion over them as it is in this day.

Nevertheless, for Thy great mercy's sake, Thou has not utterly consumed them nor forsaken them, for Thou art a merciful and gracious God. Now therefore O Lord our God our Father, Friend and Merciful One, the Great, Mighty and Lovable God who keepeth covenant and mercy; I beseech Thee, Father, let not all the trouble that has come upon us seem little before Thee, upon our kings, our princes, our priests, our prophets, our fathers, our children, and on all Thy people since the coming into the land of Babylon, America, into captivity unto this day.

Howbeit, Father, Merciful One, Thou are just in all that is brought upon us, for Thou hath done right but we have done wickedly. But Father, how long? How long will Thou forget us, O Lord? Forever? How long will Thou hide Thy face from Thy people? The captivity has been grievous. It seems to have no end. How long shall I take counsel in my soul, having sorrow in my heart daily? How long shall my enemy be exalted over me? Consider and hear me, O Lord my God: Lighten my eyes, lest I sleep the sleep of death; lest mine enemies say, I have prevailed against him; and those that trouble me rejoice when I am moved. But I have trusted in Thy mercy; my heart shall rejoice in Thy salvation. Now Father, I beseech Thee, O Merciful One, with humbleness of heart and meekness of spirit. Father, I say unto Thee, let the price be paid. Father, let it be enough what has come upon us, the sheep of Thy pasture. Father, let the price be paid! Let not Thy adversary have dominion over us. Father, let the words of my mouth and the meditation of my heart be acceptable in Thy sight, O Lord, my Strength and my Redeemer. Return unto us! Take us into Thy tabernacle that we may dwell with Thee and in Thy peace all the days of our life.

Selah

"A Prayer for Understanding"

L ord God of Israel, there is no God like unto Thee in Heaven above or on earth beneath for Thou keepeth covenant and mercy with Thy servants that walk before Thee with all their heart. I beseech Thee, have respect unto the prayer and to the supplication of thy servant, O Lord my God, to hearken unto the cry and the prayer which thy servant doth pray before Thee this day. And hearken Thou to the supplication of Thy people, and hear Thou in Heaven, Thy dwelling place, and when Thou hear, forgive; then teach them the good way wherein they should walk and be not angry with them but deliver them from the hands of the adversary, for they be Thy people and Thy inheritance which Thou brought forth out of Egypt from the midst of the iron furnace.

Lord God be with us as Thou was with our fathers; leave us not; neither forsake us. Incline our hearts unto Thee to walk in all Thy ways and to keep Thy commandments, Thy statutes and Thy judgments. And let these my words wherewith I have made supplication before the Lord, be nigh unto Thee day and night that You maintain the cause of Thy servant and the cause of Thy people Israel at all times as the matter shall require, that all the people of the earth may know that Thou art God and there is none else.

Father, Thy people are destroyed for lack of knowledge; we have rejected the instructions of God; therefore our enemies rule over us. Our glory has been turned into shame; our young men fall in the streets; we weep for our children and they are not. The daughters of Zion have been consumed by the adversary; the sons of Judah no longer provide a defense. Thy standard bearers have fallen. The enemy has come up very high, and we have sunk very low. We sought the ways of the adversary and only increased our sorrow. We have eaten of the tree of which Thou said, Ye shall not eat of it lest ye die. Father, Thou knowest and in our sorrow we cry unto Thee for we know not the way, but Thou knowest; we understand not, but Thou understandeth; we see not, but Thou seest. Teach us good judgment and knowledge; make us to understand the way of Thy precepts, for it is time to work for God.

This I recall to my mind; therefore have I hope. It is of the Lord's mercies that we are not consumed because His compassions fail not. All that pass by clap their hands; they hiss and wag their head at the daughter of Thy people, saying: Is this the people that men call the perfection of beauty? The joy of the whole earth? All mine enemies have opened their mouths against me. They hiss and gnash their teeth; they say we have swallowed her up! Certainly this is the day that we looked for. We have found; we have seen it. O Father, we have been thrown down; they have not pitied; the enemy rejoiced over us. Oh Lord God of Israel, hear, for the Lord will not cast off forever. Send Thy spirit into me like the lightning from the heavens. Open mine eyes that I may see Thy light on the path; open mine ears that I may hear Thy words and follow Thy instructions. We seek Thee O Father, for in Thee only is our salvation. We seek Thy way, for in it there is life. Remember O Lord what is come upon us; consider and behold our reproach. Our inheritance is turned to strangers; our houses to aliens. Our necks are under persecution; we labor and have no rest. Our fathers have sinned and are not, and we have borne their iniquity. Servants have ruled over us, thinking there is none to deliver out of their hand. But Thy wisdom shall deliver us; Thy knowledge shall restore our glory; Thy understanding, our greatness. Thou shall restore our soul and once again cause us to lie down in green pastures. We are Thy children; Thou art our Father. Be one again with Thy servant. For we are the sheep of Thy pasture; the work of Thine hands. Forsake us not at this the fateful hour.

Selah

"Prayer for The Black Man"

Here this, all ye people; give ear, all ye inhabitants of the world: Both low and high, rich and poor, together. I am the man that hath seen affliction by the rod of the wrath of God. Yet my soul thirsteth for God, that I might appear before Him. Send out Thy light, O God, and Thy truth: let them lead me. Let them bring me unto Thy Holy hill, and to Thy tabernacles. Have mercy upon me, O God, according to Thy loving-kindness; according unto the multitude of Thy tender mercies blot out my transgressions. Wash me thoroughly from mine iniquity, and cleanse me from my sin. For I acknowledge my transgressions: and my sin is ever before me. Against Thee, Thee only, have I sinned, and done this evil in Thy sight: that Thou might be justified when Thou speaks, and be clear when Thou judges. Create in me a clean heart, O God; and renew a right spirit within me. For in God I have put my trust; I will not fear what flesh can do unto me. Though every day they wrest my words: all their thoughts are against me for evil. They gather themselves together, they cast forth their nets, they mark my steps, when they wait for my soul. They beat my people to pieces and grind the faces of the poor. I can offer no resistance, therefore I weep sore into the night.

I have become a stranger unto my brethren, and an alien unto my mother's children. I have no honor amongst my people. My image has been cast down, it is trodden under the feet of men. The enemy has come into the stronghold of Jacob. He has thrown down; he has not pitied. In the midst of the adversary, I find no ease. Neither does the sole of my foot have rest. My life hangs in doubt before me; there is only fear day and night. In the morning I say, I wish it were evening, and in the evening I say, I wish it were morning. O Father, bring Thou my soul out of this prison. I acknowledge my sins. I have transgressed the Great Commandment. My God, my God, shine Thy light upon my path. Be merciful unto me. Let me now make reconciliation for iniquity, for what is there left of my life? I sit solitary upon the earth; I am a byword unto all that pass by. But this once, I plead unto You, lift up my face from the dust of the earth.

Renew my strength within me; bless me and keep me. Make Thy face to shine upon me, and be gracious unto me. Lift up Thy countenance O

Lord; let there be peace between me and Thee. Let the brightness of Thy coming go forth before me and the angel of Thy presence protect me. Let me fight against those that fight against Thee. O that Thou would give me strength again to show forth Thy mighty works. I would proclaim the acceptable things of God and comfort all that mourn. I would anoint with the oil of joy and give the garment of praise for the spirit of heaviness that Thy seed might be known among the strangers and their offspring among the people. Instruct me O Lord; quicken me. Hear my voice and my supplication. Incline Thine ear unto me for I will call upon Thy name as long as I live. I have thought on my ways, I entreated Thy favor with my whole heart, for Thou art my portion. I am glad that they said unto me, Let us go into the house of the Lord. I have chosen the way of truth; I will speak of Thy testimonies before kings and will not be ashamed. O Father, I am afflicted into the depths of my soul when I consider that I went astray from Thee, I whom Thou had chosen for Thy crown of gold became instead a crown of thorns. But be it known unto Thee O God that my pain has been great. My tears do run down like a mighty stream. The enemy did come against me to cut off the horn of Jacob, knowing that the strong man must be bound before the house can be robbed. But I shall yet break the chains of the captivity and bring again Thine inheritance. O ye thieves and robbers, ye that have forged a lie against me. The book is now open, the judgment is set; wake up Thy mighty men. Let your weak say, they are strong. For except the Lord build the house, they labor in vain that build it; except the Lord keep the city, the watchman waketh but in vain. It is vain for you to rise up early or sit up late, for I slumber no more. When I pray unto God then shall mine enemies turn back; this I know; for God is for me. My soul has escaped as a bird out of the snare of the fowlers. I will lift up mine eyes unto the hills, from whence cometh my help. My help cometh from the Lord, which made heaven and earth. He will not suffer my foot to be moved.

Selah

"A Prayer for The Black Woman"

O Lord my God, I have looked unto the ends of the earth and I have not seen such a thing. I have considered diligently and concluded we have changed the God of our Glory for that which does not profit.

How could one that stood so high have come down so low? I sit solitary in the dust of the earth; my crown has fallen to the ground. The enemy has entered into my gates; he has defiled the daughter of Thy people. I have cast down my defense, he sitteth at the gates of the city. Oh God, why turnest Thou away so long for Thou art my hope and my salvation? On Thee do I wait all the day. Mine eyes do fail with tears, for those I have swaddled and brought up hath mine enemy consumed. My bowels are troubled; my liver is poured upon the earth, for the destruction of the daughter of my people, because the children and the sucklings swoon in the streets of the city, and the adversary — he knoweth no pity.

Father! Where do we go from here? Teach us Thy ways O Lord, lead us in Thy paths. Show us the way wherein we should go. For Thy name-sake be merciful unto us.

Where art thou O Adam, the source of my strength? Shall we never be one again as in the garden of creation? Where art thou, O Adam? I plead unto thee that thou mightest forgive me for my error. And as for thee, O Lucifer, thou has been in Eden the Garden of God, thou didst deceive, for thou art he which covereth with darkness.

O God my Salvation; I am haughty no more, neither walk we with stretched forth necks and wanton eyes. We have seen our shame. O Father, hear, and when Thou hearest, forgive. O God, remove this reproach from us, for it is more than we can bear. For the adversary hath spread out his hand upon all my pleasant things. I have been plucked up in Thy fury, my tree does not flourish. The fruit of my womb has found no strength, therefore they cannot bear the sceptre, for they know not Thee, the Fountain of Living Waters.

They say to their mothers, Where is our portion? Why has thou made

God my enemy? I am sunk into the ground; my strength is dried up. Where are my honorable men, that I may seek counsel from them? In whose image, mother, has thou made me?

Hear me, my children! I cannot tell how you came into my womb, for I neither gave you breath nor life. Neither was it I that formed the members of your body. But it was He, the Creator of the world who formed the generation of man. He shall also have mercy upon you, that are called by His name.

My God, my God, forsake me no more! Cause Thy face to shine upon the daughters of Thy people. Bring forth Thy Holy presence in me, that Holy women may go forth as in the days of old. For I weep sore into the night; the yoke of my transgressions has made me weak before the strong; foolish before the wise, and a servant unto the wicked. Now Father, how long? My God, my Redeemer, my Saviour, how long will Thou hide Thy face from me? The enemy has chased me; he has cut off my life in the captivity. He boasteth that I am his, and shall know Adam no more, but I call upon Thy name, O Lord; Thou has heard my voice. Cause Adam to draw near unto me. Fear not, O Adam, for I shall again be one with thee. O Lord, my God, this day I commit my soul unto Thee. If Thou will teach me, I will learn. If Thou shall lead me, I shall follow. For I would rather be a doorkeeper in the house of God than continue to dwell in the tents of the wicked.

Selah

"A Prayer for The Leaders"

Blessed be the name of God forever and ever: For Wisdom and Might are His. I thank Thee, and praise Thee, O God of our Fathers, who hast given me wisdom and might and hast made known unto me what is desired of Thee. I beheld and there were no shepherds for Thy people. Wherefore, I chose to do that which was right. I will not sit in solitary; neither shall the enemy convince me that I should cease, for the hurt of the daughter of Thy people, I am hurt. Astonishment has taken hold of me, for there is no physician to heal the wounds of my people. O Lord, open Thou my lips and my mouth shall declare Thy praise. I shall cry aloud and spare not that my people may know their transgressions and the house of Jacob their sins.

The watchmen have become blind; they remove not the stumbling block from before Thy people; they are like unto dogs that cannot bark, sleeping, lying down, loving to slumber. They are shepherds that cannot understand; they all look to their own way. Everyone to his own gain from his place. But as for me, unto Thee O Lord do I lift up my soul. O my God, I trust in Thee; let me not be ashamed; show me Thy way, O Lord; teach me Thy paths. Lead me in Thy truth for Thou art the God of my salvation. Thou has proved my heart; Thou has visited me in the night. Thou has tried me and shall find nothing. Hold up my goings in Thy path; let my footsteps slip not; keep me as the apple of Thine eye. Hide me under the shadow of Thy wings from the wicked that oppress me; from deadly enemies who compass me round about. O Lord, disappoint him; cast him down. Deliver my soul from the wicked! The Lord is my rock and my fortress, my deliverer, my God and my strength, in whom I shall trust. The Lord is my shepherd; I shall not want. He restoreth my soul; He leadeth me in the path of righteousness for His name's sake. Yea, though I walk through the valley of the shadow of death, I will fear no evil for Thou art with me; Thy rod and Thy staff they comfort me.

Thou preparest a table before me in the presence of my enemies. Thou anointest my head with oil; my cup runneth over. Surely goodness and mercy shall follow me all the days of my life, and I will dwell in the house of the Lord forever. The Lord is my light and my salvation. Whom shall I fear? The Lord is the strength of my life, of whom shall I be afraid? When the wicked, even my enemies and my foes, came upon me to eat my flesh, they stumbled and fell. Though an host should encamp against me, my heart shall not fear. Though war shall rise against me, in this will I be confident. One thing have I desired of the Lord, and that will I seek after, that I may dwell in the house of the Lord all the days of my life, to behold the beauty of the Lord and to inquire in His temple; for in the time of trouble He shall hide me in His pavilion; in the secret place of His taber-nacle He shall keep me. He shall set me upon a rock and now shall mine head be lifted up above my enemies round about me.

Wait on the Lord; be of good courage and He shall strengthen thine heart. Wait, I say on the Lord. For I have heard the slander of many. Fear was on every side while they took counsel together against me. They de-vised to take away my life, but I trusted in Thee O Lord; I said Thou art my God, my times are in Thy hands. Deliver me from the hands of my enemies and from them that persecute me. Make Thy face to shine upon Thy ser-vant. Save me for Thy mercy's sake. Let me not be ashamed O Lord, for I have called upon Thee. Let the wicked be ashamed and let them be silent in the grave. Let the lying lips be put to silence which speak grievous things proudly and contemptuously against the righteous. O continue Thy loving-kindness unto them that know Thee and Thy righteousness to the upright in heart. Let not the foot of pride come against me and let not the hand of the wicked remove me, for I will declare my iniquity; I will be sorry for my sins for my enemies are lively and strong, and they that hate me wrongfully are multiplied. They also that render evil for good are mine adversary because I follow the thing that is good. Forsake me not O Lord. O my God, be not far from me; make haste to help me O Lord my Salvation; let them be ashamed and confounded together that seek after my soul to destroy it. Let them be driven backward and put to shame that wish me evil. I will cast my burden upon the Lord and he shall sustain me. He shall never suffer the Righteous to be moved.

Selah

"A Prayer for The Persecuted"

O Lord, God of Israel, Thou art God, even Thou alone. Thou has made heaven and earth. Father, who is like unto Thee? There are none to be compared with Thee. Lord, bow down Thine ear and hear. Open, Lord, Thine eyes and see that the adversary has reproached the Living God. Now therefore, O Lord our God, I beseech Thee. Save Thou us out of his hand that all the kingdoms of the earth may know that Thou art the Lord God. But it is good being persecuted by men as we look for hope from God, to be raised up again unto Him. I will love Thee, O Lord, my strength. The Lord is my rock, and my fortress, and my deliverer, my God, in whom I will trust; I will call upon the Lord, who is worthy to be praised: So shall I be saved from my enemies. But as for thee, O adversary, thou shall have no resurrection unto life. Thou has power over men in this day; thou are corruptible; thou doest what thy will, but think not that our Nation is forsaken of God, but abide a little while and behold His great power; how He will torment thee and thy seed. Be not deceived without cause, for we suffer these things for ourselves. Having went against our God, therefore marvelous things are done unto us. But think not thou (for who knoweth better than we) that as thou strive against God, that thou shall escape unpunished. In my distress I call upon the Lord, and cried unto my God: He heard my voice out of His temple and my cry came before Him, even into His ears. Then the earth shook and trembled; the foundations also of the hills were moved and shaken, because He was wrought.

Give ear to my words, O Lord; consider my meditation. Hearken unto the voice of my cry, my king, and my God: for unto Thee will I pray. Lord, how are they increased that trouble me! Many are they that rise up against me. Many there be which say of my soul, there is no help for him in God. But Thou, O Lord, art a shield for me; my glory and the lifter up of my head. I cried unto the Lord with my voice, and he heard me out of His Holy hill. O Lord, my God, in Thee do I put my trust; Save me from all them that persecute me, deliver me; Lest they tear my soul like a lion, rending it in pieces, thinking: there is none to deliver.

And I beseech thee, my people, look upon the heavens and the earth and all that is therein and consider that God made them of things that were not, and so was man made likewise. Fear not this tormentor but stand and be worthy to be called the Sons of God. Stand, I say, and be valiant for the truth! For the ungodly are like the chaff which the wind driveth away. Therefore the ungodly shall not stand in judgment, nor sinners in the congregation of the righteous. For the Lord knoweth the way of the Righteous: But the way of the ungodly shall perish.

Father, we have felt the pain afflicted upon us by the tormentor of our people. We fear not to cry for Thou has made our tears the moisture upon the soil of our people, which shall cause the plant of salvation to spring forth. So we cry, for without water the plant cannot grow. And Thou that has been the author of all mischief against our people shall not escape the hands of God. For we suffer because of our sins and though the Living God be angry with us a little while for our chastening and correction, yet shall He be at one again with His servants. O let the wickedness of the wicked come to an end; but establish the just: for the Righteous God trieth the hearts and reins. My defense is of God who saveth the upright in heart. But thou, O godless man, are of all other the most wicked. Be not lifted up without a cause or puffed up with uncertain hopes, lifting up thy hands against the people of God, for thou has not yet escaped the judgment of Almighty God who seeth all things. Thou has made a pit, and diggeth it, and shall fall into the pit which thou has made. Your mischief shall return upon your own head, and your violent dealing shall be served upon your own plate.

Father, most merciful one, hear, I pray, my prayer. Lord give ear to my supplication. In Thy faithfulness answer me and in Thy righteousness. For the enemy has persecuted Thy people. He has smitten their lives to the ground. He has made them to dwell in darkness as those that have been long dead. Therefore my spirit has overwhelmed me; my heart is heavy within me, for I remember the days of old when our souls belonged unto Thee and we loved one another. I meditate on the days we spent together; I muse in the work of their hands. Oh God, my Redeemer and Saviour, I stretch forth my hands unto Thee for my soul thirsts after Thee as a thirsty land. Hear Father speedily; hide not Thy face from Thy people, but cause them to hear Thy loving-kindness and to learn to trust again in Thee. Cause them to know the way wherein they should walk, that their souls may be lifted up unto Thee. Deliver them from the hands of the enemy; teach us to do Thy will, for Thou art God: Quicken us, O Lord, for Thy name's sake and bring our souls out of distress and destroy the enemy and all of them that afflict our soul. For I am Thy servant. Lord I cry unto Thee. Make haste to bring salvation unto Thy people. Let my prayer be set before Thee as the sweet fragrance and the lifting of my hands unto Thee as the evening sacrifice. Bring again the captivity of Zion that we may be like unto those that dream, that our hearts be filled with joy and our mouths with laughter. Hear, Father, I pray unto Thee.

Selah

"A Prayer For The Sick"

I have called upon the Lord for He will hear me. O God, incline Thine ear unto me and hear my speech. Show Thy marvelous, loving kindness O Thou that savest by thy right hand them that put their trust in Thee. Father, I suffer for my sins: I have erred; I have defiled Thy Holy temple; my pain is great, for Thy law I have not kept. I have cast Thy ways behind my back: I followed my lovers therefore I am sore afflicted. My soul it is sick. I have become weak from the sores of my heart, but surely Thine eyes are upon all the ways of the sons of men to give unto them according to their works and the fruits of the deeds of their hands.

I have become as one void of understanding. Thy instructions have been far from me. But if I return, will Thou hear me? When I plead unto you, will Thou forgive me? I acknowledge mine iniquity, that I have transgressed against the Lord my God, and have scattered my ways unto the strangers under every green tree and have not obeyed Thy voice. Who can understand his errors? Cleanse Thou me from secret faults and let the words of my mouth and the meditation of my heart be acceptable in Thy sight O Lord, my Strength and my Redeemer. Our fathers trusted in Thee; they trusted and Thou did deliver them; they cried unto Thee and were delivered. They trusted in Thee and were not confounded and as for me, I ask life of Thee, even length of days forever and ever for Thou art He that took me out of the womb; Thou didst make me whole when I was upon my mother's breast. I was cast upon Thee from the womb. Thou art my God from my mother's belly. Be not far from me for trouble is near. Remember, O Lord Thy tender mercy and Thy loving-kindness for they have been ever of old. Remember not the sins of my youth, nor my transgression. According to Thy mercy remember Thou me for Thy goodness sake, O Lord. Turn me unto Thee and have mercy upon me for I am desolate and afflicted. The troubles of my heart are enlarged. O bring Thou me out of my distresses. Look upon my affliction and my pain and forgive all my sins. Unto Thee will I cry O Lord my rock; be not silent unto me lest if Thou be silent unto me I become like them that go down into the pit. Hear the voice of my supplication when I cry unto Thee, and lift up my hand to thy Holy dwelling place.

O Lord my God, I cry unto Thee that Thou mayest hear me; that Thou mayest bring my soul from the grave, that I may not go down to the pit. I acknowledge my sin unto Thee and my iniquity I have not hid. I will confess my transgression unto the Lord for the eye of the Lord is upon them that fear Him; upon them that hope in His mercy to deliver their souls from death and to keep them alive in famine. My soul waiteth on the Lord for He is my help and my shield. I sought the Lord and He delivered me from all my fears. O fear the Lord ye His Saints for there is no want to them that fear Him. O God, merciful Father, I plead unto Thee. I lay my soul before Thine altar that Thy light may shine upon me. My wounds they stink and are corrupt because of my foolishness. I am troubled; I am bowed down greatly. I go mourning all the day long, for my loins are filled with a loathesome disease and there is no soundness in my flesh. I am feeble and sore broken. I have roared by reason of disquietness of my heart. Lord all my desire is before Thee and my groaning is not hid from Thee. My heart panteth; my strength faileth me. As for the light of mine eyes it also is gone from me. My lovers and my friends stand aloof from my sore, and my kinsmen stand afar off. O spare me that I may recover strength before I go hence and be no more. Many, Lord my God, are Thy wonderful works which Thou has done. They cannot be reckoned up in order unto Thee. If I would declare and speak of them, they are more than can be numbered. I beseech Thee, O Lord, be merciful unto me Heal my soul for I have sinned against Thee. An evil disease, say they, cleave fast unto him, and now that he liest, he shall rise up no more. But Thou Lord be merciful unto me, and raise me up that I may requite them. Behold, Thou has instructed many and Thou has strengthened the weak hands. Thy word upholdeth him that was fallen and Thou has strengthened the feeble knees. Teach me and I will hold my tongue, and cause me to understand where I have erred. Father, I know not if Thou shall heal me, but in this I am sure: I know that Thou can. My desire is that this cup be removed from me, but not my will, but Thy will must be done.

Selah

Communicators Press Publishing and Distribution

To order additional books by Ben Ammi complete the order blank below and give the others to a friend or family member that they may further their understanding about God, His People and His Plan.

For more information or wholesale requests, write:
Communicators Press, P.O. Box 26063; Washington, 20001
Tel: (202) 291-9244; Fax: (202) 291-9149; E-mail: dckog@idt.net

The Resurrection Series
by Ben Ammi

Check all that apply:

Title	Cost	Qty
❏ God the Black Man and Truth	$15.00	_____
❏ God and the Law of Relativity	$12.00	_____
❏ The Messiah and the End of this World	$17.00	_____
❏ Everlasting Life (From Thought to Reality)	$17.00	_____
❏ Yeshua the Hebrew Messiah or		
Jesus the Christian Christ?	$10.00	_____
❏ An Imitation of Life	$17.95	_____

Please send me the book(s) checked above at the total cost of $_____. Add $3.75 for shipping and handling (add $.75 for each additional book).

Name: _____

Address: _____

City, State, Zipcode: _____

Please complete the form above, include the proper funds and mail to:
Communicators Press, P.O. Box 26063; Washington, D.C. 20001

For Credit Card Order VISA, MASTERCARD, DISCOVER
or AMERICAN EXPRESS call (202) 291-9244.
or www.kingdomofyah.com/cpbooks.htm

Communicators Press Publishing and Distribution

To order additional books by Ben Ammi complete the order blank below and give the others to a friend or family member that they may further their understanding about God, His People and His Plan.

For more information or wholesale requests, write:
Communicators Press, P.O. Box 26063; Washington, 20001
Tel: (202) 291-9244; Fax: (202) 291-9149; E-mail: dckog@idt.net

The Resurrection Series

by Ben Ammi

Check all that apply:

Title	Cost	Qty
❏ God the Black Man and Truth	$15.00	_____
❏ God and the Law of Relativity	$12.00	_____
❏ The Messiah and the End of this World	$17.00	_____
❏ Everlasting Life (From Thought to Reality)	$17.00	_____
❏ Yeshua the Hebrew Messiah or Jesus the Christian Christ?	$10.00	_____
❏ An Imitation of Life	$17.95	_____

Please send me the book(s) checked above at the total cost of $_____. Add $3.75 for shipping and handling *(add $.75 for each additional book).*

Name: _____

Address: _____

City, State, Zipcode: _____

Please complete the form above, include the proper funds and mail to:
Communicators Press, P.O. Box 26063; Washington, D.C. 20001

For Credit Card Order VISA, MASTERCARD, DISCOVER
or AMERICAN EXPRESS call (202) 291-9244.
or www.kingdomofyah.com/cpbooks.htm

Communicators Press Publishing and Distribution

To order additional books by Ben Ammi complete the order blank below and give the others to a friend or family member that they may further their understanding about God, His People and His Plan.

For more information or wholesale requests, write:
Communicators Press, P.O. Box 26063; Washington, 20001
Tel: (202) 291-9244; Fax: (202) 291-9149; E-mail: dckog@idt.net

The Resurrection Series

by Ben Ammi

Check all that apply:

Title	Cost	Qty
❏ God the Black Man and Truth	$15.00	_____
❏ God and the Law of Relativity	$12.00	_____
❏ The Messiah and the End of this World	$17.00	_____
❏ Everlasting Life (From Thought to Reality)	$17.00	_____
❏ Yeshua the Hebrew Messiah or		
Jesus the Christian Christ?	$10.00	_____
❏ An Imitation of Life	$17.95	_____

Please send me the book(s) checked above at the total cost of $_____. Add $3.75 for shipping and handling *(add $.75 for each additional book).*

Name: _____

Address: _____

City, State, Zipcode: _____

Please complete the form above, include the proper funds and mail to: Communicators Press, P.O. Box 26063; Washington, D.C. 20001

For Credit Card Order VISA, MASTERCARD, DISCOVER or AMERICAN EXPRESS call (202) 291-9244. or www.kingdomofyah.com/cpbooks.htm